"Cathartic . . . something for everyone . . . You'll find the experiences of Bronson's families resonating against the music of your own. . . . These are meaty, meticulously-researched tales. . . . Bronson gives you the naked truth without exaggerating for emotional effect."

—Townhall.com

"A decent, heartening, kind and healing book . . . The integrity of [Bronson's] prose style as well as the incredible sweetness of those he writes about give him 24-karat credibility."

—*The Washington Post*

"Spellbinding."   —JOSH KORNBLUTH, *The Josh Kornbluth Show*

"Don't miss out on this celebration of the family. . . . As you are drawn into the stories, you will come across pain and suffering, but also deeply satisfying joy that comes essentially from connecting with people. . . . These are not Band-Aid solutions that you can copy-paste into your life. What they will do instead is grab you by the heart."   —*The Times of India*

"Stirring."   —*Seattle Post-Intelligencer*

"Will tighten the throat of just about any reader."

—*The Wall Street Journal*

"Heartbreaking . . . Each chapter can leave the reader in tears."

—*Orlando Sentinel*

"Compelling and philosophical . . . poignant."

—Nashville *City Paper*

"Besides breaking down all those stereotypes we harbor, what Bronson's book will do is make you think your own family is worth fighting for." —*Albuquerque Journal*

"Powerful . . . unlock[s] the essence of what it means to be a family in today's world." —*Columbus Parent*

"A powerful statement about the state of family life." —BookBitch

"Bronson is a modern Studs Terkel." —*Sunday Herald* (Glasgow)

"Gritty . . . inspirational . . . [Bronson's subjects] emerge as ordinary heroes." —*The Age* (Melbourne)

ALSO BY PO BRONSON

Nonfiction

The Nudist on the Late Shift
What Should I Do with My Life?

Fiction

Bombardiers
The First $20 Million is Always the Hardest

"Why
Do I
Love
These
People?"

RANDOM HOUSE TRADE PAPERBACKS

NEW YORK

"Why Do I Love These People?"

PO BRONSON

UNDERSTANDING,
SURVIVING, AND
CREATING YOUR
OWN FAMILY

For Michele, Luke, and Thia

Contents

Introduction: The Promise

Jerriann Massey

A few years back, a woman named Jerriann Massey was floating down a river on an inner tube when she got sucked into a hole on the back side of a waterfall. There, stuck in that hole, a very curious thing happened.

This was in the Texas Hill Country. The river was the Guadalupe, which pours out of Canyon Lake and washes down to New Braunfels. It was August; the water was shallow and limestone brown. Jerriann was along on a big family outing—twenty-four of them in all, including her husband and two children. A great gang. Their inner tubes were tied together with ski ropes into four pods. It was a lazy flotilla, complete with floating coolers and spare clothes for the kids. They had no intention of risking the rapids. When they drifted down to a spot in the river where some house boulders form a twelve-foot drop known as the Chute, they ferried to the bank and pulled their tubes out of the current. They carried their gear down a trail like pack mules. Jerriann's pod was the last to make this portage. Her husband was there with his firm hand; he grabbed the ski rope and tugged the pod toward him. The rope snapped and Jerriann's inner tube spun away, then was grabbed by the current. She was in her bathing suit with a T-shirt and hat, sneakers tight on her feet, her daughter's sunglasses in hand. She screamed, then laughed.

"See you downstream!" she cheered as the Chute sucked her in.

"Get over here!" her husband scolded her.

But what could she do? Her rump was in the water and her arms were too short to paddle effectively. She did not sense danger.

Jerriann went over the falls like a high diver, inverted, with the inner tube on top of her. She plunged straight to the bottom of the hole, felt the bottom, and pushed off to the surface as if in a swimming pool. She was surrounded by the loudest noise she had ever heard, the crashing hydraulics as the falls bent back on itself in a churn. She surfaced and gasped for air but was immediately sucked back down and tumbled topsy-turvy like a rag in a clothes dryer. She hit the surface again, managed another incomplete breath, then disappeared. *This is not right,* she thought. *I think I'm stuck.*

Her kids had already made the portage, putting in thirty yards downstream, in knee-high water. Nathan was twelve; Ashli, nine. They watched their mother flip as she went over the Chute, and then they did not see her at all amid the splashing of hairy whitewater. Imagine watching your mother drown. About a minute went by, when Jerriann's T-shirt washed downstream to them.

Then a sneaker was spit out and drifted their way.

They waited for their mother to emerge. They remember a great noise, too, the noise of chaos and panic, but they never took their eyes off that hole. Nathan began running upstream to Mom, but his dad screamed for him to go back, it was too dangerous.

A second minute ticked off.

The other sneaker followed, laces still knotted.

What was going on down there? What was Mom doing?

The third time Jerriann was sucked down, it was completely different. The noise was gone. It was extremely quiet and still, but pitch-black. A vast expanse of space was her impression, but she could not see this space. It was like being in your yard on a night so dark you can barely see your hands. The universe is palpable, just not visible. She could think clearly and hear herself as if speaking. Above herself, she saw a light. "Oh my gosh," she thought. "I'm dying."

What followed could have many explanations. Some would say her soul was saying good-bye to her bag of bones. Some would say she experienced a hallucination caused either by lack of oxygen or by calming endorphins that numb the brain to alleviate the suffering of death. But it doesn't matter, because that's not where this story is headed—it is not about what is on the other side, it's about making the most of what is on *this* side. Jerriann was at life's edge, in a dreamlike consciousness. This was her reckoning point. She was oddly, and curiously, and vividly aware.

Her life did not flash before her eyes, as the convention goes. She felt herself gliding toward the light, without any fear. The moment had the very distinctive feeling you get when you are very weary and headed home—that *I can't wait to get there* yearning. As if numbed and hypnotized, Jerriann wanted to go, desperately. She knew that if she got to that light, she would never return.

"Wait a minute!" she interrupted herself.

"Time out!" she hollered.

"Let's rewind!" she objected. "This is not supposed to be happening. Not here, not now. This is *not* what my children planned! My children did not agree to see their mother die! This is not what they came to learn!

"Something is really wrong about this," she thought.

Then the curious thing happened. Jerriann was overcome with an astounding panic as she thought, "Oh my *gosh,* I have not done what I *promised* I would do." The closest feeling she can compare this to was the time she was in a meeting at work and remembered, all of a sudden, that she had forgotten to pick the kids up from school. She has never lost her children in a crowd, but she imagines it is that same panicky feeling.

Overwhelming, this feeling. "Oh my God I haven't done what I promised!

"How could I have forgotten *that*!

"Of all things!"

It was a horrible feeling, stinging with guilt and terror.

But here's the most curious thing—Jerriann did not know what it was she had promised. In her surreal dream logic, she remembered that she had made a promise, and she remembered that it was the most important thing in her life, but she did not know, actually, what it was.

Begging now, Jerriann summoned her resolve and offered the light a bargain: "If I can go back and raise my children, I *promise* I won't forget this time, I will go back and complete what I promised."

With that, Jerriann was back in the water, alive again. But not downstream, unfortunately. Still caught in the churn, drinking water, unable to breathe. Now it was getting ridiculous. "I just talked myself back into another chance at life and I'm *still* stuck!" But she no longer believed she would die. "I'm all right," she thought. "I'm here."

Finally the river let go of her, and she washed down toward her children, sputtering, throwing up grass and muck, snorting water out her nose. The kids seemed to recognize how close to death Jerriann had come. They both needed to touch her and pat her on the back as she kneeled on the grass and continued to vomit. But the adults did not appear to grasp that they had nearly lost her.

"I almost died!" she pleaded to her husband.

"Oh, you are *fine*!" he insisted, refusing to go there, scared of admitting it.

"No, I almost died!" she cried.

He shut her down. "No, you were only in there a few minutes."

She stewed over the absurdity of his comment. Only a *few* minutes? Would he like to try a few minutes trapped underwater? Would he like to suffocate on river dredge for a few minutes?

She tried to bring it up again the next day with him. She wanted to tell him about the bargain she'd made, the promise she had to fulfill. The urgency she felt. He was uninterested. "Jerriann! You're making a big deal out of nothing!"

How could he not be interested in this mystery? How could he not be compassionate—at least for her benefit? She needed to talk about it. She had made a bargain—not with God, not with Death. With herself. She had a promise to remember, and then to keep.

But what was it?

Every time she thought about it, that same guilt and panic flooded her. It haunted her. She owed her life to it. She knew if she found it, the treasure of life would reveal itself to her.

"I made a promise," she whispered, taking Ashli to school.

"What was it?" she wondered, preparing dinner for Nathan.

This was not how it worked in the movies. In the movies, if you went all the way to your reckoning point, and you had to bargain for your life and the life of your kids, you would at least know what your end of the bargain was. You might not get it in writing, but you'd exit the negotiation with epiphany-like clarity.

In real life, though, we are meant to search. The secret to unlocking life's treasure is not handed to us. We have to look high and low for it. We have to endure, we have to experience, and we have to contemplate.

I haven't been trapped underwater, but I know a bit of that feeling Jerriann experienced—as if I, too, have a promise that I struggle to both remember and keep. I recognize that feeling Jerriann describes. It's her story, her life, but it feels a little like mine.

Life is full of promise, and we engage that promise when we take our first breath, and we remember a bit of that promise every time we fall in love, every time we go home, every time we make a new friend. Every time we cry, and every time we laugh. We live with it, just like Jerriann.

Don't you feel like Jerriann sometimes?

We are *meant* to do something.

We just don't get to know what it is.

So what did Jerriann decide her promise was?

Well, she has never stopped asking.

But she knew this, with great certainty: Whatever it was, her children were part of it. And she found herself, in the wake of her near drowning, loving her children quite differently. Before, she pressured herself to do everything "right"—never miss a Little League game, a school play, what have you. She insulated her children from disappointment and did not give them many choices. After, she loosened up. She was there to guide them and encourage them, and she started to trust their wisdom and quit fussing about their mistakes.

In the year that followed, Jerriann divorced her husband. They had been together fourteen years, but it hadn't been working for some time. She was done, like chicken falling off the bone. What killed the marriage was that she never felt *heard*. When she was a regular Texas girl, her husband was tolerant, but when she was Jerriann, with all her peculiarities, he was annoyed. Ashli supported Jerriann's right to be happy, but Nathan did not. He protected his father, and chose to live with him. But a boy needs to be heard, too. A year later Nathan called his mother and said, "I made a big mistake. I chose to live with Dad, but *I need a family.*"

A few years after her divorce Jerriann married her second husband, Doug. She thought she was done with men, but Doug listened to her like no guy ever had. No matter how weird she was, and no matter how deep her inquiries into life's riddles went, he never once treated her like she was making a big deal out of nothing. He always went with her.

Jerriann's father had to learn to hear her, too. When she was a girl, he worked in far-off cities managing insurance agencies. When he stopped traveling, Jerriann was twelve, and he didn't know what to do with the peculiar specimen of a twelve-year-old girl. They never connected. Before the near drowning, she would go months without visiting him, even though he lived two hours away. After, she drove to see him every month. Her work was changing—she moved into management—and they became friends by talking about business. Their friendship grew from that. Now he lives nearby; his workshop is behind her house, and he is around almost every day.

"He's the best friend I have," Doug said.

"There is more to my promise than just my family," Jerriann told me when we sat on their covered porch, which looked out on a small lake near Tyler, Texas. "But my family is a big part of it, sometimes the most visible part, and certainly the most immediate part. If you asked me how I have lived up to my end of that bargain I struck, the first thing I'd point to is my precious children, who have become great young adults. And I'd point to my new love for my father. And my love for Doug. My sister, my brother, my cousins—they're all in the mix. My end of the bargain is by no means complete. When I die, then I'll be done, and not a second before. But the first thing I'd point to? That's my family. They're not the whole answer to my promise, but they're part of it."

It is with that exact thought that I want to introduce this book, which is about decoding the mystery of family life so that it can become what it is meant to be—part of what fulfills our promise. Not the be-all and end-all, and not necessarily numero uno. Just part of our answer when we go looking to keep our promise. Whether *family* means the family we come from or the families we form in so many jury-rigged ways—either way, it's *part of the answer,* and not a torture, not a whirl of confusion, not a river hole that repeatedly sucks us back down. Because family life does seem that way, so often. It churns us, it overwhelms us, it nearly suffocates us.

The last book I wrote was about our individual journeys. It began with this line: "We are all writing the story of our life." As we respond to challenges and exert some choice over what interests we pursue, we are composing our own life story.

But when it comes to family, it's a little different. I like to say, "We are all constantly *rewriting* the story of our family."

When we are born we are handed this backstory, and then we spend our first decade with little control over how our story unfolds. In our second decade our understanding of the story begins to develop. We make conscious connections, notice patterns, and maybe inject some drama into the story, too. In our third decade we gain some control over where this story will go. We decide how much separation we need from the past in order to hear our own feelings. We ask very threatening questions, such as "Do I need a family? What is their purpose?" And we begin to push to create a family of our own.

Creating families of our own involves both building with new people and changing the relationships we have to those we've grown up with. On both fronts, we try to shape the story, adding new chapters as a way of changing how the old story lines turn out.

For instance, let's say one of the old story lines is "The men in my family have always been very terse and suppressed their feelings." A woman might marry a man who falls into this pattern. But they have a son, and they manage to raise him differently. This teases out the emotional side of the husband, and perhaps that of the grandfather, too. It's a joy to have a son that is expressive, but the satisfaction has deeper roots—they feel quiet pride in altering the inevitability of history. They have changed the story.

In this way, our actions today answer the past. Some old traditions are wonderful, and it's fulfilling to keep them going for another generation. Other legacies are ruinous and painful; it's a relief to end them.

Rewriting requires the ability to look at an old version of a story and see something fresh in it. That same skill is absolutely key to enjoying family life. Without it, family life would grow old very quickly, become repetitive and rote. You wake up every day, and there is your spouse, same as he or she was yesterday. You remember the day we first met him or her—how attracted you were!—but when you look at that person every day for ten years, it can be difficult to always see what was once so exciting. Or your father tries to give you advice, and it seems he's been giving you the same lecture your whole life. We fall into routines. Family tests us—it tests our ability to see the new in the old, the beauty in the ordinary. Perhaps I could even say it teaches us this ability so we can apply it to the rest of our lives. And if we have gained this skill of perception, then we can always find something fresh in the story.

There's an old saying: "You can choose your friends, but you can't choose your family." We commonly invoke this phrase to describe the struggle of family life, but I don't think it fits anymore. We may not get to choose whom we are born to, but when we grow up we do indeed choose how close to be to them. We choose whether to live in the same state, or in the same city, or under the same roof. We choose whether to call them once a day or once a year—or never. We choose which relatives to invest in and which ones to avoid. The truth is, we monitor our relationships to our given families like a finely tuned thermostat, increasing the time spent together when it's going well and withdrawing when it's going poorly.

There are many elements of family life that we can't choose, but it's not all a fait accompli. For instance, we choose the elements of our new families. We choose who to fall in love with. We choose whether to get married (though there are some unfortunate exceptions to that). We choose whether to become parents, and by what means—birth or adoption. We can choose who to call "uncle" and who best fits the role of "grandma." In fact, we can choose to do none of these things. We live at a time of increasing individualism. We have an option now. If we so choose, we can have a very fulfilling life rich in intense relationships without ever calling anyone our "family."

So if we're going to have families in this modern age, we have to choose to do so. And that choice is not always obvious. Some relationships can be saved, but some can't. And when one of those relationships is not improving, it's difficult to know how much effort to spend, and how far to expose oneself.

Let me share my goal for this book.

We get a lot of things from our families, but one of the most innately wired things we get is a template for how to give and receive love. Even if we have cut off all ties to our families, we carry this template forward in life.

Everyone has different feelings about this template. Some people feel they were taught very well how to love. Others feel they were taught terribly and given nothing but bad habits they've had to break. But most people would put themselves in the middle. They were taught some of the pieces, but others are missing.

It is the fashion of today to complain about these missing pieces—to blame our backstory for not having fully prepared us. But I think that's a mistake. I think we are all meant to search. We have all been taught some of what love is, and the rest we have to go figure out. There is a yearning to fill our gaps, to make up for what we have missed.

This is true for us, and it was true for our parents, and it was true for every generation before them. Unfortunately, it will also be true for our children. This is the nature of life. We have not been cheated. We get this chance at life, but we have to hold up our end of the bargain. We have to learn what love is, learn the parts we missed, and pass it on. That's the deal.

Is this not what drove Jerriann's changes after her near drowning? Is this not all of our story? Is this not the promise we have been trying to remember?

The goal of this book is utterly simple—to show how real people have created better families around them, whether by choosing a new family or by resolving differences with the family they came from.

In each of the chapters ahead we will meet a new person, and we will be given extremely privileged access to their story as they struggle to create a new family out of the pieces of their past. These are people I met in my travels, and they've given me permission to share their stories.

In the pages ahead, you will see these people create great families despite destructive childhoods. You will see them overcome their impulses to repeat what was inflicted upon them. You will watch them heal in their own particular way, not conforming to any fashion. You will see some relationships rescued from the brink, but not all, and you will also see the opposite—people whose lives got better only after a much-needed divorce or after a break from their parents. You will see a type of parenting that guides by setting a precedent rather than by controlling a child's choices. You will see couples create good compromises, where both get their needs met and contribute equally to the family culture. You will see people thrive not despite their differences, but thanks to their differences. You will see them use their pain not to withdraw, but to connect to others who have known pain. You will see people take responsibility for the rest of their lives, no longer letting themselves be victims of their experience. You will see people find ways to hang on to their promise and live up to it, despite unmerciful hardship.

These stories don't teach tricks or techniques. Rather, they teach more soulful lessons: compassion for what people go through, empathy for what pains people hide inside, and awareness of social factors that shape family life.

In telling these stories, I intend to show that there is not a one-size-fits-all formula to a happy family life. I will avoid the language of pop psychobabble. I'm wary of books that purport to distill the incredible complexity of family experience into Eight Simple Lessons. Reducing family wisdom to bullet points is like putting an orca whale in a small aquarium—both die in captivity. The great beauty of family, rather, is its very complexity. The past is so interesting exactly because it can be seen in so many ways, and the future is compelling because we never know how it'll turn out. In recording these stories, I listened for moments when the clichéd script for family didn't apply. I tuned my ear to the contradictions of character and action, when people behaved in ways they never would have predicted.

So the book you hold in your hands is fairly unique on a bookstore shelf. You might find it hard to categorize if you try to describe it to your friends. It is certainly not like a self-help book, though I do hope you find the stories helpful. Nor is it like the many sociological analyses of family (though on my Web site you can access seventy memos which put modern family issues in historical and cross-cultural perspective). Rather, each story unfolds like a film, raising questions and provoking contemplation as it works its way to the end. I consider the style of my work "social documentary," and these are some of the most powerful stories I've ever recorded.

I wrote this book because I fell in love with these stories, and I fell in love with these stories partially because I have been on a similar journey myself.

Today I have two healthy young children and am happily married. We live in San Francisco and our extended family is spread out over both coasts of the United States and three continents. We visit all of our relatives, often, and it is not a duty or a chore—we *like* it. My mom lives with us about six weeks a year, and my dad and I have a special connection that I would still feel if he were on Mars.

But it was not always this way. Until I was thirty-five, I never wanted children. I never wanted the burden of owning a house. I spent fifteen years keeping my parents at a distance. I used to say I would never marry again (my first marriage ended in divorce). I used to say I didn't want a family.

The things I hold most dear are all things I used to say I never wanted. So my current life has definitely been a surprise. I would assert I didn't want these things, but it's more accurate to say is that I never believed it was possible. I was stuck in that river hole for a long time, confused and adrift. I owe credit to a lot of people for rescuing me. I owe my wife, Michele, who comes from an extra-large and unusually nonjudgmental Cajun family. She has never lost her sense of family, and I borrowed some of hers to reignite my own. I owe my parents, my aunts, and my grandmother, who never gave up trying to get my attention. But more than anyone else, the one person who pulled me out of that river hole was my younger brother. The saga of our relationship is captured in the final chapter of this book.

I believe in the transformative power of stories. Through the stories of others, we revisit our own lives and learn to tell our own stories in a fresh way. We see them new again.

May these stories echo your own.

What can I do about
my problem that doesn't
require the reciprocal
acts of others?

The Cook's Story

James and Jennifer Louie

We've all lost something along the way.

In Jennifer Louie's case, what she had lost was a belief that her family was a fundamentally essential thing, a meaningful purpose worth her devotion, a principle on which to build her life. Family is like Religion: There are all kinds, but when you get right down to it, you either believe, or you're not sure, or you think it's a crock of hooey. Jen had lost her belief. She had it in China, and she lost it when she came to America. These things happen—she was moving on. She was in the right place to lose it: The United States of America has seventy-six million great families with roots around the world, but it's also one of the best places in which to move on after losing belief. It can be done here. Those "Not Sure" have plenty of company.

Then, unexpectedly, it came back. Her belief. It came back when she got to know her father, James, but not *as her father,* just as a man, a human being with feelings. She found herself loving him again, with a respect she'd not had in twenty years.

This is their story.

I had actually met Jennifer before.

"Do you remember?" she asked.

"I still have your old business card," I recalled truthfully. We would bump into each other at a South of Market club where my best friend and I used to swing-dance. What I remembered about Jen was that she spoke very directly about her emerging career as a television producer. She was ambitious and sharp. And this was memorable, because we were in a club where (1) businessy career conversations seemed out of place, not to mention hard to hear, and (2) Jen was working as a Lucky Strike cigarette girl, in costume, giving away cigarettes. Her second job.

It was amusing to listen to the beautiful, fiercely independent Chinese Lucky Strike girl going on about her successful day job for a cable channel in the big city. It always stuck in my memory, a multiculti Mary Tyler Moore moment. Yes, she was in Lucky Strike costume, but she moved around the nightclub with the body language of a manager in an office, armed with business cards, never missing a chance to network. When she mentioned her family, she always painfully waved the topic away. "They just don't get me," she would say, or "They don't approve of what I'm doing with my life," or "They're living their life, I'm living mine." Unable to please them, she'd stopped trying. She treasured her career passion like a good secret, it being the only part of her life that was hers alone to ruin or shape into something grand.

Then, one day some six years later, after I made a presentation at a business conference (about the heroic courage required to find a meaningful career, no less), Jennifer came up to me, wondering if I remembered her. She said she'd just moved back from New York. There was something different about her, a peacefulness to equal her confidence. It intrigued me. We agreed to meet for a glass of wine after work the next week.

With Jen, there's so much to attract the eye. She puts the double H in hip-hop. Blond streaks highlight her black hair. A mountain lion tooth dangles from her leather choker. Metallic powder-blue eyeshadow, umber lip liner, and rose-tinted sunglasses add color to her visage. Pin-striped pants, a snug T-shirt, and black boots with two-inch heels proudly show off her curves. But while I noticed these details, my eye fixed on the one accessory that didn't fit. On her left wrist was a delicate bracelet of beaded hooks, with a single gold heart dangling from the chain. It was solid gold, but somehow raw—shiny, but without the luster of contemporary jewelry. It looked fragile. This was not the sort of bracelet folks bought in Soho. An heirloom?

"Is it a locket?" I asked, referring to the single gold heart.

"No, it's not a locket," Jen answered, "but it's very perceptive of you to notice this, of all things. It never leaves my wrist."

"There's more to it than that, I can tell from your voice."

"I didn't see this bracelet for twenty years. Now a whole story is *represented* to me by this bracelet."

A locket after all.

Over the next year I spent many afternoons with Jen and her father, James. He's fifty-three, relaxed in the face, but often looks down in contemplation. He is not a formal man; sometimes I found him in a Sacramento Kings T-shirt and flip-flops, at other times in an open-necked dress shirt and dress slacks, but shoeless. We laughed together, and hugged unself-consciously, which was not something Jen had seen him do with anyone in America except his immediate family. I think of physical affection as a sort of fourth dimension: You can get through life without ever knowing it's there, but it sure adds something to the experience when you open up to it. I guess James was demonstrative with me as a way of reaching across the limitations of language. When narrating facts, he spoke Cantonese, with Jen translating, saving his sparse and humble English for the very few concepts or feelings he was desperate to communicate. Often he needed to say it to Jen once, get the English translation from her, shake that off like a pitcher might a catcher's sign, modify it, test a better word on Jen, and then be the one who delivered this translation to me, warm from the oven of his heart. When communication slows down—when the data rate slows down— we can *feel* more. In fact, it was my practice to go over the same material repeatedly, often forcing a source to retell the story five to eight times until he had lost track of his codified "safe" version and was spilling out untapped remembrances that made him feel it all again.

At one point James had said something that made him laugh almost silently to himself. Because laughter is infectious among friends, I giggled impulsively.

"What'd he say?" I asked Jen.

She repeated in English, amused, "This must be a world record."

"For what?"

"For the longest anyone has ever listened to a fry cook."

———

Before leaving China, they had hidden the gold.

The gold had been forged into necklaces, bracelets, and rings. Their fortune fit into the flat, round plastic cases of two powder compacts, their makeshift treasure chest. One of the bracelets was a family heirloom passed down from a great-grandmother—a string of beaded hooks with a single small gold heart dangling off the chain. It fell over on itself in a double loop in the compact case. A fold of silk kept the jewelry from rattling.

It's traditional for migrating families to convert their savings to gold, since it's a reliable currency accepted everywhere. But James Louie didn't bring the gold with him to California. He brought all his cash, five hundred dollars, but he hid the gold in the house he was leaving. In this moment—in this very untraditional and revealing decision—what heartwarming, charmingly hopeless love of home! James Louie stashed the gold because he fully intended to come back. Frequently! He anticipated making enough money in America to return every few summers on vacation. The house he, his son, and his daughter had been born in—a brick-and-cinder hovel in the rice commune of Tai San (house number 18 in case you're ever in the neighborhood)—would become his summer home. While there was no plumbing whatsoever (they scooped water from the river) and no stove (cooking instead over small fires of fig leaves and branches), the house had been supplied with electrical current ten years before, and recently James had wired a television—the only one in the village. On Thursday nights James's daughter, Jennifer, all of eight years old, would sell tickets to people from neighboring villages to watch the only Chinese television show they could receive.

James had farmed rice almost every day of his twenty-nine-year life in a village where barter, not money, was the primary currency. He had been to high school, where he had met his wife, Kim, but that was it. His peasant's life did not resemble that of the doctors and academicians who had been thrown into the rice fields during the Cultural Revolution, torn from their children and spouses. Even if James—like everyone else—wanted a ticket out, communism had never scarred his family. Occasionally the communists showed up and hauled away the stored rice. They were not an everyday presence. They let James plant vegetables in an unclaimed corner of a field and keep a pigsty and chicken coop across the street. James Louie was a simple man. His love for Tai San was not complicated.

So he ordered the pots to be left hanging from their hooks. He told his family to take some clothes, but to leave others folded neatly in chests. The heart and soul of the home was an altar of framed photographs of family members going back a few generations, with James's mother dominating in the middle. He harvested very little from the altar, only the smallest mementos.

"I will be back, Mother," he said, bowing before her photo.

This was July 1980. He was in southern China, 120 miles from Canton City, 200 miles from Hong Kong, 7,100 miles from California.

He slipped the gold into the red compacts and pried loose a wood panel from the brick. Jimmying a white block forward with his fingers, he opened his secret hiding place. Behind the wall was a wormhole just wide enough for his arm to snake down into. At the end of his reach, he wedged the gold. (He was the tallest man in the village, thus his arms were longest. The few extra inches might make a difference.)

The whitewashed brick and wood panel were set back in place. The door to number 18 was locked, and James entrusted the lock's skeleton key to his best friend. They paid one last visit to his mother's grave in the rice fields, and then James told his grandfather—the man, now in his eighties, who'd raised him—that he would return the following summer. James held back the tears and the fear that it would probably be three or four years before he returned. He knew that he might be seeing his beloved grandfather for the last time.

Jennifer had been given a pink princess dress and a Dorothy Hamill haircut for the occasion. (Somehow, the Dorothy Hamill bob with blunt bangs had made it to China.) Jennifer remembers fretting about whether this American ice skater's haircut would be sufficient to allow her to fit in, but her father seemed confident in what he was doing. In their culture there was no such thing as questioning your father. "Your cousins will teach you," he promised. His own father, sister, and brother had gone to San Francisco twenty years earlier. By now they were thriving. The family would smooth their transition.

They didn't. The family was caught up in their own lives.

They treated the new Louies rudely, mocked them for not speaking English, and overlooked them at Christmas. The new arrivals were never "emotionally claimed," to use James's phrase.

Way too soon the new Louies were on their own, living in Sacramento, running restaurants, sacrificing, trying to assimilate, hoping their children would attend college, maybe even—if they were a very lucky family—the University of California at Berkeley. Which is exactly where Jennifer went. All that unfolded like the great American Dream, but they never knew it would work out like that. In any given moment, they were terrified and powerless and felt like failures and took it out on one another in the way only families can: cruelly. On paper they appeared a success, but financially the extreme hardship never relented. Emotionally, they became dire enemies.

James: "The father my daughter knew was bitter . . . controlling . . . *rough*." He knows this now, abuse being an American concept he's had to learn.

Jen added, "He also now knows it was illegal to have left his children at home unsupervised every afternoon and evening."

James corrected her, "No, I knew then. I knew."

Jen absorbed this; then, worried her father was shouldering all the blame, offered her own confession: "The daughter my father knew was *selfish,* she thought only of herself, she was embarrassed by her Chinese heritage, she refused to speak in Cantonese to her parents anywhere in public. In ninth grade I won an award for a poem I had written about my great-grandfather unwillingly letting us go on our last day in China. I didn't even invite my parents to the awards ceremony. I told myself it was because they couldn't come anyway, but the truth was, I was afraid they'd show up in their communist pajamas and embarrass me." Jen dug out the poem from a paperback book her high school had published. I read it quickly. I sensed James's interest. I handed the book to him. He read it as only a man fifteen years too late can read a poem.

In her poems and journals young Jen had started to carve out her own secret life. In high school she lied in order to see boys and go to dances. Her parents sensed all this, and in their minds they had already lost her. Nothing they said or did could keep her from becoming Americanized. When they telephoned her at Berkeley, all they heard was "Yeah Dad, yeah Mom, okay, yeah."

In graduation photos, forced to stand with her parents, she looks positively gloomy.

Then the *ultimate* indignity: After college their daughter went to work for pennies as a producer for a new cable show, Q-TV, an issues and entertainment show for gays and lesbians. They knew their daughter wasn't a lesbian, but if she had been that might have made more sense. Occasionally she showed up with videotapes, proud of her hard work, hoping to share.

Imagine this scene! Imagine what her parents were feeling. They left their homeland at middle age, their siblings sabotaged their attempt to assimilate, they both worked double shifts for fourteen years to put their daughter into one of the best colleges in America, and what did she do with this incredible opportunity? Not buy a house, not buy a new car, but rather—*she created a great seven-minute segment on the hot new gay comic!*

She had no steady boyfriend, no real income, but *she'd gone to Palm Springs and sat by the pool for two days interviewing lesbian conventioneers about how, exactly, they practice safe sex!*

And did she even get paid for this work? *Not enough that she didn't have to sell cigarettes to make her rent!*

Oh, they were thrilled.

And try to imagine this without the benefit of your complex understanding of how things usually work out one way or another in America. Try to imagine this from the point of view of a village peasant in a strange land, a man who has had no experiences that give him confidence it'll be okay, no family to tell him she'll be all right. A man who's never been in a nightclub and has only his wildest fears to conjure what might go on in one. There's nothing that will keep a man like James Louie up at night like the fear that he can't save his own children. How did this happen? How did it come to this?

James Louie's greatest dreams had come true, but so had his greatest fears.

Several years seemed to disappear, thrown away faster than they were lived, down into a black hole of memory. Jen had cut off her roots, emotionally if not in practice. Her parents now vested all their hopes in her brother. Jen would drive out to Ocean Beach and sit in the sand looking toward China and cry. She'd lost something, back across that ocean. She'd left it there and she was never going to get it back. Did anyone but her even remember? Could anyone in her family ever remember those days when they did not yell at one another?

It seemed as if far more than the heirloom gold bracelet had been forgotten in that wormhole in the wall in Tai San. When they came to America, they forgot that their childhoods had been happy. They forgot the charm and innocence of belonging to a place and a community. They forgot the joy of running down the street chasing a friend on a tricycle. The rocking chair James had carved for his daughter by hand. What it was like to play hide-and-seek in the long grass while the parents worked the rice fields nearby. They forgot what it was like to love one another.

Could anyone even remember that feeling?

It was as if their love had all been traded for gold, then forged into bracelets and rings and stuffed into a wall rather than brought with them.

They had left it behind, in two red compact cases.

And somehow, the Louies found it again. There is that bracelet, which Jen never lets leave her wrist. She adores her dad, and the feeling is mutual. So the question we want answered is, *How?* How'd they do it and, more important, can the rest of us do it, too—can we get that feeling back?

The Louies didn't go to counseling, though perhaps they should have.

And Jen didn't give a big speech that all of a sudden convinced her parents to stop judging her.

And nobody said to anybody else *I'm sorry* or *I forgive you,* though in the way they relate today it's apparent they *are* sorry and they *have* forgiven each other.

And they did not dig their heels in, stubbornly refusing to see one another until one side or the other broke down and agreed to change— that was not how it happened.

What happened was, Kim Louie went into the hospital. This was a big deal because while she complained for years of aches, she didn't believe in Western medicine and was too proud to ever see a doctor. So if she was in the hospital, she was really sick. With what nobody was sure. Kim believed she had contracted an illness from drinking rice field water in Tai San. When Jen was born, James had to buy blood for Kim from neighboring villages.

Anyway, only one thing is certain when you go to the hospital: You get billed.

The bills piled up. They didn't ask Jen outright for money. It was more like they criticized her clothes, picked a fight, and then, in the heat of the argument, said things like *We sent you to college and you're still no better off than we are! We're still washing dishes and can't pay our medical bills, and look at you, you have nothing!*

One day—completely out of the blue—Jennifer decided to apply a sort of reverse psychology on her parents. She can pinpoint this decision to a very particular place and time. She had just walked into a popular hip-hop radio station to interview for a job as a radio producer. She had noticed all these sweet rides in the parking lot—Mercedeses, Lexuses, BMWs. During her interview, she happened to ask the senior producer, "Which one is yours?"

The producer laughed. "Me? You gotta be kidding. Those all belong to the advertising salesmen."

Something clicked. "Then I'd like to interview with that department."

She had an idea that she'd do it for one year, and send a truckload of money to her parents. This might finally get them off her back, and then she would be free of them. Her obligation would be fulfilled.

So she did it. "Just to be clear on my motives," she explained to me, "I didn't want to *take care* of my parents. I just wanted to shut them up. I wanted them to stop yelling at me."

In this way she met both her own criteria and theirs: She managed to be insolent and obedient at the same time. *I'm just doing this to shut them up!*

Jen turned out to have a work ethic much like her mother's. But selling advertising is a lot more lucrative than washing pots. Jen paid her mother's medical bills. A year went by. She paid off her parents' mortgage. Another year. She discovered—to her total surprise—that it felt good to support her family. She went looking for a little house of her own. When her brother and his girlfriend got pregnant, she bought a five-bedroom house and let them live there, keeping her apartment. Mind you, there had been no apologies. There had been no forgiveness. But it seemed petty to harbor resentments with Mom sick. While Jen told herself she would soon go back to her passion, now that her family life wasn't so outright contentious it didn't seem so crucial that she be pursuing her passion every minute.

One day at a business brunch, Jen bumped into the mayor of San Francisco, Willie Brown. She had interviewed him about gay politics a few times during her Q-TV days, and he remembered her. He was about to embark on a ten-day tour of China with a delegation of business leaders and dignitaries.

"Where in China?" she asked.

"Southern China."

"Which provinces?"

He listed a few, and then added, "Guangdong."

"That's where I was born," she said proudly.

"You weren't born here?"

"No, I only got my citizenship last year."

"Have you ever been back?"

"No."

"You must come with me. Bring your parents."

Mom was too sick to travel, but Dad agreed to go.

"You have to understand how big a deal this was," Jen narrated. "My parents had never taken a vacation in their entire life. You have to understand—in their first ten years here, they never took a single day off from work. Not one day. I am not exaggerating. Forget about the fact they'd never been back to China, never been to Los Angeles, never been anywhere. They simply had never left the kitchen of their restaurant. For my dad, to go on a vacation was like winning the lottery."

From the couch, James rocked and nodded in memory.

"We flew to Hong Kong, and the first night, we're put up in a hotel, I think it was called the White Stallion, overlooking Hong Kong Harbor. The view from the patio is incredible. 'Dad,' I say, 'let me take your picture out here,' I say. 'No, no,' he says, 'take my picture in here.' I go in, and he's sitting at the hotel room desk. 'Take a picture of me sitting here,' he says. 'Why, Daddy?' 'Because this desk will make me look important.' He had never worked at a desk in his life. Then it was the bath soaps, the little plastic-wrapped soaps. He was enchanted by them. Never seen them before."

"Never seen hotel bath soaps before?" I asked.

"Well, he'd never stayed in a hotel room before."

"Never in his life?"

"No. It was his first time. In the mornings he would make our beds. Finally I said, 'Daddy, you don't have to do that, the maids will do that for us.' He didn't know there was maid service in hotels."

"Wow, a real innocent."

"Exactly. I'd never seen innocence in my father before. To me he was always the authoritarian. He always told me how to do things. But it turned out he didn't even know how to tie a tie. I caught him standing at the mirror fumbling with it as we got ready for the first night's banquet with the delegation. Something was wrong."

"What, Daddy?" Jen asked him.

"I don't know how to do this," he said.

"You've never worn a tie?"

"When would I have worn a tie?"

It took half an hour for Jennifer to make his tie presentable. They agreed to buy him a clip-on the following day.

"I do not belong here," he said glumly.

"You do, too, Daddy. We were invited."

"*You* were invited."

"Daddy, you are a successful businessman."

"No," he corrected her. "I am just a cook."

"You must understand," Jen explained, "that shattered my heart to hear. My father was always such a proud man. And now, to see him *afraid*—when he had always made sure I was afraid of him. You must understand—whenever I spoke back to my parents, I was whipped with bamboo lashes on my butt and hands, or sometimes hit with a shoe. There were times I could not walk. Up until the age of twelve I was abused. This is just the way it's done in China. Sometimes I threatened to turn them in. 'They're going to come get you,' I would say, but I never did because I was afraid of being orphaned. I was scared of my father. Now to see fear in him . . ."

Fear that he would embarrass himself and his family. Fear the other delegates would see right through his tie and his suit jacket and know this poor man was no dignitary. *Why, this is no businessman! Look at his tie! Anyone can plainly tell—he's a cook! He sweats over a fryer sixteen hours a day!*

"I had never seen that vulnerability in my father," Jen said. "It was the beginning of learning that my father had feelings of his own, feelings that he had always been too proud to reveal."

James stirred from the couch, coming forward to pick up the story: "At the dinner, she was not the daughter I had known for twenty years.

All these dignitaries treated my daughter with such respect. She was so composed, so confident."

"She had turned into a lady," I concluded.

James nodded. Then he felt it important enough to offer, humbly, "I stood in back."

"He stood in back because he did not think he belonged," Jen clarified. "I had turned into a woman and he had turned into a little boy. That night was the first time he ever told me he was proud of me. But then, over the next few days, it was very interesting. Most of the dignitaries—though of Chinese heritage—had been born in California. As we moved through the provinces and into the villages, they started to feel like tourists in a strange land. They became insecure. But my father's confidence grew. He knew the language, he knew the country, he knew the mind-set of the people. He seemed so comfortable. There was a manhood about him that I'd never seen. He was reclaiming a dignity he'd lost. I'll never forget the day the Red Army came out to shake hands with everyone in the delegation. My father was so emotional. He left as a peasant rice farmer, and now the Red Army wanted to shake his hand. In that moment everything he had sacrificed for was finally recognized. There was a parade, and all these schoolgirls lined the street, yelling 'Welcome! Welcome!' in English. They were wearing the same red school dress I used to wear at their age. Then the delegation moved on, but we had arranged for a car to take us to our village."

Tai San is a tiny village, with only about a hundred people, and it had barely been touched by time. As their car rolled down the dirt road, children ran behind it, screaming.

"What did you think would happen?" I asked.

"We didn't know. We had told nobody we were coming. They had heard about the parade in the province but of course had no idea we were in the delegation. We thought we might just take a look around and go. You know, it could have been very disappointing, and we were ready for that. We didn't know who was alive, or who had moved away. Just like anybody goes back to their childhood house. It's mostly symbolic. In your heart, you know it's all changed. You know it's not going to be the way you left it."

"Did anyone recognize you?"

"Oh, it was so funny. They recognized Dad the second he stepped out of the car. They crowded around him, ecstatic, until I got out of the car. Then it was dead silence."

"Why?"

"They thought I was his mistress. They thought he had left his wife, and that was why he had never returned. They didn't recognize me. But then I said, in perfect dialect, 'I'm no mistress, I'm Louie Louie Wah.' That's my Chinese name. I was so in love with my father that moment, being cheered by our village, and for the first time I could really see how far he had come. I could see how much sacrifice it had taken to get us to where we were. There was a young woman there, a peasant girl, who looked at me in all my glamour with such envy, like she was seeing a movie star, but I was looking at her with envy to equal hers, craving what she had—simplicity, family. We wanted to trade places, and for a moment, I would have, if I could have had my dad with me like she had hers."

Then the entourage went walking up the road, taking in the village. Soon they were outside number 18, their house. There it was.

James asked the villagers, "Who lives there now?"

Everyone laughed.

"What's so funny?" he insisted.

"But *you* live there," he was told.

Surely that was not possible. Surely people had moved in, people had moved out, life had gone on? Surely the Party had transferred the house to another family?

"Oh no," he was told. "We wouldn't let them."

It had been seventeen years since he had even written anybody in the village a letter. James was dumbfounded by their loyalty.

"I'm sure everything inside has been taken," he suggested to his longtime neighbors. For doubtless, in a village this poor, all the clothing and furniture would have found better use in someone else's home.

"See for yourself," he was told.

James asked who had the key.

Nobody knew.

James knew.

A moment later he was in the village machine shop, where his best friend was making bolts. They embraced, tried to get over the shock, and another moment later James had the skeleton key in the door to number 18. He and Jen entered alone.

There was dust everywhere. James pulled back the curtains to let in the light.

"*Nothing had been touched,*" Jen remembered. "It was all there. The pots from the hooks, the clothes in the drawers, the altar of photographs. I was shaking. It was—it was like a dream."

James went right to the altar and bowed three times to his mother.

"I'm home, Mom."

Jen looked at the photo he was bowing to, and to her surprise, it was like looking in a mirror. Her grandmother—whom she'd never met—looked just like her. So young.

"Daddy," she asked him, "how old was your mother when she died?"

"The same age you are right now," he answered.

She was shaking.

"Daddy, why did the villagers think I was your mistress?"

"They didn't really think that."

"Yes they did. I heard them say it. I heard the women whisper, 'Just like his father.' "

"My mother died of a broken heart," he said. "When she washed Dad's clothes, she'd find letters and photos from other women. I heard these stories growing up. Mom died when I was only one year old. You are all I ever had of her. I never knew my mother."

I never knew my mother.

For Jen, this was an unbearable confession to receive. Because while Jen knew this fact, had picked it up through osmosis, she'd never heard her dad mention it. Her dad's long silence had implied he did not recognize it as material. His long silence had always suggested such things simply didn't matter. But now she knew that *he knew*—he had known all along, and he had suffered silently, stoically. Jen had grown up believing her father simply didn't have an emotional inner life. For twenty years his pain hid behind this proud façade.

"My father—" James went on, "my father did not leave with my sister and brother when I was nine years old. He actually left right after Mom died. He went to Hong Kong. He came back when I was four, for a while, and then again when I was nine. He was going to take me to America. At the last minute I was scratched, because I was not old enough to work. I was left behind by a father I never knew. I waited to be sent for. I did not understand why it took so long. Why, why did it take so long for my dad to send for me? He was sending money, he was doing well, why did he not send for me? Why did he not come for me? Why, why did it take so long?"

James looked at his daughter, who was unable to control her tears.

"Now I know," he said sadly. "Now I understand. For it has taken me every bit as long."

James removed the wood panel. Then the brick. His arm snaked down into the wormhole.

Out came the two compact cases.

Jen remembered, "There was a huge smile on my father's face. It was the first smile I had ever seen on him. He was so excited. That it was still there. Despite years and years and years of neglect, it was still there, still perfect, wrapped in silk."

He thumbed the jewelry, momentarily that boy again, then removed the bracelet that had belonged to his mother's mother. He gestured for Jen to extend her wrist.

"This, my daughter, this is for you."

Despite years and years and years of neglect, it was still there, perfect.

We have all lost something along the way. And we've moved on. There's no point going back for it. We're surviving just fine without it. So much pain has shattered it to dust, surely. If not, someone has stolen it, surely. Put it to other use. Besides, we've tried before to get it back and never made progress. Why dig up all that guilt? Why provoke old animosities? We simply don't have the energy for it. We have all lost something along the way.

These things happen.

It's been shattered.

We're not sure if it ever was really there in the first place.

But maybe—just maybe—in that place in our souls where the roads are still dirt, and where the houses are still cement and cinder, and the paint has long ago peeled from the door, under all that dust, despite years and years of neglect, it is still there, waiting for us, perfect. Waiting for us to let it out.

I'm reminded of a passage from a book that once helped me through my divorce. I was a wreck. I absolutely believed that I was ruined, tainted, broken for good. I would never really be able to love anyone again. Then I found this book about Buddhism, and I stumbled onto a single page that has never failed since to soothe me. The passage insisted that believing we are broken is a mistaken perception of our true nature. We are all, it went on, inherently virtuous and noble, but time covers us with layers and layers of experience. We often act badly, for the world is confusing. And we are often hurt, because others get confused, too. And when we look in the mirror—when we build a mental image of ourselves—we see only these layers upon layers. We conclude, *I am not a good person,* or *I have been hurt very badly.* But we are mistaken. This is not our true nature. Inside us all, under all those layers, despite years and years of neglect, there is still a virtuous and noble person, waiting to be let out. We don't *become* good people. We simply cease, slowly, to be deluded by the layers.

That page—just two paragraphs I'd underlined, really—became my calm in the storm. It reminded me that the start of a better life was not out there somewhere, out there in the freak-show universe of spiritual guides, but rather, that the start of a better life was my own goodness, and *it was already inside me.* It had been there all along, under all those layers. Waiting for me. I just had to calm down, stop looking everywhere else for answers, and start letting it out.

I do not mean to turn this true story of the Louies into a parable. I'm not suggesting we all need to take a trip with our dad, or that we all need to be more devoted to our parents, or that our families all need to kiss and make up, because that's not going to happen. This is about each of us and our core beliefs. This is about choosing the principles upon which we build our lives. This is about what we find meaningful enough to devote ourselves to. This is about what we find fundamentally essential. With stakes this high, isn't it worth considering that we have let our bad experiences cloud out the good ones; that we might treat one another badly, but we are still good people; that there is an emotional inner life inside each of us no matter what we see on the outside, and that culture and poverty and hardship explain a lot of what happened?

Is it possible that it's waiting for us, still there, perfect?

No sooner was the story told than the Louies wanted to retell it. They insisted I come back the following week.

Spread out on the glass coffee table were maybe fifty photographs, most of them reprints of old photos from the altar and drawers in Tai

San. Jen had another fifty of the trip in a plastic ziplock bag, and then a few from high school and college. We went through them again.

Jen was afraid she had not communicated how hard it was on all of them. "You must understand, my parents left every morning at six A.M. for their restaurant, and did not return until eleven-thirty P.M. They both worked two shifts a day to avoid hiring more workers. Every afternoon and evening I babysat my brother and cousin. I missed my parents terribly. I wrote in my journal that I had been orphaned. I was not allowed to go to movies or dances. Instead, my brother and I were sent out to gather bottles and cans for recycling, digging through public trash cans. The only times I saw my parents, they were yelling at me for what I'd done wrong, or yelling at each other. I told them to get a divorce. They told me I think like a white girl. But they fought constantly, usually over money."

James spoke, and Jen gave me the gist of it. "My parents," she explained, "believed in two opposing Chinese values. My mother believed in saving for the future, for a house and college tuition, so she sewed us clothes, which we refused to wear. My father believed in maintaining face, so if we kids needed new clothes from Macy's to fit in, so be it. He was proud and wanted to be seen as taking care of his family. These Chinese values were in a permanent clash."

Jen added her own memory to her father's analysis. "The biggest fight I ever saw was when Dad bought jumbo shrimp for my brother's birthday, to spoil us, when we didn't even have money for new shoes."

After this, there was a shame in the room. The past had returned, slipped in the back door. Jen chased it away with another story. "You must understand, I never had respect for my parents' relationship. I wanted romantic love, not what they had. Theirs was not a marriage, it was a merger. Mom and Dad were matched not because they had longed for each other from afar, but because Dad's father was in San Francisco and Mom's father was in Canada. Their marriage was a ticket out of communism. They stuck together, building a life together as equal partners. Since our trip to China, the biggest change has not been my relationship with my father. It's been Dad and Mom finally falling in love. That dignity he recovered there, he brought it home. That manhood about him, he came home with that. The confidence. He started to be openly affectionate with her. Every night he rubbed her shoulders and feet with Chinese therapeutic oils. He treated her with an old-fashioned chivalry you don't see in modern men. Most children watch their parents grow out of love. I've watched mine grow into it. I used to never want a relationship like my parents'. I wanted a glamorous life. Now I want exactly what they have."

The next day Jennifer called. She was frustrated at not having gotten something right—it was left unspoken, perhaps implied, but it should be articulated just to be sure. It was humbling to go to China. It was humbling to behold that kind of loyalty and devotion. She thought she "got" what loyalty and devotion were, but this was on another scale. Imagine, these poor villagers, taking care of the Louies' house for twenty years, when they had not heard from the family for seventeen. Out of loyalty to her dad. And to see her dad in front of his mother's photograph—to see he'd been devoted for nearly fifty years to a woman he'd never known other than in that photograph. Jen laughs at her own foolishness, to think she ever presumed to know what devotion was. Her parents were willing to wait thirty years for the love to enter their marriage. It was so humbling, so *calming,* so reassuring. She realized she could never drive her parents away. She realized nothing she ever did would truly cause them to give up on her. For they knew mountains. She thought she knew mountains but no, oh no, she did not. *They* knew mountains, nothing like she had ever seen.

Do we need

to have been taught

what love is to give it

to someone else?

The Trial

Rosa Gonzalez, at home, in Mesa, Arizona.

Here's the most noteworthy thing to remember about Rosa Gonzalez: *She never wanted children.* She never got that basic imprint of motherly love, what some might call that "childbearing gene." Her life, as she forecast it, just wasn't going to involve needy toddlers. She wasn't even a very good aunt. She held her siblings' babies only when forced, and they unfailingly burst into tears in Rosa's awkward arms.

Now, there are cities full of professional women and men who wholeheartedly echo this feeling. They go around saying things like *I'm too selfish to be a mother,* or *I'm not a baby person,* or my favorite, *I love my life too much to do that to it.* A friend of mine calls them the Petrified Forest—people who would freeze their life in time if they could. "Manhattan's turning into a Petrified Forest," my friend mocked. I winced when she said this, because I used to be one of them. When the Petrified Forest imagines parenthood, their hearts are flooded with the feeling of doors closing, not opening. If you ask, many will explain that their own mothers had to put up with too much—the mothers' lives seemed *compromised, underattained.* A smaller group will confess that they admired their fathers more than their mothers. While motherhood is still revered in places to the north, south, east, and west of the big cities, within those cities a career has become the metric by which a woman's life is often measured. In London or Los Angeles a woman who manages to be a good mother *and* have a progressive career is put on a pedestal by her friends and worshiped as a demigod. For a moment, the Petrified Forest swoons. But then the evidence is tabulated. Every account is weighed—every account of sleep deprivation, diminished sex life, a promotion passed over, and social events missed. The Petrified

Forest sits like a jury, considering the facts, making their calculations, collecting more evidence. In our society today, parenthood is on trial.

But can those analytical calculations ever truly account for the experience between a parent and a child?

Few in the Petrified Forest would imagine that their fear was once shared by a poor Mexican girl in a Texas border town. But Rosa did not go through their extensive calculations. What she knew was this: She was the youngest of eight siblings; her father was sixty-five when she was born. Her mother was forty-four. They'd met at the copper smelter as migrant workers. Later, Rosa's mother treated her mental illness with heroin and alcohol. Her father doted on his only daughter, but when he died at seventy, Rosa's mother went off the deep end. When Rosa was seven, she ended up in her oldest brother's care. She learned to call her brother "Dad" and her sister-in-law "Mom." She cried a lot. *Other than that,* it was a completely normal tough childhood, in a very family-oriented town. In their neighborhood of El Paso, everyone wanted to have kids. By the time they hit puberty, most girls had names for their future children picked out. Most had put a few of those names to use by their mid-teens. So Rosa *really* felt like she didn't fit in.

It was beyond Rosa's horizon to dream of a career or an education. She didn't fully know those things existed. But there was a girl down the road, on the other side of the street, who would invite Rosa over and offer to comb her hair when Rosa was little. She was nineteen, the only girl on the block over the age of fifteen without a baby. What she did have was something Rosa had never seen anywhere else: a really nice mirror dresser, wood stained blond with a thick glass top on which sat combs and brushes and bottles of perfume, perfectly organized. A long jewelry box with three smoothly gliding drawers sat beside a round tub of after-bath powder. Oh, it was nice. It was heavenly. Something about this dresser—the thing you could have if you didn't have children—hinted to Rosa about all the things out there in the larger world. The dresser was a portal to the unimaginable. Rosa loved to sit there, having her hair combed, pretending a dresser like this would someday be hers.

That says everything about the kind of world young Rosa lived in: A mere dresser symbolized the good life. Not a fancy car, not a big home, not a college diploma. A glass-topped dresser.

Children, no, but love, yes. Well, if not love, then sex. It was for sex that Rosa married for the first time, at nineteen. Soon after they were married her husband hit her, busting her lip; the next time he came after her, she jumped up on the bed, announced, "Come on, death match!" and dared him to get in the ring. The marriage was over in less than six months.

At twenty-three she met David Gonzalez at the Texas Instruments plant in Dallas, where she handled a soldering gun as an electrical repair technician. He soon proposed. Vince was an accident. Rosa went home to visit her sister-in-law mother that Christmas, and Rosa left her birth control pills at home because she didn't want her mom to know she was having sex before marriage. When Rosa returned to Dallas, she had to wait a couple of weeks before going back on the pill. They took a chance anyway.

They moved their wedding plans forward, marrying a month later at Little Church of the West in Las Vegas.

Rosa's pregnancy was complicated. It turned out that rather than having two kidneys, hers were joined at the top—a single kidney shaped like a horseshoe. This malformed kidney couldn't filter the doubled volume of blood in the late stages of pregnancy, so her baby was yanked out two months prematurely. David named their son after Vince Ferragamo, the quarterback for the Los Angeles Rams. Rosa's family gathered in the hospital corridors to discuss what to do. "How can Rosa be a mother?" they asked. "We all know she is no good with kids. Does she have any idea what she's gotten herself into?" The doctors noticed this, too. Rosa was not a natural with babies, to put it kindly. Before they let her take Vince home, they made her work two eight-hour shifts in the intensive care unit to learn how to handle a newborn.

By all accounts, Vince was a hyper and relentless toddler who never gave anyone quiet time. Babysitters quit on Rosa routinely. Vince was extremely sensitive to fabrics. He chewed the collars on his shirts. He was so lacking in hand-eye coordination that he fell off chairs. And Rosa, having so little experience with kids, didn't realize any of this was abnormal. She found solutions. She took him to the mall, where he could run around. She developed a way to get her distracted little boy to pay attention: She touched her face every time she said his name. With a touch of her face, he would settle briefly, and she could communicate an instruction. Whenever they went to someone else's house, they sat in the car beforehand and rehearsed what to do inside, how to adjust to the new environment. She never disciplined him in public, but that meant she left a lot of half-full grocery carts in the Safeway aisle in order to drive home immediately. No book instructed her to do this; it just seemed the best way to handle it. Motherhood was turning out to be pretty much what she'd expected it would be—incredibly hard and thankless work. Rosa was strung out and often at her wit's end. But she loved her son; they learned together. She kept on touching her face. She and David chose to have a second child, and this baby, a girl, was significantly easier. They assumed it was the difference between boys and girls.

One day, when Vince was in second grade at Beasley Elementary School, Rosa was called in for a "conference," which turned out to be more of an ambush. She was ganged up on by the school principal, the school counselor, Vince's teacher, and his teacher from first grade. All of them sat on one side of a long conference table. They did not let Rosa take a seat on the other side of the table. Instead, they offered her a chair on the other side of the room. A shrimpy second-grade plastic resin chair with metal legs. They put her in that chair, her knees nearly to her chin. The court had convened, and Rosa was on trial.

She will never forget the insult of that chair.

Here, Mom, this is what we think of you. You get the kiddie chair.

The intimidation was intentional.

We know better than you.

"We're going to move Vince down," they said. "He's in a Level Three program for math and English. We're going to move him down to Level Four. Special ed. It's really for the best. He's really got problems."

To which Rosa said angrily, "So why am I here? If you're going to go ahead and do this, why have you called me off work? Why have you not already done it?"

"Mrs. Gonzalez, he can't concentrate. He stares out the window. He falls out of his chair. He can't look his teachers in the eye."

She did not back down. "What I asked was, *Why am I here?*"

Reluctantly, they gave her an answer. "Because you need to okay it. You need to sign the transfer."

Rosa sat there, stewing in her anger. *You think because I speak more Spanish than English, I am just going to roll over?* she thought. *You think because I work in a factory, and because I am not educated like you—you think because there are four of you and only one of me—you think because I am down here by the floor, and you are up there on your pedestal, I am just going to say, "Okay, you must know best"?*

"My son is smart," she insisted.

"Something's wrong with him," they said. Then, rudely, "He's very emotional. Is there something going on at home? Are you by chance pregnant?"

She let that one pass, but not easily. "He needs to be challenged," Rosa answered sincerely, expressing what she believed.

"He disrupts the class. He belongs with other kids like him."

Rosa stood up. She rose up from that kiddie chair and gathered herself defiantly. "No," she said resolutely. "I am his mother, and the answer is no." *I dare you to get in the ring with me!*

Rosa called Baylor Medical Center to ask for help. They sent her to Easter Seals, which was testing children for disabilities. Her seven-year-old was put in a room behind a one-way mirror and presented a series of cognitive exercises including arranging blocks, putting pegs in holes, and drawing a copy of a simple line illustration. The whole time, he had his parka pulled up over his head, zipped high, and he looked out through the tunnel of his parka collar at the far wall. He was utterly unable to sit still. Arms akimbo. To the doctors who know these things, Vince's brain dysfunction was blatant: He had severe ADHD, attention deficit/hyperactivity disorder.

ADHD is a highly controversial disorder. Ritalin (and drugs like it) are often administered to children with borderline symptoms who have been "diagnosed" by teachers or parents, not doctors, and the cavalier reliance on drugs has drawn criticism. As a consequence, those with severe symptoms, such as Vince, end up being looked at skeptically. There is, in the air, a suspicion that ADHD is an excuse, not a condition.

Rosa and David Gonzalez did not want this label on their son. To them, he was just a kid being a kid. They didn't want the principal of Beasley Elementary to see the Easter Seals results. They didn't want anyone to have that ammunition to use against their son.

"It was my absolute lowest point," Rosa remembered. "It really pushed me off the ledge I'd been clinging to for so long. *Nobody* wants their kid labeled."

Did she ever worry that somehow she was responsible for her son's behavior?

"Plenty of other people blamed me. I was too busy defending myself. But I did wonder if I could blame it on a chemical in his brain."

Yet if there was a treatment for Vince, how could she deny it to him?

Indeed, she asked herself, *If my son had diabetes, wouldn't I give him insulin?*

Didn't she want her son to learn to catch a ball?

Didn't she want her son to be able to stand with his feet together without falling over like a board stood on end?

Didn't she want him to learn?

Didn't she want him to stop eating his clothing?

Rosa and David gave Vince the Ritalin during the school years, not in the summers. "I wanted him to deal with it," Rosa said. "Now I know how cruel that was. He needed it all the time, of course. But it was *so* controversial back then. No mother wants to have to make this choice."

"Did the drugs make much difference?" I asked.

"Some. He was still up at five-thirty every morning. To guide him through his evenings and mornings, we had checklists and special blue binders. I gave up on him picking up his room. Oh, I tried it all."

Symptoms include: constant night terrors.

Solutions include: applying "magic" lotion that makes them go away.

Symptoms include: inability to get dressed.

Solutions include: setting clothes out on floor in shape of a person the night before.

Symptoms include: saying hurtful things to other kids.

Solutions include: scripting "nice" phrases.

Symptoms include: perpetual lateness.

Solutions include: warm towels, chores set to timers, rewards.

She tried it all. She went to support groups. She took Vince to neurologists. They told Rosa that if she could just hang in there, Vince would likely grow out of it. Would he ever, really?

Many parents of children with severe ADHD, as well as parents of children with other disabilities, develop not so much a different *kind* of parenting as a different *level* of parenting. A different intensity. They do the same things as regular parents, but a lot more frequently. If parenting is a 24/7 responsibility, then parenting a child with a disability is a 60/60/24/7 responsibility. They are on call every second of every hour. They never take their eyes off the child. They come up with solutions—language, games, goals. They reinforce what they said a thousand times before. They parent an eight-year-old like they might a three-year-old. Parents get so overwhelmed, they run out of steam. Many are on the verge of simply giving up on their kid. They're desperate to know if there's a light at the end of the tunnel. *Will my child truly be better for all this effort I'm putting out—or is that just something I want to believe?*

Symptoms include: utter hopelessness.

Solutions include: prayer, shopping.

Symptoms include: marriage strain.

Solutions include: counseling, eating.

Symptoms include: anger.

Solutions include: tutors, hiring attorneys to fight schools.

Rosa had survived her father dying, her mother going crazy, her first husband bloodying her lip, her son being unexpected, her son being premature, her son being hyperactive—now she would have to fight the school system. Her son needed all sorts of inventive systems just to make it through the nights and mornings at home, but what he really needed was to be pushed at school—to be challenged by his teachers. To be in the hardest classes. He was smart—*she knew it*—that was the only thing he had going for him.

Once her son was labeled, every new situation was a reenactment of that trial at Beasley Elementary School. Every teacher, every school, every summer program. Rosa did not give up. She kept on touching her face, grabbing Vince's attention, using that special bond to steer him in the right direction. Eventually, around his sophomore year of high school, his D grades suddenly turned into A's, he was moved into the honors classes, and he began working with autistic children. He was appointed to the youth legislature of the National Hispanic Institute, where he was urged to consider great things. By that, the mentors meant something tougher than the community college Vince planned to attend. He listened. A year ago he graduated summa cum laude from Arizona State with a degree in religious studies. The ceremony was held in the late morning at the campus basketball arena. Rosa and David and their daughter, Bonnie, stood in the stands, surrounded by family and friends. Rosa soaked a lot of tissues. *Summa Cum Laude!* With Highest Praise. That was a label she didn't mind.

Rosa had always believed her son had it in him. She just hadn't always believed that she had it in *her.* It took her twenty-two years to discover that she had been a great mother all along. Twenty-two years to find out maybe you don't *have* to start with a desire to be a mother, maybe you don't *have* to be experienced with kids, maybe you don't *have* to have had someone show you how to love. Maybe you just need to give yourself a chance to grow into the role.

The decision to be a parent is a personal one. Nobody should intrude on that process of discernment. But it is a mistake to assume that the decision can be reckoned with tools of analysis—with a scorecard—when it is fundamentally a mystical experience.

Rosa wishes she'd had a chance at more in her life. She worked, she raised two children, and she remained married to the same man. She wishes she had another purpose in addition to her children. Her whole family wishes that for her. They wish she did not have to struggle through so much. But life gave her *this* chance, and she ran with it.

Rosa did not just develop into a great mother for her own children. She helped kids in the neighborhood get through their gang problems, suicide attempts, drug addictions, and comings out of the closet. "Every one of my friends considers her a mother for them," Vince assured me. "My mom is an irrepressibly lonely person who will always want children, always want to give parts of herself away. She cries at a light breeze. She has a heart bigger than her chest. *Everybody* is her child. My sister and I just have good seats in the auditorium."

Three months after graduation, it was time for Vince to move on. David took him to IHOP for breakfast while Rosa helped pack the Budget truck. David bought him an atlas; Rosa bought him a cooler packed with high-energy cola. His girlfriend's parents came over. Everyone cried, and then Vince got in the truck, girlfriend beside him, and they waved good-bye.

They moved to Chicago, where they found a small apartment off Des Plaines Avenue in Forest Park—suburban Chicago. The el rattled along behind their building. Vince came to Chicago to continue his work with autistic children, only to discover his Arizona certification was not valid in Illinois. He landed at the local Olive Garden. This was good for him; the grind of busing tables forced him to admit a few things. First, that he wanted to marry his girlfriend; they were soon engaged. Second, that he really wanted to be a religious scholar, and so he would be. The day after we met in Chicago, he flew to Israel to study Hebrew for eight weeks. Then his mom flew to Chicago, and the three of them—Vince, his fiancée, and his mother—drove to Atlanta, where Vince began the master's program in Jewish mysticism at Emory University.

Vince Gonzalez, on the morning before his trip to Israel.

Any parent would be proud to have Vince as a son. He is discerning, never unthinking. He is remarkably willing to peer into the mysteries of human experience. Not a day is taken for granted. He is not interested in shortcuts. There is an integrity to the way he engages with life.

Though studying Jewish mysticism, Vince has not converted to Judaism, and in fact he is not affiliated with any religion at all. "I am to religions as an auto mechanic is to cars," he explained. He works on them all. He is interested in the question of how different people throughout history have experienced God—"What is God if you're a thirteenth-century Spanish Jew, versus a twentieth-century California New Ager?" Articulating people's spiritual experiences will be the thrust of his research at Emory.

His skillful analysis made me wonder whether his interest was entirely intellectual—did *he* actually believe in God? To answer this, Vince shared a story from the Book of Acts, of when Paul traveled through Greece. The Athenians built temples and made sacrifices to many gods; they even built altars to nameless gods, sort of a pagan Player To Be Named Later, to make sure the yet-to-be-discovered gods would not be angry with them for being ignored. Paul stumbled across one of these altars, inscribed TO AN UNKNOWN GOD, and was fascinated by it. When he reached Athens, Paul claimed that it was their Unknown God who made the world. It was from their Unknown God that all things—life and breath—came to us. (This idea appealed to the Athenians, but Paul later lost the crowd when he brought up resurrection.)

Vince now makes his prayers to an Unknown God. He does not name this God, or claim it under a religion, as Paul did. Rather, the appeal is in admitting *it is unknowable;* it cannot be defined one way for all. "If there were a being out there, it makes sense that this being would be interpreted six billion ways by six billion people." Thus the thirteenth-century Spanish Jew interprets God differently from the twentieth-century New Ager—but they are both experiencing the same unknowable God. Vince draws a parallel between the way an autistic child experiences his teachers and the way we experience God. The autistic child spends most of his life in a haze of distraction. Now and then a teacher or parent gets through, and for a brief moment this child feels gloriously in touch with a higher power who seems to know everything. In this same way, we experience God. We get moments. Not miracles, but moments where God simply seems to be saying, *Pay attention.* Lately, God has been saying this a lot to him.

"The gods speak a language to which we are all autistic," Vince summarized eloquently.

Imagine being the mother of this child. Imagine being a forty-seven-year-old Spanish-speaking Mexican American woman, a factory girl whose parents were migrant workers in El Paso—imagine you're Rosa Gonzalez, and this is your son: He is speaking like a prophet, using big English words, making free-form extrapolations and radical theoretical connections. He is engaged to be married, he has direction, he pays his bills. He is not out drunk in the bars, or standing on street corners, or sleepwalking through life. He is all this, and he is only twenty-three. Rosa is thinking one thing: *He came from me? I made something this beautiful?*

It makes you wonder.

It made *me* wonder how Vince got so interested in spiritual experience in the first place. Was there a teacher at school? Did Mom drag him to church a lot? Did he read a particular book? But it was nothing so secondhand as that.

"Oh, I have had spiritual experiences my whole life," he answered.

"Your whole life?"

"Oh yes. Ever since I was a little kid."

"Those 'moments,' as you describe?"

"Precisely."

I was a little surprised, because Rosa had not mentioned her son's spiritual experiences. Not once, in some sixteen hours of interviews. How could Vince have been having spiritual experiences his whole life, and his mom—with whom he was extremely close—not know about it? For some reason, that old trick question popped into my head: A man and his son were in an automobile accident. The man died on the way to the hospital, but the boy was rushed into surgery. The emergency room surgeon said, "I can't operate, that's my son!" How is this possible?

The surgeon was his mother.

I saw on Vince's face a smile of recognition.

Before he left Arizona, Vince gave his mother a book. In the frontispiece of that book he wrote a note. In the middle was this phrase: "Remember, mundanity can be elevated to art by perception alone."

Vince knew his mother had been concerned about her appearance lately, as well as concerned about how her appearance reflected on her life. Vince wanted her to know what he thought—he was reminding her that her life was beautiful, that she was art, that she was beautiful, and later in the letter he said exactly that.

We all have a choice whether to see the mundane or to see the beauty.

Most of the time, our family life is dangerously mundane. Most of the time, we are in the living room, plopped on the couch, and it all seems pointlessly ordinary. Now and then we get flashes—we feel tapped into a very intense parallel universe of unbearable feeling. But we do not hang out in that state of connected grace for very long. We tend to forget about it. We are back to the living room couch. We ask,

What is it all for? So we could sit on the couch together doing nothing particularly significant?

Do not be fooled by those incredibly ordinary stretches into believing it is not something profound. Do not be fooled into forgetting about the special moments.

We all undergo this trial. We are all tested by this very situation. Routinely. The routineness of this test is part of its trick.

What Rosa remembers about her son's childhood is being at wit's end, thinking she could take it no more, feeling perpetually out of steam. She remembers it being a grind she could not escape.

But Vince remembers it in a different way. He perceived something else entirely. This is what he was trying to tell me; this is what it was like for him:

"I have had spiritual experiences my whole life."

The child spends most of his life in a haze of distraction. Now and then a parent gets through, and for a brief moment this child feels gloriously in touch with a higher power.

Rosa is touching her face. "Vince."

We get moments.

God is tapping his shoulder. "Vince, pay attention."

The surgeon is his mother.

God speaks a language to which we are all autistic.

It's all a blur. Then:

"Vince. Vince."

This is important. Pay attention.

Don't be fooled.

What is God, to a seven-year-old hyperactive boy running circles in a mall?

Is that God really unknown?

For much of our lives we have all been that boy, distracted and confused by all the incredible opportunities, wondering what to make of our lives, tossed around by endlessly shifting circumstance, hopping restlessly, flickering like a candle in an open window, processing our calculations—until someone who loves us comes along and says, "Hey, I need you."

For this, we should thank them.

Let us take a lesson in finding purpose from an orphan girl who just wanted a glass-topped dresser.

Let us take a lesson in perception from her twenty-three-year-old son.

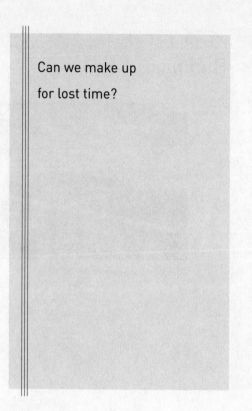

Can we make up

for lost time?

Bumpkin

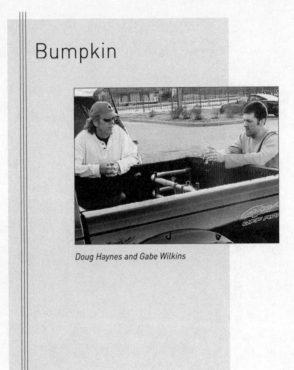

Doug Haynes and Gabe Wilkins

The Ozarks don't quite reach as far north as St. Louis, or as far west as Tulsa, or as far south as Little Rock, or as far east as Memphis. They are a place best reached by car or bus, and the drive is through dense, shady forests of sycamore, silver maple, sweet gum, and oak. Occasionally you'll pass scenic lakes created by electricity dams on the White and Black rivers. Many of the people you meet can proudly tell you the exact population of their towns, quoting numbers like "4,321" (Carl Junction) and "2,261" (Horseshoe Bend). Some other telling statistics: In the rural counties, the population is often 95 percent white, with per capita income around fifteen thousand dollars annually. Ten percent of residents might have a college degree. People in the Ozarks get married *and* get divorced at nearly double the national rate. The way to a better life does not necessarily involve moving north or south to a big city to get an education. Ozarkers don't have a culture or tradition of migration. They are as planted as the sycamores. Hardship is persistent and passed down like a surname. A better life, to them, means giving yourself over to the Lord and letting Jesus redeem you from your sins. The region is the epicenter of conservative Christian fundamentalism. Springfield, Missouri, was once dubbed "the buckle of the Bible Belt." Church offers hope where hope is hard to find. In this way, religion and poverty are interlocked as the constructive and destructive forces acting on people and their families.

The western descent of the Ozarks is anchored by a former lead-mining town of forty-six thousand people named Joplin, Missouri. Joplin is where Doug Haynes and Gabe Wilkins hail from.

Doug is Gabe's biological father, though for fourteen years Gabe didn't even know that Doug existed.

There are parts of this story that make Doug squirm, parts that took him a year to completely own up to with me. For a long time he's had to live with his shame, and the thing about shame is, it doesn't really wane. No matter how you might have redeemed yourself—no matter how many good deeds you have stacked up to counterbalance what you once did—the shame of it is still scorching hot. The better a man you've become, the more godawful it sounds hearing what you once did. Once it's out, you'd like to do nothing but crawl under a rock. Shame has dragged many a life right back down. For this reason, most men run from their shame and run from anything that might remind them of it. It is extremely hard to stand straight and own up to your mistakes and believe you still have the authority to discuss how anyone should live his life. So I respect Doug Haynes. I've come to respect him for a lot of reasons, but let's start with this one: He has owned up to his mistake.

It happened when Doug was eighteen. He met Wendy at their Southern Baptist church group and fell for her instantly. She was getting out of a bad marriage, but wasn't out yet. Both were very active in the evangelical wing of their church, which had prepared them only to avoid this very situation, not to deal with it. Doug was shocked when his friends—even his pastor—told him to pretend the baby wasn't his, wasn't his problem. This angered Doug. It bewildered him.

Since Wendy was not yet divorced when the baby was born, her husband was listed as the father on the birth certificate. That was just a convenience—everybody knew. Everybody, that is, but the boy. Wendy gave Doug more than a fair chance. They loved each other as much as two nineteen-year-olds can. Yes, they were young, and yes, the situation was chaotic, but she was willing to make it work. She wanted Doug to marry her. Doug worked at the cheese-processing plant, which provided a steady paycheck but not enough upside to properly support a family. "I was just an Ozark bumpkin," he said. "You know, *white trash.*" But by all accounts he was also a spiritually hungry young man and a fair observer of people, an otherwise good kid way in over his head. When Doug looks back at that time, he wishes there had been a stable man in his life to steer him right. That's all it would have taken. His dad, a trucker, had died when Doug was nine. His mom was protective of her son and didn't think Wendy was good enough for him. So Doug waffled.

Wendy put up with Doug's indecision for about two years. She let Doug play with the baby now and then, even let him take the baby out to the country one weekend.

"My heart wanted to be with Wendy and Gabe," he said forlornly, looking back at his inaction. "But there were a lot of people back then telling me that what we had done was simply not right, and the professed 'right' thing to do was to stop the relationship, not continue it. That was the atmosphere all around us. I did not think Wendy and I really had a chance of succeeding under those circumstances.

"For years I have blamed the people around me. But the truth is, part of me just said, *No thanks.* I didn't want the responsibility of real fatherhood and marriage. I was not able to step up to the plate. I only admitted this to myself recently. Saying it to you makes me feel really tiny. But it's important for me to be honest."

"Would you have married Wendy if not for Gabe?" I asked. "Was it taking care of a little kid that scared you off?"

"That's a fair question, but I have never asked myself that. I always thought of them as a pair, to tell you the truth. I still do."

Doug and Wendy remained friendly. Doug paid child support—it wasn't much, but it was the figure they had agreed upon. At church and at picnics, Doug watched the toddler grow into a little boy. It killed him to keep his distance, but he respected Wendy's reasoning—being a boy's parent is an all-or-nothing deal. Wendy wasn't going to let any guy break her son's heart by being an intermittent figure. Eventually she met another man and married him quickly, craving stability. At that point, she refused Doug's child support and asked Doug not to come around anymore, per her husband's wishes. This sent Doug into a depression, which he hadn't seen coming. He thought he'd just been liberated from a load of problems. He figured he'd been cut free. Instead, he was saddled with regret and confusion. He kept slugging it out at the factory, cutting wheels of cheese into blocks for grocery stores. He attended church every Wednesday night and twice on Sunday. He had a reliable job, and he had his faith, but his soul was in turmoil. Yet he did not see what he could do about it.

Several years later Doug pulled into the parking lot of a convenience store outside Joplin. Wendy happened to pull up at the same time. She looked good, as always. Seeing her gave him a lift. Gabe sat in her backseat, playing with the window crank. He was six years old. His blond hair was trimmed into a pageboy and he still had some baby fat.

Wendy had news for Doug. Her husband had signed up with the navy. They were packing that day to move to Tennessee for basic training. When he'd completed it, they could be shipped anywhere. Her husband didn't want her in touch with Doug, so she would not write or call. She delivered this news tenderly, aware it was hard to handle. There was not a drop of animosity between them, just a gallon of regret.

"I guess this is it, then," Doug mustered. He stepped over to Gabe. "You've sure gotten big. I bet you're strong, too. Why don't you give me a big hug to show me how strong you are? C'mon, show me how hard you can squeeze."

Gabe, unaware this was his own father talking to him, believed Doug was an old friend of Mom's who hadn't been around for a couple of years. Being a polite kid, he stepped out, put his arms around Doug, and squeezed forcefully.

Doug hugged him back. "Yup, you're sure strong, all right."

Gabe climbed back in the car.

"Take care of yourself, Doug," Wendy offered. She turned over the engine and pulled out, heading in the direction of town.

Doug watched from the parking lot, his long lanky body wilting against his car, reaching a new depth of helplessness, wondering how it had come to this.

"It was hard to deal with," he recalled, his eyes wetting with the memory. "You see, I was never okay with not being his father openly, and in fact it still sticks in my craw that her first husband was put on the birth certificate. But at least during those first six years I knew where he was. Now, not only did my son not know who I was, *I would never know where he was.* If I thought it was hard before, I was wrong. I had created my own hell."

The absence of Gabe became a black hole. "Every single day, I wondered where he was, if he was happy, if he was safe. Had he had any bad accidents? Any health problems? Had he been abused or mistreated? Was he suffering in any way? Was he getting through school okay? Did he need me? Or—a very real possibility—was he better off without me?"

Seven years went by, but during those seven years the constant sorrow had a transformative effect on Doug's life. Pain opened his heart and made him ready to learn. Realizing he was going nowhere fast, he left the cheese factory after eight years there, and at twenty-seven began freshman college classes. He painted houses in his free time, pocketed fifty bucks a week manning the register at a convenience store, and bunked at his mom's. He earned his bachelor's degree in four years from Missouri Southern, but equally important, he grew confident in his own intelligence and competence. After college he drove a delivery truck for a year. That stiffened his resolve to keep pushing himself. By the age of thirty-three he had completed a year of law school at the University of Texas at Austin, and was beginning his second.

But he couldn't study. He simply couldn't concentrate. When he stared at the casebooks the words turned to a jumble. He decided to clear his head by taking a walk. Being in Texas, and this being early September with temperatures in the mid-nineties, he went for his walk at the Barton Creek Square—a mall.

The mall was crowded. Kids of all ages were shopping for back-to-school clothes. Wait, what was that? In a herd of junior high boys, Doug saw a face—blond hair, green eyes, nose beginning to hook down— *Naw, can't be.* He stopped, looked again. *Naw, he's too thin.* Doug shook it off and continued strolling. Gabe could be here, or he could be anywhere. *Wait, there—nope.* Getting out of that car, coming out of that store, face after face, so many faces, so many kids, so many voices, each one mapped to his memory of that six-year-old boy in the backseat of his mom's car. In every one of those kids, Doug saw *need*. They wore their needs on the outside, as visibly as new duds. They needed confidence. They needed encouragement. They needed someone now and then to steer them right. It was welling up in Doug and he could deny it no longer. Every day for seven years he'd been looking in every young face that passed. It was absurd to pretend that he was moving on with his life when he'd been on edge nearly every second. Walking through that mall in Austin, Doug became obsessed with the possibility—*What if he needs me? He's thirteen. What if he needs me right now?*

He had to know, and he had to know *now*.

It was time to own up to his life.

He composed Wendy a cordial letter, not wanting to cause trouble, just hoping to learn whether Gabe was all right. The letter eventually reached Wendy by way of her mother and sister. She wrote back from Jacksonville, Florida. At first she put up a front: Gabe was fine. He was playing sports and his grades were satisfactory. She didn't want him to know about Doug yet. But she offered her phone number, suggesting Doug call during the day before the kids came home from school. When he called, she was amiable.

Encouraged, he called occasionally, and he learned that chaos was brewing in Gabe's life like a storm coming up from the Gulf. Wendy's marriage was falling apart; she had three children now, and her husband did not really have a close relationship with Gabe. She was no longer confident about her ability to provide a good environment for her son.

Wendy dropped hints to Gabe that she'd been talking to his birth father. "There's this guy . . . ," she would start in. Gabe had never asked about his biological father, and it had never occurred to him to ask. He considered his stepdad his father figure and had called him "Dad" for five years. This guy Doug was a complete stranger. But Wendy very gently encouraged Gabe to get to know him, and Gabe grew curious. Everyone took it slow, unsure how to handle it, but that caution gave them time to get comfortable with the situation. One evening Wendy telephoned Doug and said, "There's a boy here who'd like to talk to you."

"I remember my first words very clearly," Doug narrated. "When I heard his voice, I said, 'Man, I've been waiting for this day for a long time.' He said, 'Really?' I think it surprised him to learn I cared. But it meant a lot to him. He was at an age where he needed someone to take an interest in him. On that first phone call, and every time thereafter, I never forced it. All the men who'd ever entered Gabe's life were there because they were interested in *his mom,* not in him. I knew I was a stranger to him, but I tried to let him know that no matter how hard it got around that house in Florida, there was a man out here who cared about him."

Gabe was skeptical. He was not looking for an emotional bond with Doug. But his parents were splitting up after ten years together, and that confused him greatly; Doug seemed to be the only guy he could talk to about it. The best thing about Doug was that he was wonderfully calm. He just listened.

Doug was invited to visit for Thanksgiving weekend in his third year of law school. It was not a tearful or poignant reunion at the airport. To Doug's surprise, Gabe's hair had turned dark and he was tall and thin. It took an adjustment to associate these brand-new features with the telephone voice. They cooked the turkey together. Doug slept on the floor of Gabe's bedroom. The next day they took Wendy's car down to St. Augustine for the day. Doug could tell that Gabe was at that age when boys are choosing who to run with, who to be. He was losing direction, and he did not know where to turn because the adults in his life were pretty much at a loss, too. He needed someone who wasn't drowning in confusion. Doug didn't get through to Gabe that weekend, but their time together was peaceful and pleasant. The night before Doug left Florida, Gabe asked him for a hug.

They stayed in touch. A few months later Wendy told Doug she was afraid she was going to lose Gabe to a bad road. She asked if she could send Gabe to live with him. "I had never crossed that line with her, never touched the subject, for fear of threatening her," Doug remembered. "But I'd been thinking it." He and Gabe discussed the possibility. Doug assured Gabe that he wanted to do it, but he believed they would have a better chance of success if they waited until Doug finished law school. "Hang in there. I want to be in a position where I can be a real father to you."

That summer Doug moved to Colorado and took the bar exam. Gabe flew out to live with him. They attempted to be friends, finding fairly generic things to do together. Partly because it was summer and he was fourteen, Gabe described it as "like a vacation." Doug was unable to find a law firm to hire him, so at the end of the summer they moved back to Doug's mom's house outside Joplin. They lived on unemployment. Gabe had a slouchy, urban smart-ass attitude he'd picked up on the streets of Jacksonville, and he clashed with Doug's mom. It was a big adjustment for Gabe; even though Doug was trying to be a friend more than a parent, the rules of the house were a lot stricter than Gabe was accustomed to. The weather was similarly oppressive. Gabe admitted, "I didn't really move there to form a bond with Doug. I just wanted to get out of the situation in Florida. I really missed my mom and sister. I tried it with Doug; it didn't feel right."

"The graft was not taking," Doug recalled. "It was very apparent that biology was not enough to create a bond. I was a stranger. It was very stressful."

After six quick months, the experiment was called off. Doug drove Gabe to Springfield and put him on a Greyhound to Florida.

"I failed," Doug said. "I had the miracle of a second chance with my son, and I didn't get through. I lost him."

The day Gabe stepped onto that bus to Florida was also the last day Doug had any faith in the Southern Baptist doctrine. He'd been pulling away from his church for years, partly because he was increasingly uncomfortable evangelizing, pushing his views on others. He no longer believed that the Bible was the one and only Word of God; he believed it was one of many very intelligent interpretations of how we transform ourselves into good people. Doug has always been a searcher for meaning, and since his mid-teens he has tried to reconcile religious doctrine with what he feels in his heart. When Gabe left, Doug did not blame the Lord. In fact, he did the opposite. He did not see God's hand in Gabe's departure—he saw his own hands. He felt personally responsible. His own actions had led to this. His own choices. According to his religion, as long as Doug kept his faith, he was saved—he was in a state of grace. His life had been redeemed by Jesus, two millennia ago, through sacrifice on the cross.

But when Gabe left, that notion was unacceptable. It was absurd to consider himself *saved,* incongruous to consider himself *redeemed.*

It was time to redeem his own life—and nobody, not even Jesus, was going to do it for him. The only way to return to a state of grace was to ensure that his son turned out all right. Doug could no longer trust his son to God, or trust his son to the poor example of other men, or trust that his kid would be all right because he carried Doug's genes. He was not going to leave something this important up to fate. Doug had let circumstance play too great a role in his own life and that of his son. He had let guilt and shame come between him and his purpose. Doug took a new vow, this one to himself: *Whatever it takes.* The future would be decided by his actions today.

Doug took the Florida bar and hunted for attorney positions closer to his son. He called Gabe frequently, which was excruciating because Gabe's situation was spinning out of control in a hurry. While he'd been away, Wendy and her husband had split up. To save money, she shared the rent on a place with another soldier in her husband's unit. They ended up involved. He liked to drink more than a little too much. He had kids, too; spouses and ex-spouses were forever fighting in the house. Gabe's sixteen-year-old sister had gotten pregnant. There were eleven people in the house, and Gabe's mom and sister were caught up in their own problems. Nobody made Gabe go to school. Nobody kept him from trying drugs.

"I realized I needed to get out of there," Gabe said. "Doug had kept the door open, always assuring me that if I wanted to come back, I could. I realized that Doug was a decent guy. To hear that he was trying to move down to be near me—that he wasn't giving up—that kind of effort on my behalf was something I hadn't had, and it was something

I needed. I called him and told him I wanted to move back. That was the first step to actually having a father."

Gabe moved back into Doug's mom's house in Missouri. They didn't know if they'd end up there or in Florida. Doug's mom quarreled with both of them. She wouldn't tolerate Gabe's mouthiness, and she was driven to anger seeing her son turn his back on their church. Doug popped down to Florida for a week to scour for a job, and when he returned Gabe was gone. Mom wasn't talking. Doug found him at a relative of Wendy's.

"I could see my mom's side," Doug said. "Gabe was a kid few would love, at a time in a boy's life when it's hard to find a lot there to love. My mom has a short fuse. He pissed her off."

His mother laid down her terms: Doug was welcome back but not Gabe. She wanted him out of the house. Doug was livid. (Their relationship has never quite recovered.) Doug went to Gabe and told his son, "We'll go live in a hole in the ground if we have to, but we're staying together. I have traveled too long a road to get you back, and nothing and no one is ever coming between us again. Whatever it takes. If that's what you want. We are a team."

Gabe did not hesitate. No man had ever said anything like that to him. "Yeah, that's what I want."

Despite having only unemployment for income, Doug found an apartment and the two moved in together. Gabe had his own bedroom. A month later Doug finally found work, there in Missouri. They bought a black leather couch.

"That did it for me," Gabe said. "That triggered the bond. It convinced me to stick with this guy. He'd proven he really cared, proven he was serious. He was willing to fight for me. It meant a lot."

Doug struggled to steer Gabe onto a good path. Treating him as a peer had already failed. Yet Doug had only started to earn Gabe's respect, and Doug did not feel entitled to be an authoritarian. It was a thin line to walk. He had to show consideration for Gabe's boundaries, too. So this time, there were no absolute rules. Doug tried to lead by example. He drank very rarely, and only in moderation, because Gabe had seen a lot of irresponsible drinking. When Gabe brought home D's and F's on his first report card, Doug made it clear that he wasn't mad and he understood that in Florida nobody had even made Gabe go to class, which hadn't been permissiveness but neglect. Ensuring Gabe did his homework was a way of caring and looking out for his son, not being a hard-ass on a power trip. Gabe seemed to get this idea, didn't rebel, and responded quickly. Even though Doug was parenting by feel, on the fly, he believed that communicating carefully—making those little distinctions—made a significant difference when added up over time.

Gabe slowly found common ground with the new man in his life. One day they went to a car show. Doug suddenly saw his own stepfather at a distance, and pointed him out to Gabe. "You've got a stepfather, too?" Gabe asked.

"I haven't seen him since I was fourteen," Doug answered.

"Should we go talk to him?" Gabe offered.

Doug returned, "No, he was kind of a bastard." Doug's mom had married the guy when Doug was twelve. He was a drunk, and when drunk he would challenge Doug to fight. Doug never took the bait. Gabe realized he and Doug had very similar experiences of being fourteen years old.

Gabe also came to understand why his father had never married. Doug offered a variety of answers, but they always ended up with this logic: "I was afraid to get close. I didn't want anyone to take your place. I was always afraid if someone else entered my life, I would lose you forever."

They only had one big fight. Gabe was sixteen. He had gone somewhere without telling Doug, and did so in a way that flouted the only principle Doug had—that they let each other know where they were. Doug went out hunting for him in his car. Eventually he found Gabe at a friend's and dragged him home. As they came into the kitchen, Doug explained why it was important to call, how they needed to work together. Gabe continued being a butt and a smart-ass, resentful of being yanked away from his friend's. Doug lost his patience. He grabbed Gabe's shirt, held him against the counter, and told him to respect whose house they were in. Gabe pushed back and the shouting match took off. Within a few exchanges, Gabe became enraged, and finally his real accusation came out, something he'd needed to say for so long:

"Where were you all those years! Why were you not paying child support?"

"What?!"

"You heard me!"

"You'll have to talk to your stepfather about that! I *was* paying support. I *was* around. And not because some court ordered me to do it. I did it because it was the right thing. Then I was told to leave. Your stepfather wouldn't let me be in your life."

"That's not what I heard! I heard you didn't want me!"

"Is that what he told you? I know your mom didn't say that to you! She knows I was always a good man."

"I was never in your plans!"

"You were a surprise, but not a mistake! Your mom and I loved each other!"

"Then where were you?! Where were you?"

Gabe stomped upstairs. Doug fell on the couch and cried. Thirty minutes later, Gabe came back down and stood half defiantly at the bottom of the stairs—a peace offering. Doug immediately apologized.

"I just want to be a good father, Gabe. I'm trying to be a good dad. I'm sorry if I'm doing a lousy job. Please, help me figure this out."

"I'm sorry, too. I didn't know the facts."

"No, you've had a right to ask and you never have. I know I've hurt you by not being there. I can't change it and will never pretend I have. I'll always be making up for lost time. You not being in my life was entirely my responsibility."

Doug did not date while Gabe was in high school. He saw nothing inherently wrong with doing so, but he wanted to ensure that Gabe had a stable environment after so long without one. He wanted Gabe to know that he was all that mattered. They worked out together at the gym, and played tennis and basketball. Doug became a great listener.

Gabe learned to talk to Doug about anything. He discovered that Doug was unlike other men—nothing Gabe did or said ever made Doug fly off the handle. One time Doug came home early from a trial in Fayetteville and found Gabe hosting a party. Doug took one look and said, "Oh. All right. I'll be in my room if you need me." Everyone slapped Gabe on the back. His dad was cool! The party never got out of hand. Another time—later, when Gabe was eighteen—he got drunk and drove home, stupidly, whereupon he was slapped with a ticket for reckless driving. When he reached home he waited in his truck outside for an hour and a half, trying to sober up. Finally he dragged himself up the stairs to face Doug. Doug just put him in bed and advised that some community service would be a good way to deal with the ticket. Doug understood that people make mistakes, and he trusted that his son was developing good judgment and using it most of the time. He needed to learn for himself what crossing that line felt like, and how the anxiety of being over the line wasn't worth it.

A few weeks later Doug was noodling on his guitar in bed when he heard Gabe come in with friends. Doug plodded downstairs and found two girls with his son. Doug made enough small talk to be polite, then gave them their space and headed back to his room. Later, Gabe came up.

"What'd you think, Doug?"

"Of what?"

"Of Jen."

"She seemed nice. I barely talked to her."

"No, man! Did you see her legs?"

The eighteen-year-old was in love. Doug knew what that was about. He also knew how hard it is to turn young love into a stable adult relationship. He and Gabe talked at every turn—how not to be threatened, how to give each other room, how to tell the truth, how not to expect her to be the same as you in every way, how to take a break when you're about to say something you don't mean. Gabe married Jen six years later, and they've been together nine years now. They own a fairly big new home on a cul-de-sac. She works for a regional bank, and he drives a delivery truck for Anheuser-Busch, which is a better living than you'd suspect. They are in no rush to have kids.

For his part, Doug has worked as an attorney doing Social Security law and family law, and he's taught at Crowder College, and he's written grants for the United Way. He still lives in that same apartment he moved into with Gabe. He is still single, still careful. He is reading Taoist texts, from which one line resonates most: *"The Tao guides without interfering."*

Doug and Gabe have a strong relationship today. They talk all the time; they're best friends, kindred spirits. "He's the best man I know," Doug said. "A man of quality and character. A better man than I was at his age, a much better man."

Gabe returned, "He has never judged me. He has encouraged me in everything I did. He has never forced preconceived notions on me of what a son should be like. He is happy for me to be my own original self. He mostly just listens. So the few times he does have something to say, it always means something, and it's always an influence on my decisions."

When pressed for how he did this, how he created such a bond with his son, Doug thought about it awhile and said, "All I did was provide a stable environment and a constant presence. The rest I let him figure out."

Both Doug and Gabe are observers. Neither is the first in a crowd to offer an opinion or make a statement just to hear his own voice. Their lives are quiet, and contentedly so; the chaos in their past barely echoes anymore. Gabe is developing into an articulate person, but Doug is truly there. He's not eloquent in an oratorial sense, but rather, he chooses his words carefully to pin down exactly what he feels. Being a father by feel taught him this. The word *fortunate* comes up a lot. It's a privilege to have this relationship with his son, a kid he basically walked away from—it's beyond anything he could ever ask for. He considers himself a very lucky man. He's grateful to Gabe. He's grateful to Wendy, who encouraged Gabe to have a relationship with him, and who has never lacked forgiveness for what happened when they were eighteen.

Not bad for a couple of bumpkins.

Redemption had come.

Doug reflected, "Most sons work so hard to earn their father's respect. I worked so hard for six years to earn my son's respect. When I finally had that—when I was worthy of his admiration, when I'd redeemed myself in his eyes—my whole life collapsed into a moment. It broke my heart. I *did* it. I managed to be someone he respects. That's all I need."

The week before I visited, Wendy moved back to town and, needing a bed, she took Gabe's old room until she could get settled in her own place. That morning, she was gone before Doug awoke. A couple of hours later she walked back in wearing her new Wal-Mart uniform. It was her first day on the job, but nobody had been there to train her.

"She looked as good as ever," Doug could not help saying. "She looked great."

Gabe paused and chuckled softly. He knew what Doug was really saying. "Doug, I figured out you were a one-woman man a long time ago."

When I left Doug and Gabe, I hit the highway, hoping I might make it to Kansas City and thereby catch an earlier flight in the morning. I missed my son terribly. I wanted to tell him we were a team, and I wanted to tell him this in person. I didn't make it to KC; I ended up in a twenty-nine-dollar motel by the highway, the kind where the royal-blue carpets seem eternally moist. I sat on the bed beside my thirty pages of fresh notes and drank half a gallon of green Gatorade. You can get sad very quickly in a place like this, and I was in a lot of places exactly like it that year. But on that night I was not sad. I seemed impervious to sadness. I had Doug and Gabe with me, as memories. I could not figure out why, exactly, they were sadness's silver bullet. But I think it is this:

Every single man knows some version of what Gabe must have been feeling as a young man. We have all ached for a man to come along and prove he cares for us. We have all longed for a father who would just listen.

Women know this feeling, too.

In a world that often obsesses over deadbeat dads and emotionally distant fathers, many men *do* care, and when coached well they can express their care in a very healthy way.

Something drew me across the country to Doug. I guess I just wanted to meet him, meet the dad who, to me, symbolized the great arc that we as a society are going through as more and more men discover how to be emotionally present for our children. He had longed for a father himself, but he had walked out on his son, and then he'd discovered that he cared after all. He cared so much the pain broke his life into Before and After, and then he did something about it. He found his son and made good.

Which is sweeter,

getting what we always

wanted or getting

what we never asked for?

The White Guy

Steve, Jo-Jo, and Aubrey Tabayoyong Murphy

Sometime in the late 1800s, a big happy Irish family by the name of Murphy landed in New Orleans. No one's sure whether they were fleeing famine or seeking fortune or just hoping to enjoy a humid climate. They held tight to their culture and religion and prospered. Inevitably, as it happens, a few generations later one of the Murphys decided to have nothing to do with his family, and he moved to Los Angeles, forever severing ties. He got a woman pregnant, married her quickly, and separated from her soon after their second son was born. He died unexpectedly when this second son was nine.

This second son, Steve Murphy, barely knew his father, and knew almost nothing of his forebears. He once sat down with a surviving aunt in New Orleans, but she provided only names and birthdays—none of the *story,* nothing about how it unfolded, or who his Murphys were.

Steve's mom had grown up during the Great Depression. Her father had worked for Northern Pacific Railroad, and she had gotten from him the idea that they were better off if they kept moving. So as a child, Steve got used to constant change; in the fifth grade alone, they moved three times. His mom also clung to her Depression-era frugality and relentless work ethic. During the summer, rather than pay a babysitter while she worked, his mom would drop Steve off at the movie theater in the morning. Steve would sit through *Mary Poppins* four times in a row, then his mom would pick him up. By his high school years they had landed in Spokane, terrain familiar to his mom from her childhood. When his older brother got into drugs, Steve kept his distance. Later, his half brother died in a motorcycle accident.

The Murphys were down to two.

When Steve obtained his driver's license at sixteen, he took a long solo trip through the American Southwest. The way he chose a college was simple: Eastern Washington University was local, and it was cheap. After college he went to work at Kmart in management, and the company moved him to Phoenix. He described himself then as "the least Irish Murphy there ever was." He had been to church only twice in his life. His sense of culture had been extinguished, and so had any sense of family. He spent most holidays alone, and it did not bother him. He thought nothing of this. He sent a card; that was enough. He called his mother four times a year. He enjoyed his privacy and independence. At his house in Phoenix, he had everything to himself. He had the pool to himself, the bathrooms to himself, the kitchen to himself. If you had visited him then, dinner would have been awkward, because there was only one wood chair seated at the dining room table, and only one place mat in front of it. The others were in storage. One set was all that was necessary.

That year, he made a decision: He was never getting married.

"Who needs a wife?" he asked, and his empty house did not argue with him.

He was good-spirited. He did not feel he had lost anything, because the way he was raised, family was never emphasized. He held no grudge about this. You don't miss what you never knew.

That summer he took yet another vacation by himself, two weeks alone in Yellowstone Park. Then, in late October, he flew to San Francisco for the wedding of his one friend from Spokane.

And at this wedding he met a woman, a college roommate of the bride.

Perhaps he should have been suspicious, for her last name was Tabayoyong. Pronounced just the way it looks. First name Jo-Jo.

Jo-Jo Tabayoyong was Filipino. Her family moved to Chicago when she was four.

He didn't ask any more about her family, and she didn't ask about his.

But something opened in him the moment he met Jo-Jo. He doesn't know where it came from. Around her, he felt instantly at ease.

They wrote and talked by telephone for a month, and then Jo-Jo flew to Phoenix for a three-day weekend. Both felt what they had found was acutely special, and neither wanted to part. On their last night together Jo-Jo asked him the dreaded question: "So, when's the next time I get to see you?"

Steve's answer shocked him: "Well, we could do that, we could plan the next time we'll meet. Or—or, I suppose, we could also just get married."

In this way, Steve sorta proposed, and Jo-Jo sorta accepted, and they were happy.

Jo-Jo did offer one caveat, though. "You know, before we get married, you're going to have to come to Chicago and meet my family."

"Sure, sure," Steve replied, cluelessly. "Of course."

Her dad actually telephoned about two hours later, just to check in on his daughter. Perhaps Steve might have thought this odd—a dad calling a boyfriend's house, on his daughter's second date, a *grown* daughter, with her own apartment and job? But this oddity was lost in the excitement over Jo-Jo's big announcement, which she immediately shared with her father. Quickly Jo-Jo handed the phone to Steve.

This man was talking with such a thick accent that Steve couldn't really make out what he was saying. But his tone was welcoming and enthusiastic, so Steve was giddy. To this day, he is not sure what Jo-Jo's dad's speech was about, but he thinks it concerned what makes a good marriage. Steve just kept saying "Yes, yes, yes" at every pause, and they seemed to get along great.

In early January, Steve flew to Chicago to meet the Tabayoyong family. Right before he left his house, Jo-Jo called. "When you change planes in Dallas, some of the Dallas contingent will be there to meet you."

The Dallas contingent?

Sure enough, when Steve got off the plane at the Dallas–Fort Worth airport, two of Jo-Jo's cousins were at the gate to greet him and escort him to his connection. It turned out there were at least a hundred Tabayoyongs in Dallas. They were curious about this man their cousin intended to marry. At this point Steve thought the greeting committee was cute and endearing. It made Jo-Jo exotic. The cousins were talkative and friendly. Though they were there to judge him, oddly he did not *feel* judged. There was something about how Jo-Jo's family assessed a person that was very different from the way Steve's family did. All families are judgmental, but not all families are judgmental to the same degree. Many families judge people like they are vetting a candidate for the Supreme Court. Every fault is magnified and scrutinized. There's another way to do it—more like the way people are patted down on the way in to a rock concert. As long as you're not bringing in any handguns, knives, or alcohol, you're welcome to join the party.

Steve's undersized family looked for often petty reasons to exclude someone. Jo-Jo's sprawling family found reasons to include anyone. From their point of view, this newcomer Steve had a job, an education, and he made Jo-Jo happy. That was good enough for them. When Steve got on his next plane, they called ahead to Chicago.

"Thumbs-up," they declared.

In Chicago, Steve walked into a party that had been gathered on short notice. Not many could make it. So there were only six cousins, two parents, a grandparent, a handful of aunts and uncles, and a dozen or so friends from their church. They embraced Steve like a long-lost brother, which was awkward for him, because in his family there were no outward displays of affection. Dozens of new names were thrown at him, in one ear and out the other, but luckily Jo-Jo had briefed him on the usage of *lola* and *lolo* for grandparents, *manang* and *manong* for cousins. Aunts and uncles were just "Auntie" and "Uncle." These are titles of respect, and they are always used when addressing an elder, so it was not odd to use them as shorthand.

And then the good-byes! It was not sufficient to yawn and point to the coats and simply wave the guests away wholesale. It had taken Steve the whole night to meet everyone, and now he had to say good-bye to every single person there—and each of *them* also had to say good-bye to every person there. Filipino good-bye rituals can last an hour easily. Steve was overwhelmed, but still game. Jo-Jo's aunts sent him home with an ice chest packed with *lumpia,* a type of egg roll. He had passed the Family Test.

Were they genuinely judging him? Or was it a formality just to make her family feel included?

Jo-Jo said, "I joke about it as the Family Test, but it was not so much about their approval as their opinion. I really wanted to know what they thought of him. I had made a few mistakes with boyfriends in the past, guys whose faults I didn't see coming but they spotted from the start. So I trusted their judgment, whether they liked him as much as I did."

"And they liked him even though he was not Filipino?"

"I had been coached for years to marry a Filipino, but the moment they met Steve that expectation vanished and never returned."

"So on what basis did they judge him?"

"His character. He is open and forthright and has a sense of humor and is easygoing. My aunt said the moment she met him, she took pity on him, but that's really a botched translation from Ilocano, our dialect, where the word means something more akin to 'compassion.' Her heart went out to him. 'Simpatico' is what a cousin said she felt. He was a man they were going to enjoy sharing life with."

"If they had not liked him, what would you have done?"

"I don't know. It would have made it very hard. At that time, my parents were going through a rocky patch in their marriage, and so I was hyperaware of not wanting to make a mistake in my choice. If my family did not love him as I did, I would have been very careful."

In March, Steve moved in with Jo-Jo, into her Gold Coast studio apartment. Kmart allowed a transfer. The wedding was planned for late May. However, there was a glitch. All of Jo-Jo's siblings moved in with them, too. They did not want to live with their parents while the parents were fighting. So there were six people living in one studio apartment. Can you imagine what this must have been like for Steve? From a ranch house all to himself to a *studio* with six adults sleeping on every inch of floor? From a family he rarely saw to a gaggle of strangers putting rock salt on their fruit and charring fish on the stove and stuffing the refrigerator full of food he could not recognize—greasy sausages and green mangoes and something called *"baboong"*? He joked that they were "the Boat People," and the others took up the joke in good spirit. They liked "the White Guy."

Still, though, Steve did not really understand what he was getting into. In the haze of romance, he did not put it all together. He figured her siblings would move back to their parents' soon enough and he and Jo-Jo would have their own life. It really only sank in when they started premarital counseling through Jo-Jo's church. Steve attended this counseling with the attitude *Sure, whatever, can't hurt.* But Jo-Jo took it very seriously—again, because she trusted her pastor's input. This pastor had known the Tabayoyongs for decades. In their first session he looked straight at Steve and drilled him.

"Do you realize what you're getting into with her family?" By this he meant, rhetorically, *Son, I don't think you do.*

"What do you mean?" Steve asked.

"Do you even know the *size* of her family?"

"I've met them."

"No, you have met just a small part. There are several hundred Tabayoyongs in the United States alone. Do you know what this will mean for your marriage?"

"I guess not," he admitted.

"You are not just marrying Jo-Jo, son. You are marrying this family. They will become *your* family. They will be in your life, in your business, help raise your children, and expect you to care for them when they're in need."

Steve sat back and really thought about it for the first time. Until then, he had assumed that he and Jo-Jo would have their own life—her extended family would be in the periphery, and he and Jo-Jo and any children they had would be his family. But he had fallen in love with *an oldest daughter,* who has certain obligations in a Filipino family. Jo-Jo took these obligations seriously: She is one of two in the family who knows everybody's birthday by heart, and always sends a card. Several hundred birthdays are magically stored in her brain.

The pastor's speech daunted Steve. "But I loved Jo-Jo and wanted to be with her. There was some trepidation on my part, but never did I once consider not going ahead with it."

If there are two camps in our society—one that includes extended family, another that shuts them out; one that puts family above everything, another that declares family is important but rarely acts like it—then there has never been a wedding that has better represented what can happen when these two camps are thrown together. There were 125 guests crammed into the small wedding chapel. If that church had been a car, the passenger side would have scraped the street. If that church had been a boat, it would have capsized. Only two guests were from Steve's family—his mother and her husband. They represented two-thirds of his *entire* family (his stepsister was grounded by an airline strike). The other guests were from Jo-Jo's family. They represented only a third of the *American* Tabayoyongs. Jo-Jo has fifty-two first cousins. Steve has none. Steve's family was prompt and on time and staring at their watches within minutes. Jo-Jo's family was on island time, give or take an hour. In Steve's family, they can barely make eye contact. In Jo-Jo's family, they squeeze and hug and wave grandly and kiss easily.

It was only a semi-traditional Filipino wedding. Jo-Jo did not inflict on Steve's family many of the rituals distinct to her culture, such as the passing back and forth of thirteen gold coins or the wrapping of a cord in figure eights around their necks. But when the bride and groom took their first dance, Jo-Jo's family members darted out and pinned money to the newlyweds' dress and tux. Steve loved this! He loved it!

You might wonder how Steve had managed such an amazing turn-around in a mere seven months. In the back of his mind there remained a notion of marriage he had developed over time. In vowing to never marry, he had been vowing to never have a marriage that resembled this unpalatable notion. And so every curiosity and novelty that Jo-Jo's family threw in his way served to build a new path, a way around that obstacle. His marriage to Jo-Jo did not resemble the thing he had rejected. This big happy family, the siblings on his studio floor, the long good-byes—he had never imagined such things. They breathed new life into a tired idea. They made his marriage *original;* they transformed marriage and family into an adventure. So when his new in-laws—his *family*—began pinning twenties and fifties to the tails of his tux, he was thrilled, because weddings can feel like you're buying into some ancient crusty pact (reminiscent of that old notion), and the money dance reminded him that he was *not.*

So many newlyweds are discouraged when their wedding and their marriage turn into something they never expected. Steve had the opposite reaction. The less it resembled what he expected, the better.

In truth, Steve was an easy convert. He did not have to be won over. Like most people who have decided family is not important, he simply needed to be shown that the family he would create did not have to imitate the family he came from. From there, warm feelings evolved naturally, without effort.

"I've adopted them as the family I never had," he said. But that wasn't strong enough. "The Tabayoyongs *saved* me," he added. "I've learned so much from them. They've given me an impression of what family can be. I wish I'd had these ideas in my background." Still, this didn't manage to capture what he feels, so he tried this: "What we have, as a family—despite the problems and rough patches—it's paradise for me. I consider this paradise."

Pressed to elucidate what it is, exactly, that's so great, Steve boiled it down to something simple. "They *care.* They genuinely care about each other. So when I walk in a room, they *light up.* They burst out of their chairs, their faces beam, they are enthusiastic. I have never had that in my family. Never seen a whole room light up just because so-and-so walked in. When Jo-Jo and I travel, there is always a relative nearby who wants to see us. Not out of duty, or habit, but because they care—because the sight of us makes them happy."

This is how Steve talks today, but it took a few years to get used to, and he and Jo-Jo were forever discovering new depths to the contrast between their family styles. For instance, when Steve's stepfather died, Jo-Jo was shocked at how the funeral unfolded. The family sat behind a sheer curtain, and the visitors filed past them without a word or even a glance. If anyone cried, you sure couldn't hear it. There was no body to pay respects to, just a photograph and an urn. At the brief reception afterward, people made small talk, ate a cocktail plate's worth of food, and left. Not long after, one of Jo-Jo's cousins in Dallas was killed in a car accident. At this ceremony, relatives took pictures of themselves with the deceased in his open casket. They wailed openly. When he was lowered into the ground, the entire family sobbed and only managed to remain standing by gripping one another. Each person went to the head of the casket and told a story. Then they went back to another cousin's house and told funny stories late into the night. All of the cousins chipped in some money, up to five hundred dollars each, to pay for the funeral and help his family.

Just as the Tabayoyongs grieved, they fought—they let it out rather than holding it in. In the first years of marriage, Steve and Jo-Jo found that their jobs had them working different schedules. This upset Jo-Jo, because her father—a doctor—had worked long hours, and she did not want that pattern to repeat itself in her marriage. So one morning she lit into Steve about his work hours. Later that day, he showed up at her office with flowers and a big apology. He really thought they were on the brink of separation. She laughed. To her, it was just a fight. She was letting off steam.

"You mean, you're not leaving me?" he said.

"You *believed* me?"

In fact, one of the notions Steve needed to learn was how *invulnerable* their marriage was. In his family divorce was common. His mother was divorced twice, his stepsister once; even his brother had managed to get divorced before dying. So he considered marriage to be enormously fragile. If you consider it fragile, you're wary of rocking the boat by expressing your needs, so those needs go unmet, which is far more dangerous in the long term. In Jo-Jo's family divorce was unheard of. And while her parents fought through many hard spells—fought loudly, dramatically—they never considered splitting up. So Jo-Jo had no qualms about speaking up or expressing herself, because according to the notion in the back of *her* mind, nothing could really threaten her marriage to Steve.

The best aspect of having a huge extended family emerged when Jo-Jo gave birth to Aubrey. Steve had those memories of sitting through *Mary Poppins* all day, and he sure didn't want his daughter to experience anything like it. He needn't have worried. The way Jo-Jo had grown up, she barely learned to walk because there was *never* not a pair of hands to hold her. And so it would be with Aubrey. Jo-Jo kept working until Aubrey was three, so Aubrey practically lived with her grandparents, who were only seven miles away. Just as Jo-Jo had an intense bond with her maternal grandmother, Aubrey had a bond with Jo-Jo's father, who doted on Aubrey in a way he never had with his own children. This made raising a baby much less overwhelming to Steve. The new responsibility was never daunting. Steve never had to worry who would care for his child if something happened to him.

Over time, Steve made several attempts to spread this new spirit into his mother's family. For the most part, his efforts failed to change anything. Right after the wedding, he began calling his mom weekly (rather than quarterly), but he admits his true motive was more to impress Jo-Jo than to get closer to his mother. The regular calls had their restorative effect, though, and his mother began visiting Chicago four times a year. This culminated in a big trip to Disney World with Jo-Jo's parents and Steve's mom and stepsister. The week was an absolute disaster. The contrast in styles made everyone uncomfortable. The Murphys and Tabayoyongs were like oil and water. It was in Orlando that Jo-Jo learned the Murphys do know how to fight after all—at least with one another. As the story of that week was told and retold for years, it took on a nickname: the Great Experiment.

More experiments were conducted over the years, but the gains were temporary. Steve has remained close to his mom, but to him the remnants and shards of his past—primarily his stepsister's family—are not worth fighting for. One family can often heal its in-laws by osmosis, but in Steve's case the gap was too great between what he expected, now that he's a Tabayoyong, and what the Murphy side delivered. When he flew to Reno, where his mother and stepsister lived, the room never lit up. He predicts that when his mother dies he is likely to let that connection to her side go.

Though Steve had a lot to learn about family from Jo-Jo, he also had something to teach her: She had never learned how to say no to her family.

She had never insisted they respect her borders. They had not let her become an independent adult. By this measure, she and Steve really had opposite pasts. Consider how Steve was allowed to drive throughout the Southwest by himself at sixteen. Jo-Jo's father did not even allow her to get a driver's license at that age ("You're too young, it's too dangerous!").

Then consider the way Steve was allowed to find his own way academically. He was never pressured, and as a result he's always enjoyed his work. It's his; his motives are in the right place. Jo-Jo was ordered to follow her father and become a doctor. She was sent to Stanford as the family's "Great Hope." Not only did that not work out, but Jo-Jo credits this overbearing pressure with her failure to ever find her own soulful connection to work. Today she has a job behind the register at a drugstore; she's great at it, but it's not her passion.

Her real love is music. She plays the harp. She, like all her siblings, was raised to the sound of *harana* on their father's guitar, and they spent their childhood in front of a piano. As teens, they "rebelled" by switching to the violin. Music had been their father's first career; he only took up medicine because his parents told him his jazz combo was no way to provide for his new family, even though he was fairly successful as a musician. (Medical school is what brought him to Chicago.) And so he passed this same warning on to his children. They were encouraged to play, but music was to be a hobby, not a profession. He meant it. When one of Jo-Jo's brothers moved to Los Angeles to make it as a musician—and inevitably struggled (who doesn't at first?)—this caused a great rift. He was treated as an outcast and did not speak to his father for *five years.*

That *never* would have happened in Steve's family.

Perhaps it was inevitable that at some point Steve was going to butt heads with Jo-Jo's parents. It was only a question of when, and of whose side Jo-Jo would take.

Their pastor had been dead-on during marital counseling when he predicted Jo-Jo's family would "be in your life, in your business." This *intrusiveness,* let's call it, is characteristic of Filipino families in general, but by no means limited to Filipinos—I have heard this trait described hundreds of times, by families of every size and from every country. I interviewed a sprawling Sicilian family that was on the verge of exploding like a grenade under the constant pressure of being loyal to its patriarch, but I also interviewed a mom-and-pop duo in coastal Virginia who had driven their two adult children away by never respecting their independence. The size of a family does not correlate with whether or not it respects autonomy. Not to do so is a damaging trait. It destroys more families than it preserves.

Where does it come from? From tradition and imitation, partly. But it's exacerbated by fear, usually the fear that the family will fall apart or fail if the rule by an iron fist is not maintained. So families that migrate internationally often bring with them a tradition of patriarchal control, but it can get much worse in the new surroundings.

The Tabayoyongs' intrusions were minor compared with other stories I heard.

When Jo-Jo's daughter was born, her parents stepped in. At first this was great. When Aubrey was three, Jo-Jo decided to work part-time. By the time Aubrey was four, Jo-Jo realized her daughter had been allowed to become a spoiled brat. She had assumed her parents were teaching her daughter obedience and respect, as they had Jo-Jo, but apparently they'd thrown all that out the window. They were raising a princess. Jo-Jo recognized she had to take control and chose to stay at home full-time. She needed to discipline her daughter, but did not want to spank her child as she had been spanked, so she and Steve began taking parenting classes. The classes were so great that Jo-Jo went from being a student to a teacher-facilitator. She had learned to say no to her daughter, but still hadn't learned how to say no to her parents. Was there a class for that?

Missing their granddaughter, Jo-Jo's parents began showing up uninvited at Steve and Jo-Jo's house. Not once in a while, which would have been charming, but *every single evening.* Once there, they routinely criticized the way Jo-Jo treated her daughter—and not in private, after Aubrey had gone to bed. At the time, Jo-Jo and Steve were trying to wean Aubrey off a bottle.

"If she wants the bottle, give it to her. What's the harm?"

"*Mom,* I'm trying to establish some rules here."

As a child will do, Aubrey sensed the lack of a united front, and she turned into an expert negotiator, twisting every *no* into a lengthy debate. The grandparents remained Aubrey's primary babysitters—they were quick to volunteer—but Jo-Jo eventually figured out that her parents were not respecting the new rules. They gave her milk in a bottle, then let her stay up late. One step forward, two steps back. Jo-Jo screamed at them, but they thought they knew better.

It got to the point that when Jo-Jo's parents knocked on the door in the evening, occasionally Steve and Jo-Jo hid upstairs and pretended they were not home. The third time this happened, Steve looked at Jo-Jo and said, "When Aubrey grows up, do you want *her* to hide from *us*?"

It came to a head on the verge of Jo-Jo and Steve's tenth wedding anniversary. Steve was taking Jo-Jo to Boston for a romantic weekend, so they dropped off Aubrey (then seven) with her grandparents the night before they flew east. A few hours later, Aubrey called in tears, terrified, begging to come home. She had seen her grandparents argue quite often, but she had never seen them fight *physically*. Steve and Jo-Jo were incensed. In their minds, that was it. They picked Aubrey up and took her to an aunt's. They were up most of the night, stewing with guilt over letting it get this bad.

"It's got to stop," Steve insisted. "In the morning, you're going to call them."

"They don't listen to me."

So for the first time, Steve called them. He had no trouble putting it in a way Jo-Jo never could: "This is my family; that is yours. Please don't taint mine. Do not call here, and do not come here. We will let you know when we are ready to let you back into our lives."

Oh, the scandal! Immediately, the phones were buzzing.

"Can you believe what that *husband* of Jo-Jo's said to his elders!"

Steve was suddenly the outsider, the White Guy again. Jo-Jo stood beside him (or maybe a little behind him). She might not have been able to stand up for her own needs, but she would protect her daughter.

For three months the grudge did not budge. Both sides waited for an apology. Finally Jo-Jo's father got sick, and Steve immediately took his family to visit. They were at the hospital every day. No apologies were offered, either way, and the issue was buried.

"My family is great at pretending things never happened," Jo-Jo explained.

After that, Steve made a rule: The grandparents could come over, but they had to call first. It was a small demand, and one they obeyed forever after, but not without a lot of collateral griping to Jo-Jo's siblings.

"If it were not for Steve," Jo-Jo said, "I never would have learned how to have my own life. He taught me we don't have to *always* give our bedroom to visitors, and we don't have to show up at *every* family event. I never knew I didn't *have* to put up with it. I tried, but they always wore me down. Steve protects me. He offers the perspective of an outsider, one who isn't Filipino and chained by the expectations that come with that heritage."

When I began my research for this book, the first trend that jumped out at me was how common it is for modern couples to bring very different notions of family into their marriage. If you were to take a poll, almost every couple would say it is true, if to different degrees. Every couple is a hybrid.

People are mingling more. Colleges and workplaces no longer discriminate or segregate, so people of different ethnicities meet and inevitably fall in love. Prejudice is fading, so potential partners are not screened out based on race or culture or class. Families have become so spread out—particularly in the United States, which is so big geographically—that often, when a couple falls in love, their families aren't even around. The introductions come later. We have largely abandoned the premise that a romantic match is based on who your family is. A new couple has its own chemistry, then tries to hang on to it when families are brought into the picture. In many cases the different backgrounds are not an obstacle to love, but rather the secret source of it—each partner longs for something unavailable from his or her own family.

Often the traits that attracted two people to each other become the very traits that drive them apart. At some point the old gyroscope takes over, past habits set in, and we find ourselves wishing we had a little more in common with our spouses. It's like buying leather pants. At first we're attracted to the exotic, but by the time we get home we wonder what we were thinking.

While it creates challenges for every couple, this cross-pollination is an unmistakably good thing for our society as a whole. Ecologists emphasize how important diversity of species is to survival. In our society there are many varieties of families, with many different notions and expectations. The long-term effect will inevitably be a new generation of families that are healthier and better equipped to cope. While some families will fall apart (such as Steve's), their remnants may get adopted by others (such as Jo-Jo's), and in turn bring with them a few good ideas. There's a tendency today to look only at the families that are falling apart and deduce all sorts of false conclusions from this myopia. We hear assertions that our society has lost its way because the basic building block of civilization—the family—is being undermined. In truth, we're not trending toward chaos. We're evolving. Hope is being restored as fast as it's being lost.

This trend is too broad to be represented by just one couple, but Jo-Jo and Steve are a striking example, because their contrasts are so memorable. I will never forget the image of their wedding chapel, our world in a microcosm. They are also a great example of how it works when it works best—both spouses contributed important lessons to the creation of their own family. They learned from each other. They'll celebrate their twentieth anniversary this year.

Jo-Jo summed it up this way. "Far from being a problem, I think the fact Steve and I came from such opposite backgrounds has been the secret to our success. We've never been able to fall into a pattern, never had a chance to fall asleep at the wheel. Our contrasts have made us conscious, made us stay attentive."

"I think that's true," Steve echoed, with a glint in his eye. "But I don't know if I'll ever get comfortable with how your family likes to have their picture taken with the dead person at a funeral."

This tickled Jo-Jo, who added, "Or how we carry a pig's head on the plane when we visit cousins?"

"Yeah, I'm happy in this family, but I'm never going to win the White Guy Game."

The White Guy Game was Jo-Jo's sister's idea. They were down in Dallas for a reunion, and she decided to put on a contest, a mock version of the game show *Jeopardy!,* testing all the "white guys" in the family on Filipino culture. In addition to Steve, the contestants included a Mexican spouse, a longtime boyfriend, a niece's fiancé, and Jo-Jo's younger brother, who was born in Chicago. They were instructed to count to ten in Tagalog. They were then given a couple of ingredients and asked to name a traditional Filipino dish that included them. Obscure relatives were pointed out, and anyone who could identify them scored a point.

Questions were thrown out to the contestants:

"Can you use *opallo* and *wag* in a sentence?"

"What plant is a *Barong Tagalog* made from?"

"How do you hail somebody across a crowd?"

The family roared with laughter as the contestants guessed.

"Seventeen years we had been married," Jo-Jo teased, remembering the contest. "You seemed to have absorbed so little."

"Sometimes it does feel like we just got married yesterday," Steve remarked.

Jo-Jo replied, "That's a good thing."

Do our actions
need to come
from desire,
not just obligation?

Dorothy's Child

Jarralynne Fletcher-Agee,
posing for her high school graduation picture.
It is the earliest photo she has;
no photos survived her childhood.

Jarralynne Agee liked to think of herself as just another bright young woman who found her mother embarrassing. Her girlfriends echoed this feeling—they appreciated their moms, but sure didn't want to turn out like them. These women wanted to take bold chances with their careers, and then allow their professions to get healthy head starts before they had children. They would choose husbands who valued this same plan—men who wanted to be equals at work and home. And because of their goals . . . because they wanted so much *more* than their mothers . . . because they and their mothers seemed symbolic of entirely different eras . . . their relationships with their mothers were inevitably awkward. They took their mothers with a grain of salt and rolled their eyes when Mom went old-school on them.

That was just the way it was.

Doesn't every mother sometimes drive her daughter crazy?

So Jarralynne Agee could console herself with the way her feelings toward her mother seemed parallel to everyone else's. She could hide in plain sight, her secret intact. Nobody had to know that her story was theirs *but in extreme.* They had moms whose lives had not worked out the way they had planned, and so did Jarralynne. They had to step from their mother's shadow in order to succeed, and so had Jarralynne. This symmetry provided an effective camouflage. Nobody had to know.

But in August 1999, Jarralynne's past could no longer be kept from sight. She was forced to deal with it, and in doing so she slowly came to own it. Now, five years later, she's no longer ashamed of where she came from. She can say proudly, *This is me; this is my mother; this is us together; this is our life.*

Her mother is Karen Fletcher.

———

When Karen Fletcher was a girl in Dayton, Ohio, her parents considered themselves to be the black bourgeoisie, part of a proud middle-class renaissance. In that culture, *bourgeois* did not have the capitalist connotations ascribed to it by Karl Marx; the phrase had descended from pre–Civil War usage of *bourgeois noir,* when it meant "a black free-man," as opposed to a slave.

Her grandmother had been part of Miami University's elite. Her aunt had married a respected doctor. Her father was the assistant principal at Dunbar High School in an era when teaching at Dunbar was as prestigious as being a university professor might be for a white man. Karen's mother, Dorothy, was very fair-complected, and this, too, conferred status. Her father was very protective of his wife, and he often repeated that people did not think he deserved a woman as beautiful as she. They lived on Stolz Avenue, on a street where six other Dunbar teachers lived.

But from her front door, Karen could look up past the streetlight to the neighborhood known as Sugar Hill. Those on Sugar Hill had only a little more money, but it was a time when a slight difference in income made a big difference in how people thought of themselves. People who lived on Sugar Hill belonged to black professional societies such as the Links and sent their children to social organizations like Jack-and-Jill. They were doctors and lawyers or had management jobs at Frigidaire and NCR. They parked their Cadillacs in driveways beside houses with nice porches. Their children wore expensive shoes and skirts. Karen was born on the border of this upper-middle-class black society. Her parents and family had the education to match, but not quite the income. Sugar Hill was more than a temptation or aspiration; Karen considered it her destiny, her right, her natural progression.

On the night of her junior prom, Karen Fletcher's date was a nice boy from Trinity Presbyterian named James Kirk. Karen and James went down the street to meet all the neighbors and show off her dress—that was how it was done back then. They were all expecting her. At one of these houses there was a family of three boys, one of whom was barred from the prom because he'd been suspended from school. "You think you look so cute in that dress your momma bought you?" he taunted, cruelly. "Well, she's not really your momma. You're adopted."

When she arrived at the prom, Karen reported the taunt to her mother, who was there as a chaperone. Her mother in turn reported it to her father, who was there as an administrator. Both seemed to watch her all night, protectively. It dawned on her that there might be some validity to that boy's accusation.

In the morning Karen's parents sat her down. They told her that they loved her and that Karen should be glad someone had wanted to adopt her. But Karen was devastated. Back then, being adopted was something that nobody spoke about. That the secret had come out, publicly, in front of her prom date, was horrifying. The stigma attached to adoption back then made an adopted child feel second-rate, never able to be loved like a biological child. Once she went looking for the evidence, Karen could find plenty to support her fear that she was not loved like a "real" child. Her shoes came from a thrift store and her clothes from a discount store—was this not proof that her parents did not care enough even to dress her like the other kids?

Karen looked elsewhere for love and attention. By the fall of her senior year she was pregnant. This scandalized the neighborhood. Karen's father insisted she should put the baby up for adoption. He had raised his daughter to marry a rich man; her chance at that was already ruined, but perhaps some of her life could be salvaged. Every week of the pregnancy, Karen's father dragged her down to the Community Chest building to meet with the executive director, who counseled Karen on how they would place the baby with another family. However, the director insisted that the choice was Karen's. She eventually decided to keep the baby. She had a daughter, Jackie, in August 1967, right before she was to begin college. She had been accepted to Kentucky State University in Frankfort. The university kept calling, wondering when Karen would make her deposit on her dorm room. Her father punished her by refusing to pay. He eventually called the school and told them that his daughter had "fallen from grace."

Her father kicked her out and cut her off. Karen responded by having three children from three different fathers by the time she was twenty-two: Jackie, Jarralynne, and James. She got an apartment three blocks away. During this period her mother, Dorothy, snuck her money and looked after the children while Karen worked at Ohio Bell as a telephone operator. When the youngest was one month old, Karen's mother suddenly and unexpectedly died. A neighbor came to her door to tell her. Karen stumbled out into the street and wailed. She looked to the heavens and asked God why he had taken her. In one moment, Karen lost everything. Her mother was the one who cared, the one who listened, the one who loved.

"The rest of our days have been ruled by the loss of my mother," she recounted.

Quite suddenly without child care, and having a salary that covered rent or food but not both, Karen begged her father for help. She knew he did not want to see her, so she limited her pleas to only the worst emergencies. He complained that all his daughter wanted was money. Karen and her kids became "those needy people."

In his eyes Karen had fallen from grace. Then she kept on falling, with no bottom in sight.

Without any options, Karen applied at the housing agency for a place to live. They told her she could move into the Metropolitan Apartments south of town, which were brand-new. But in the meantime, while the Metropolitan was being finished, she would have to move into the cold cement hulks at the Parkside Homes, the nastiest housing project in Ohio.

The day she moved into Parkside, her television moved out. In the year that followed, a neighbor was shot on his doorstep. Another mother's baby was killed when her boyfriend dropped the child. A five-year-old girl was molested. The housing agency never lived up to its promise to let Karen move into the Metropolitan.

"It was a shocking transition," Karen remembered. "I was completely unprepared. I was a society girl. I was not used to being around people who drank alcohol. To this day I have never tasted a drop myself. Every night the neighbors fought. I have never gotten over this."

Rarely could Karen find a babysitter for her children, so she sometimes left them in the care of her oldest child, Jackalynne, who was only five. One night Karen came home and found the apartment reeking from smoke. There had been a fire when Jarralynne tried to warm up a can of pork and beans on the stove. Amazingly, the postman had saved her children. But Children's Services had been telephoned. They began an investigation. Trying to avert a disaster, Karen took her children down to Head Start.

Head Start evaluated each of the children, and then considered Karen. Head Start told her they could care for her children, but that Karen needed help, too; they believed she was showing signs of mental illness, perhaps set off by the loss of her mother. They offered to steer her to the proper agency. Karen considered this to the fullest extent of her capabilities. The potential benefit did not seem to outweigh the risk of some doctor declaring her unfit to care for her kids. So she insisted she was not ill, she had simply lost her mother. Before they could stop her, she grabbed her kids and left.

PHOTO: © BRUCE MANSON

Karen Fletcher

When Jarralynne was a young girl, her mother seemed constantly overwhelmed. Then there were times Jarralynne thought her mother was suffocating under the burden. As if she were on her last breath. Like on the night her mother put Jarralynne in the backseat of the car with her little brother, Jamie, and her older sister, Jackie.

Karen drove and cried and muttered. Jarralynne was accustomed to Mother crying, but it never failed to scare her. Where was she taking them? To a restaurant to beg for food? To Granddaddy's house? She rubbed the fogged windows with her jacket to look for clues.

When the car turned onto North Main Street, Jarralynne and her siblings became stone silent. Mother parked the car in a lot beside some brightly colored bungalows. The sign read SHAWN ACRES. Jarralynne knew what it was. She had known kids who had been there. Shawn Acres was a county foster home for troubled children and orphans.

Her mother's tears went from dribbles to sobs. "Lord, give me strength," Karen bawled.

Karen climbed on the seat back and reached to hug and kiss each of her children.

"I'm so sorry, children. I have to let you go. I can't do it anymore. I can't."

"No, Momma," Jarralynne cried. "We're sorry. We won't cause you any more trouble."

"I could have had a life if not for you all. You've been my chain. Don't get pregnant young, or your life will be over like mine was."

"Momma, we're sorry!"

"I can't do it, children. You'll be better off. You won't go hungry."

"We're not hungry, Momma. We're okay! Please, Momma."

"Lord, please Lord. Give me a break."

Karen did not say anything for a long time. She just slumped over and cried. Jarralynne and her siblings huddled and continued to make promises. They wanted their mother to be happy. They would do anything to make their mother happy. But they were not getting out of that car.

Hours seemed to go by. Then Jarralynne realized her mother had not made a sound in a long time.

"Momma?"

Jarralynne looked over the seat. Mother was slumped across the front seat. She didn't seem to be moving. Jarralynne noticed that there was a bottle of empty pills on the floor in front of her mother.

"Momma! Mommy, wake up!"

The kids reached over and shook her. Nothing.

"Mommy, don't die! Mommy, wake up!"

They pounded on her and shook her until her eyes finally opened again. The crying resumed. Then their mother said, "We wouldn't be hungry if my mommy was still alive."

Finally Karen restarted the car.

"I'm sorry, children. I'm sorry for scaring you. Momma's just so un-happy, I don't know what to do. I need a break. Pray for Mommy. Please pray for Mommy."

In the backseat, Jarralynne prayed.

If there was a bottom, that was it.

But this happened more than once.

This scene recurred maybe four times a year, up until Jarralynne was about ten years old.

Karen would come out of those harrowing decision points outside Shawn Acres with some determination. Karen was the working poor, which meant she was jealous of those on food stamps, who at least had something to eat. So she'd get creative. She would dress herself up real nice, drag the kids to a restaurant, and announce, "Oh my God, the check didn't show up! But it'll be here tomorrow. The kids gotta eat, though."

If that didn't work, Karen would tell her girls to go up to a nice lady somewhere and ask her to "be my godmother." Karen knew they would think it was cute, and some handout would come of it.

Karen's father had remarried and moved from his house on Stolz Avenue. But he kept the house, and even kept it heated, so Karen would sneak her kids in through the window at night. When Karen's father found out, he called the police and had them removed. They took to sleeping in their car because it had a heater. But Karen did not carry insurance on the car, so when it was stolen it was not replaced.

In time, Karen married Gene Fletcher. He was about her equal, meaning he worked and yet had problems on a par with hers, and he was not able to add much stability to the situation.

Whenever Jarralynne was invited to dinner at another girl's house, she would make herself as busy as a maid, hoping to get invited back. When she was thirteen, she began working evenings at Huffies Bar B Q, which allowed her to bring leftovers home for her hungry family.

Most children in Jarralynne's situation develop a sense of the world in which they are not prime movers—they believe they are utterly unable to affect their environment. Everything they experience seems outside of their control. The miracle in Jarralynne's development was that she was very good at letting go of so many bad things and very good at hanging on to the precious examples of situations in which her own effort paid off, such as at school and at work. She was a victim of tragic circumstance, but she pretended she was not, and she proved the virtue of this lie. By pretending she was in control, she constructed an identity that served her well. She remembers that she logged people as either Nonbelievers or Believers, according to their faith in her. She ignored the Nonbelievers and basked in the confidence of the Believers. Her biggest cheerleader was always her mother.

Despite her fall from grace and her debilitating depression, Karen Fletcher hoped her children could enjoy the same benefits she once had as a child. Even though she could not feed her kids, Karen insisted that they learn all the skills proper children learn. She signed them up for every group and summer program that the middle-class kids went to. Jamie was on the boys' swim team; the girls were entered in beauty pageants and later joined female sororities. Karen used friends' addresses to enroll her children in the best public schools. She insisted her children act in school plays, and when Jarralynne had to memorize her monologues for *Porgy & Bess,* her mother also learned every single line and rehearsed it with Jarralynne to perfection. All of the children were entered in speech contests. They joined the student government and in high school were voted student body presidents. The kids were expected to go to college. It was not an opportunity, not a choice. It was an expectation drilled into them since they were young.

Jarralynne could never figure her mother out. On the one hand, the rent would go unpaid and they would be publicly evicted. On the other hand, her mother was the only parent who knew how to do taxes correctly, or fill out a college application, or get somebody's son out of jail. For this wisdom, her mother was highly respected by other parents. The Karen Fletcher they knew stirred hearts when she sang "You Light Up My Life" in church. To this day, Karen Fletcher is *revered* in the African American community of Dayton. If this is hard for us to imagine, knowing what we do about her struggles, think of how much harder it was for Jarralynne to reconcile. She never knew which mom was going to be there at night.

When Jarralynne was a junior in high school, she carried around a brochure for a summer study program at Washington & Lee in Virginia. She knew her mother could never afford it, but the pictures on the brochure entranced her. She kept the brochure close to her heart, and stared at it in private moments.

One day her mother said, "You're going."

Huh? "How?"

"I called them and persuaded them to take you."

Partly because of her performance in that summer program and the people she met there, Jarralynne was offered a full scholarship to Fisk University in Nashville.

Jarralynne did not stop at her bachelor's degree. She earned her PhD in psychology in California, then did her internship at Georgia State in Atlanta. She met Bob Agee there; he was studying to be a sports medicine physician. On their first date they decided to spend the rest of their lives together. Bob was from a family completely unlike hers. His father was a respected army surgeon. When she went home with Bob to visit the Agees their first Christmas together, there were more presents under the tree than Jarralynne had received in her entire life. To her surprise, every single one of the presents was for her. She had no idea how to take this: She had some practice learning to accept food given to her, though she always offered to work for it; she had some practice receiving a night in a warm house, though she had always tried to tidy up as a way of repaying that, too. She thought she knew how to receive, but she did not, for this was a kind of abundance she could never repay.

In August 1999, Jarralynne was twenty-nine years old and living in Atlanta. She and Bob were completing their studies with graduate-level internships. It was the end of a long haul for both of them, and they were looking forward to the future. Once they finished their internships, she and Bob intended to find jobs, buy a charming house, and raise a family. Jarralynne did not want a better relationship with her mom. Mostly, Jarralynne just wanted her privacy. She had earned her freedom. She deserved her own life.

She felt a responsibility to her mom, but she did not really want to have to *see* her. She did not want her mom close by. She did not want to be emotionally vulnerable to her mom's antics.

So Jarralynne managed her responsibility with frequent phone calls, holiday visits, and money wires. She had no trouble sending money. When she was twenty-two, Jarralynne gave her brother a car. When she was twenty-four, she gave her mom a car. She often paid their phone bills and rent. Though scraping by on graduate school stipends, she and Bob still managed to assist her family.

No, if all that was required was wiring cash by Western Union now and then, Jarralynne had no trouble with it.

It was as if Jarralynne had been planning a party for twenty-nine years, and the day for the party was just around the corner, and when she looked at the invite list she realized she did not want her mom present. Her mom had ruined too many events before. At Jarralynne's bridal shower, Mom called Jari "rich bitch" and "evil heifer" right in front of Mrs. Agee. At the state oratory competition, right in the middle of Jari's speech, Mom stood up and whooped like Arsenio Hall.

When Mom was summoned to Jarralynne's high school by the principal, she showed up in her bathrobe and slippers with her wig on sideways. Mom had a knack for making sure nobody else was the center of attention. So when it came to the future Jarralynne imagined—Bob, the house, the kids—she was not going to risk Mom making it all about her.

By then Jarralynne's mother and stepfather had moved to Greensboro, North Carolina. Jarralynne had run out of excuses for not paying them a visit. So in August 1999, shortly before her school year resumed, Jarralynne flew to Greensboro from Atlanta. She found her mom crawling on her knees in the driveway beside her Honda. The car's doors were open.

No greeting, no hello. "I can't find it!"

"What, Mom?"

"It's here. I know it is. Help me find it." Mom was frantic.

"Okay. What?"

"Don't 'what' *me*."

"*What* are you looking for, Mom?"

Karen paused, thought about it. "I'll remember when I see it."

"*Mom.*"

"I can't remember, Jari."

"Your keys?"

"No!"

"Lipstick?"

"No! It's something *important*." Said like, *Would I be on my knees looking for lipstick?*

Karen switched from combing the pavement to digging through the car. Scrunched-up yellow wrappers filled the seat wells, keeping the Big Gulp cups and knee-high socks company.

"Mom, why do you smell?"

"I'm *looking*, Jari. Don't bother me."

"Mom, you're *dirty*. What are you wearing!"

"Not everyone's rich like you."

"Mom, will you go get some clothes on?"

Jarralynne went into the house to find her mom some clothes, but her closets were emptied. There was no food in the refrigerator, either.

"I was mortified," Jarralynne remembered. "I could not help but feel like she was doing it to embarrass me. She was playing me somehow. She was always good at acting the fool to get what she wanted, which was sympathy and food and clothes and money and more sympathy."

Did she think it was an act?

"It was easier to think it was an act than to consider the alternative, which was something I absolutely did not want to face."

Jarralynne drove to the grocery store to fill the refrigerator. She decided she could not bear to stay with her mom, so she rented a hotel room. Later, Mom showed up at the hotel. Jarralynne was getting ready to go out with one of her college roommates who had moved to Greensboro. She was looking forward to spending the evening on the town with someone sane.

"Mom, what are you doing here?"

"Let me stay here, Jari."

"No, you can't stay here, Mom."

"I won't cause any trouble."

"No. My girlfriend will be here in a minute to pick me up. And you're not staying here without me."

"Why not?"

"Because you're acting crazy! Go home, Dad needs you."

"Please, Jari. Please let me stay. It's so nice here."

"No, Mom. Go. *Go home.*"

"I'll come later, then."

"Mom, this is *my* hotel room. *Mine.* I will see you tomorrow."

It was too much. After ushering her mom back to her car, Jarralynne blew off her friend. She went straight to the airport and flew back to Atlanta under the cover of night. She knew her life would never be the same. She knew the future was never going to look the way she had pictured it. Her mom had always been a time bomb and was now down to her final ticks. Jarralynne knew she would be right back in Greensboro soon. So she escaped to Atlanta to enjoy the last days of her privacy, the last days of her new life before it turned back into her old life.

"I ran because I was scared," Jarralynne said. "I was scared of how she was acting, and I was scared of all it meant. She was clearly out of her mind."

Six days later a nurse called from the hospital in North Carolina. They were unable to reach Karen's husband because his phone was out, so they called Jarralynne. Her mother had suffered a massive stroke.

"That was it," Jarralynne says as a way of summarizing that day's impact. She recognized what really mattered and brought her mom to live with her. Or so that version goes. When Jarralynne is not rushing the story and plays it out piece by piece, the truth turns out to be far more complicated. In fact, the circumstances of her mother entering the hospital flipped Jarralynne's feelings from oh-my-gosh *responsibility* to how-could-I-have-been-so-callous *guilt.* Karen had been admitted to the psych ward after a 911 call five days earlier—the morning after Jarralynne fled town. The doctors on the psych ward had trouble diagnosing her, but now that she'd suffered a major stroke, they realized in retrospect that she'd been having repeated minor strokes for more than a week. Her brain had been misfiring. *Transient ischemic attacks* is the condition's clinical name. In other words, Karen had been having those strokes the day Jarralynne found her in the driveway.

"I'm a psychologist! If anyone should have seen the signs, it should have been me," Jarralynne recalled, scolding herself. "I should have taken her to the hospital. Maybe the big stroke would have been prevented if she'd been put on blood thinners sooner. Instead, I ditched her. I really thought the way she was acting was somehow *about me,* just the next act in her saga, refusing to comport herself like the *normal* mother I always wanted her to be. All I could think about was all the times Mom had embarrassed me. I will live with the guilt over that weekend forever."

On blood thinners, Karen recovered reasonably well, though her legs remained fairly immobile and she was stuck in a wheelchair. Jarralynne and Bob could not consider taking her in, because they did not have a place of their own. So they paid to set up Karen and Gene in a series of apartments in North Carolina.

Over the course of a year, it became clear that no amount of money was going to guarantee the Fletchers' safety. Each of their tenancies was marred by mystifying neglect. The money that was sent was often misused. Her parents did not pay their electricity and did not eat properly. One building they were renting was scheduled to be torn down; the day demolition was to begin, her parents were still in their apartment, oblivious, despite an eviction notice pinned to their door. Jarralynne moved them to a new place and paid the bills herself. After a storm, the pilot light in the furnace needed to be relit. Gene just thought the gas bill had gone unpaid, so they froze and did not complain. The plan to care for them by wiring Western Union worked about as well as using a T-shirt for a blanket.

The word for what Jarralynne felt was *dread*. "I kept thinking, *Oh no, it's going to follow me again. I'm chained to them. I'm never going to leave this behind.*"

When they finished their internships, the Agees found jobs in Northern California. Bob was hired as a sports medicine physician at Kaiser Permanente in Union City and as a doctor for the University of California athletic teams. Jarralynne received a fellowship in the student counseling center at U. C. Berkeley. She was pregnant when they arrived. They needed a house, fast. Bob's parents were willing to help with the down payment. The only question: how many bedrooms?

Jarralynne reflected, "If I had been married to someone from my own background, his attitude would have been *To hell with your mother, she's not living with us. Nor is my mother. This is* our *life.*"

But Bob's father had taught his son to look out for others. This was partly the creed of being a doctor, and partly personal—Bob's father was an only child, and he had always wanted more family. So he embraced people. Bob remembers "Aunt Martha" staying with them during the Christmas holidays; she is a widow they knew from church.

Bob wanted to take Jarralynne's parents in. He believed in love and medicine. They'd get Mom better medical attention, get her the right drugs, put her in physical therapy, shower her with love, and heal her soul. It might take a little while, but soon they'd be living as one big happy family.

"We've just got to love her through it," he advised.

Jarralynne discussed the prospect with her siblings. They were aghast. "Are you crazy? You don't owe her your life! We're not expecting you to do it. Don't do it." They had not been much help the last year; her brother had not even visited Karen. Their grandfather had died during the year—their mom's father—and he bestowed about a hundred thousand dollars on his family. However, no one was willing to allocate any of their share to helping Bob and Jarralynne care for Karen.

"I felt dumped on," Jarralynne said. "Once again, the problem was entirely mine to deal with. I had *just started* my life."

Jarralynne realized that she would be taking care of her mom one way or another, in North Carolina or Northern California. It might as well be right close by. She and Bob did not consider long-term care, because it was extremely expensive and her parents were only in their early fifties. A decision was made, more out of inevitability than choice. They had located a nearly completed house in a new subdivision off the interstate half an hour north of their work. They paid fifteen thousand dollars to have part of the main floor converted into another bedroom, requested cheaper carpet throughout the house, and canceled the two-door stainless refrigerator on order.

And here's the thing about *inevitability*. When you have no choice, it is natural to start looking for the silver lining. As scared as she was, a part of Jarralynne got excited at the prospect of having a big old-fashioned extended family. Mom and Dad would be able to help with the new baby, who was due in a month. They would babysit in a pinch, or at least hold the baby when Jari cooked. They would have Sunday meals together. Her children would know their grandparents. She started to look forward to it. She told her parents to get rid of everything. Which they did. Karen was excited, too. She felt like the family in *The Jeffersons*. "We're moving to California!"

It was a great feeling to have—*We're family, we'll work it out.* It was going to be fine, just fine.

Karen and Gene arrived from North Carolina by plane and moved into the bedroom on the main floor of Bob and Jarralynne's new home. They were welcomed with open arms, but living under one roof inevitably brought out tensions.

"Mom, you already had one brownie. The doctor told you to cut down on the sweets."

"Don't tell me what I can and can't eat."

Just about anything became potential fodder for an occasional dig—deciding what to watch on television, or choosing furniture for the new house, or picking what to serve for dinner.

Jarralynne gave birth to her first son a month after her parents arrived. It was a glorious moment in their life, but taking care of a baby added to the stress. Jarralynne and Karen were on each other's nerves.

So when Karen started peeing on the carpet, Jarralynne could not help but feel it was somehow her mom's way of getting even for whatever bickering had occurred an hour earlier.

"I'm *incontinent,* Jari."

"You can't wear a diaper?"

"It was an *accident.*"

"Accident, my ass."

Jarralynne did not employ her doctorate-of-psychology skills in handling this. She handled it like any thirteen-year-old girl ticked off at her mom. She got furious. *She's peeing on my new life!* The more time Jarralynne spent around her mom, the less she felt like the successful working mother she was and the more she felt like a thirteen-year-old girl again.

Then Uncle Jimmy and his wife came to visit from Ohio. Uncle Jimmy was Karen's brother, younger by six years. He was oddly stand-offish in his preparations for the trip. He refused to stay with Jarralynne and Bob. Instead he rented a hotel room in San Francisco. Jarralynne did not know what she could have possibly done to upset her uncle. When he showed up at their house, he took one look around and confronted his sister.

"You told me they had you *in the basement.*"

"It *is* the bottom floor."

"You made it sound like a dungeon!" He apologized to Bob and Jarralynne. Karen had complained endlessly to him, so he had planned to come rescue her.

That *really* hurt Bob, after all he had done for his mother-in-law.

Uncle Jimmy laughed now that he saw what was really going on. "We're going sightseeing. Man, I wish *I* lived this well."

It turned out that Karen had been pleading for sympathy at her church as well. Jarralynne noticed that her mom started to get a lot of letters. Then food started being sent to the house. The congregation from Mom's church was sending get-well cards with twenty-five-dollar checks. They imagined Karen was having strokes again, which she was not.

Jarralynne and Bob organized family meetings to address Karen's behavior and set goals. For instance, they wanted her to stand and go to the restroom, and pick up the remote control herself. She tried, but couldn't manage it. When Jarralynne tried to persuade her mom that it was just a matter of will, that Mom's block was *mental,* Karen would cut her off. "Don't you try that psychology stuff on me! I see you're doing that! Don't *analyze* me!"

Over the course of the year, it started to get weird for Jarralynne. She felt like she was living in the past. Her past had taken over the guest bedroom, unpacked its bags, and announced it liked the weather in California so much it was never going to leave.

Every time Jarralynne opened her refrigerator and saw all the food stuffed onto the shelves, she had flashbacks of being a girl standing before their empty refrigerator, knowing she was going to go hungry again.

Jari would get up in the middle of the night to breast-feed her son. Climbing back into bed, trying to fall back to sleep, her earliest memories would find their way up from the darkest recesses of her mind. One of those nights, Jarralynne wrote me a letter by hand. It was about a winter they survived after living in the Parkside projects, in a place in Highview Hills that the kids nicknamed "Little House on the Prairie."

> The lights were off and that meant the heat was, too. We were in a poorly insulated house with a dirt floor in the kitchen and bathroom. Somehow the carpet eroded into the earth—I have no clue where the foundation was. Jackie, Jamie and I would squeeze ourselves into sleeping bags on the floor—two of us together and one in another bag. It didn't keep us that warm so we put stray kittens in the bag around our feet. The kittens had fleas. The sleeping bag got fleas, we got bit all night by fleas. So we slept on the floor and tried to keep the kittens inside. Some kittens scratched us bad and then found their way out of the bags. Those kittens died. We were sad because we had tried to save them, keep them in that bag for their own good. It really is a wonder that we survived with the flea scars that were so bad that we wore socks with sandals for years and I had the scars from scratching until I started grad school years later.

When the memories first started returning, Jarralynne thought, *Oh, this is good. I'll revisit the past and I'll heal.* But that turned out to be naïve. The process of remembering was much like when she was a little girl, looking out the window at an Ohio blizzard. The snow was coming down. Big, soft snowflakes. It seemed so nice, so beautiful, that she wanted to open the door for a second, let just a little in. The second she opened the door, the blizzard bit her like only freezing cold can, punishing her for being so stupid.

So it was with her memories of childhood. Her mom's presence had cracked that door, and soon the blizzard had Jarralynne out there freezing with it.

Stay warm, she was discovering. *Don't crack that door.*

"They can't stay here anymore, Bob. Please, Bob, I mean it. I love them, but it's not working."

Bob relented. "All right. We'll get them their own place."

Jarralynne found an apartment five miles away for her parents, and with that the blizzard weakened, then gave way to spring. Today they have arrived at a workable equilibrium—Karen and Gene are close enough to be looked after, but not too close. Karen's Social Security check pays the rent. Jarralynne and Bob pay for the utilities, their van, and their groceries. They also want to provide for Karen's physical therapy, but she refuses to go.

"Bob talked to the doctors, Mom. They say there's no reason you can't walk again."

"*They* don't know what my legs feel like."

Karen misses her independence. This topic makes her shed tears like a sprinkler. "There are so many ways I would like to be a part of the community but am unable to do. In Dayton, I was *so* involved." She listed two worthy social programs she directed and a Christian organization she participated in. It would fill a page to include all the credentials of the people she met through those community activities. "Here, my only outlet is watching channel five and CNN," she sobbed. She also has her church, Sojourner Truth Presbyterian, and does get to sing there occasionally. She is fifty-five years old, but going on old age.

"I'm back in the ghetto again," Karen remarked.

Jarralynne piped up. "*Mom,* this is *not* the ghetto. These are very nice apartments."

"I miss the cable at your house."

"It's the *same* ninety-five-dollar-a-month cable as we have there. Both bills are charged to my card."

Karen has trouble being appreciative—she can't help it, because Karen sees her daughter having the life Karen was *supposed* to have, and was raised to expect. As she put it, "In some way, even as I am grateful that Jarralynne is doing well and married a rich man, it serves as a constant and grating reminder of the life I was going to have, and was set up to have."

To get a sense of the world Karen once belonged to, you only have to hear her voice. While she stammers a little, and sometimes she can't find the word she's looking for, it is otherwise the voice of a very *proper* woman, a woman who has been to finishing classes and cotillions. She draws on an extensive vocabulary. All her descriptions are front-loaded, leaning hard on people's credentials: "Nobody else had graduated from a revered place like Miami of Ohio University," for instance, or "It was a very *elite* church; the pastor was involved in the *NAACP*." She will always inform you who so-and-so's parents were, and how respected they were. When Karen talks, it's like that prosperous middle-class black renaissance of mid-century is brought back to life. Make no mistake: This woman was once a *lady*.

Karen has a deep need for someone, anyone, to understand what she has been through. She showed me the Bible she carried during the hard years in Dayton. In every margin are scrawled prayers to the Heavenly Father thanking him (in advance) for the help she hoped he would send her way. These prayers are extremely specific, mentioning heating bills and car payments and clothes her daughters needed for school.

I asked Karen, "So I guess you've been in need of medical treatment probably since your early twenties?"

"Oh yes. Absolutely. I sure did. I look at antidepressants, and I wonder how they might have helped me back then. But of course that was not how they treated mental illness at that time."

"You were afraid they might take your kids if you pursued treatment?"

"Oh yes."

A month later, I had lunch with Jarralynne and asked about her mother's mental state. Jarralynne could now finally speak about her mother like a psychologist, not a thirteen-year-old girl. She believes her mother still demonstrates classic post-traumatic stress disorder, stemming from the death of her own mother, Dorothy. She explains that her mother is now on Paxil, which helps, but that Karen exhibits *perseveration,* which is a type of repetitive fixation. Her mother hears things in the news involving death and incorporates them into her own story. So after a rash of murders in Oakland, Karen wanted to move to Oakland and kept saying she had to "get to Oakland."

"So was your mom always mentally ill? Was she having strokes all along?"

"We think the poverty, and the repudiation from her father, and eventually the strokes all obfuscated the situation, kept anyone from realizing that she suffered from mood disorder and chemical imbalance."

"What would the diagnosis be?"

"Probably dysthymia with histrionic features. Dysthymia is chronic depression due to incessantly overwhelming negative episodes, really one bad thing after another."

"And it's better now?"

"We haven't had one single shouting match."

All things considered, it has been a lot better since Karen moved into the apartment. It's doable. It is going to work. There are occasional wrinkles. For instance, last month Karen racked up *six hundred dollars* in 411 calls, not realizing how phone companies have changed since her Ohio Bell days.

Both Karen and Jarralynne hit crossroads in their twenties where they felt like freedom was within reach if only they were not shackled to each other, if only they did not have the other to care for. This is how Karen felt when she drove her children to Shawn Acres, and this is how Jarralynne felt when she found her mother acting crazy in the driveway. Their desire was gone, and their will was weak, but the chain held, unbreakable.

It is common for us—people of every income and plight—to go through a period in which we're convinced we'd be free, if not for the family chained to us.

The Fletcher-Agees suffered a tragic and harrowing fall, but despite the devastation managed to return to prominence a generation later. It strained them but did not divide them. They have hung on to each other when others have not; they have found a way through it. Yet there have been times that I've been around them when I wondered, *Is this success?* Is this success, if Karen is jealous of her daughter and often can't be nice? Is this success, if Jarralynne and her siblings talk on the phone all the time and yet never mention the inheritance from Karen's father that was not put toward her care? Is this success, if Jarralynne takes care of her mother but can't really *enjoy* doing so? If providing for her mother doesn't fill her with "a sense of purpose"?

Many times Jarralynne calls me to express this very same frustration. She usually has just come away from some unsatisfying encounter with her mother or one of her siblings. These really eat at her—they bug her far more than the burden of supporting the family. In other words, she doesn't mind having to help out so much as she minds that her family cuts one another down a size when they get a chance. She misses the days when they were united, "The Fletchers Versus the World." As a psychologist, she is trained to view a very normal amount of carping in her family as something wrong, a problem. But is it?

Perhaps these are just the scars of survival. Is a little bickering and denial worth being so offended by, particularly when we understand where it comes from, and how it could have been so much worse? I suggest to Jarralynne that complaining about bickering and denial may be quite a privilege. It's not that I've lowered my expectations. But I'm learning to understand the bigger challenges that families face.

And this is what I tell Jarralynne when she calls. She has endured poverty, hunger, a mentally unstable mother, neighborhoods racked with drugs and violence, and cruel neglect from a grandfather. If the only legacy of her childhood is a tendency to take a few cheap shots when times are good, I consider that fairly amazing.

It always helps Jarralynne to hear this, and it often helps her find her pride again in their bottom line. "My mother's marriage to Dad has lasted nearly thirty years. All three children are college graduates. We have all had our hard times. Yet my sister, Jackalynne, is a lawyer. My brother, James, is in real estate in Ohio. He is married with two children. Every single boy in our old neighborhood—every single boy—is either dead or in prison."

Jackalynne, Jarralynne, James, Uncle Jimmy, and Karen

Every family has had its trials. Very often, the complaints we hear today—*My mother was never very loving*—have their roots in those trials. We are witness only to the fading reflection of something that happened long ago. And while I would never say the past is an excuse, I do think it helps to have done your research. Give people credit for what they've had to cope with. Bringing an *appropriate* expectation to your search for harmony is the first step to getting that expectation met.

Is the Fletcher-Agees' story ultimately sad and dark? Most people would think so. That the family has succeeded is overshadowed by the tragedy they had to endure. The pain of their story is so deep that it can be hard to feel happy for them. But *do* be happy for them. They aren't sad for themselves. They came from a community where those problems were common. They feel lucky.

Jarralynne could have handled it so differently. She could have been one of those young career women who simply ran away from her troubled family and started fresh on her own. She could have pushed her childhood down into the frozen iceberg of all things forgotten. Her family could just be "those people" she never talks to anymore. To the Fletcher-Agees, that scenario would be the truly sad one.

Jarralynne and I talk about something else for a while, and when we come back to the topic of her mother, Jarralynne is no longer the psychologist. She is back to being the daughter, contemplating her mother. I notice that when Jarralynne remembers with her family all around, there's a sort of safety in numbers, and she manages to laugh at all the old stories. But when I interview her one-on-one, the same stories scare her stiff. Jarralynne is remembering one now.

It was after she had ditched her mom in North Carolina, and a week later the nurse at the hospital had called. The nurse had pestered Karen for days, insisting they needed to call her family, they needed to call someone to come help her. Karen kept providing a name without a number. But then, finally, Karen remembered the number. So the nurse dialed. But the nurse did not ask for Jarralynne.

Instead, the nurse asked, "I'd like to speak to Dorothy. Is there a Dorothy there?"

And in that moment, Jarralynne knew.

Why do we do things

we know we shouldn't?

The Tree

Julie and Andrew Ervin Bennett

This will sound like a fable, but every bit of it is true.

It starts with a story about a remarkable tree, an American elm with a lush green crown that spreads more than sixty feet across. Its trunk is now about twelve feet in circumference, so the tree is surely over a hundred years old, perhaps much more.

This elm is next to a barn, at the bottom of a hill, beside a cherry orchard, on forty-seven acres of a family farm. This farm is three miles outside a town named Beulah, near the northwestern tip of Michigan's Lower Peninsula. Beulah is so tiny that it says WELCOME TO BEULAH on both sides of the sign.

Back in the 1950s, the family that owned this farm kept its cattle bull chained to this elm. All day long the bull would pace around the tree, dragging his chain with him. The iron chain scraped a trench in the bark that circled the trunk three feet off the ground. Over the years, the trench deepened into a gash.

Then the family sold the farm. They took their bull but left its chain, cutting the next-to-last link so that what remained resembled a stub necklace, a chain loop now nearly embedded in the bark, with a single link dangling down.

For a few years the farm was dormant. Then a family arrived. Two grandparents, their adult son-in-law, and his two boys, one eleven years old, the other only four. The four-year-old boy found the elm right away, and he felt a kinship for this grand old being with its horrific scar and its curious dangling link. By then the bark had started to grow back, and it nearly met itself as it reached over the iron links. This boy, too, had a scar: His mother and his sister had recently been killed by a drunk driver.

The next year, the boy's wound got deeper. His father remarried and moved away, taking his older son with him but not the boy. There were reasons offered, but none that made any sense to the boy, who simply understood that his father and stepmother did not want him. The boy remained on the farm to be raised by his maternal grandparents. He rarely saw his father again. But his grandfather was loving and playful, and the boy glommed on to the old man.

The next years put the great elm in jeopardy. Dutch elm disease, a fungus carried from tree to tree by beetles, proceeded to wipe out nearly all the elms along its spreading path through North America in the 1960s and 1970s. The county was terrified, because these American elms were ubiquitously used for shade. Surveyors were sent out to forecast the likely damage. The elms lining the road up to the farm, a road made of tar and wood chips, died quickly. The grandfather figured the old great elm would be next. There was no way the tree could last, between the encroaching fungus and that chain belt strangling its trunk. He considered doing the safe thing, which was to pull it out and chop it up before it became diseased and fell onto the barn in a storm.

But the grandfather could not bring himself to uproot the elm. He and the boy had spent so much time in its shade, the darn thing felt like a family member. So he let nature take its course. Miraculously, the tree did not wither. Year after year it continued to bloom great cathedral-like canopies. Nobody could conceive how this was possible. Word of this elm traveled throughout Michigan, and plant pathologists and horticulturalists from Michigan State University were dispatched to examine the curiosity. The boy was ten by then. He well remembers the crew from the university that came out that summer. They were not sure what to conclude. By then the tree had thickened, and its bark had completely grown over the chain; the descending lip of bark turned out as it met the ascending lip, creating a fat seam the boy could run his finger along. The chain inside was as rusty as a shipwreck, its single dangle now partly immersed. The university crew had only one theory to offer. Somehow, this scar, this chain, which for years everyone thought was going to kill the tree, instead had saved the tree's life. They suggested that by absorbing so much iron from the chain, the tree had become immune.

To the boy, this offered a powerful metaphor. Perhaps his scar was not going to kill him, either. Perhaps someday, when everyone expected it to destroy him, it might save his life.

With the grandfather's extensive encouragement, the boy studied magic tricks, and in public he adopted the persona of a performer. This hid the pain of his loss. Then, one April day when the boy was seventeen, the grandfather went down to the barn beside the elm and shot himself. Nobody ever asked the boy about this, and the boy did not want to talk about it. That was the way it was handled back then in that part of the country. The boy's scar was just another notch deeper. It was miracle enough to stay alive. He carried on with his grandmother and their inspiring elm.

Today the elm dwarfs the barn. The chain is completely covered with bark, and may even have decomposed inside, though the scar is still there.

PHOTO: © JOHN KALNINS

The picnic bench in front of the trunk gives some sense of the tree's proportions.

The boy, Andrew Bennett, grew into an adult. He was handsome, and women considered him sensitive and open. Men liked that he had grown up on a farm and knew how to hunt and fish. He advanced quickly in his field, business consulting. In all these ways he resembled a man, but his heart was still that of a boy. It was ruled by a desperate longing to be swallowed by love—which made him overly romantic, needy, and self-centered. He attempted to deal with this responsibly; he sought out therapists. But *awareness* was no antidote. Knowing that his weakness was rooted in his childhood—and being able to ascribe theories to it—did little to affect how he reacted when under pressure.

On the very night I met him, Andrew was in trouble.

For nine years he had lived peacefully with his wife, Julie. They lived in Ann Arbor, Michigan. Andrew was in his early forties, Julie in her mid-thirties. They were ready to get pregnant and become parents, or so they thought—until he inexplicably started to balk. He became critical of his wife, finding fault in her, making her miserable. Self-employed, he withdrew from his work and began living off their savings.

Last June I met Andrew in Ann Arbor. Having only a short amount of time to spend with him, I listened to the story of his childhood, and how his career needed a jolt, but I could sense that his distress sprang from something far more immediate. I took notes and promised to stay in touch, perhaps return. I later learned what was really going on that night. Not two hours earlier, he had told Julie he needed a break. Reluctantly, Julie granted him his space. She could use the peace. They did not label themselves with that loaded word, *separated,* but that was their status, at least in Andrew's mind.

After our meeting, he went off to live at a friend's lake house, where he numbed himself with beer for a few weeks, weakening his judgment and drowning his guilt. Then, as he had secretly anticipated all along, Andrew began seeing someone else.

Many affairs begin as flings; at least at first, there is no intention of the affair ever leaving the bedroom. But this was not casual for Andrew; he believed he had finally found the soul mate he had always been searching for, a woman who was his equal. She had been an acquaintance for months. The tension had built. It felt *right*.

In late July he went to talk with Julie at their condominium. She sat down on one of their matching couches. He sat down in the high-backed chair close to the door, then came right out with it: He wanted a divorce. This was not what she was expecting *at all*. She thought he was going to sort himself out, not *quit*. She suspected this must be about another woman, because she knew his pattern. Twice before—when he was twenty-seven and thirty-four—he had fled a lengthy relationship. Nine years ago, Julie had been the woman whose arms he had escaped to. She was no fool.

"No, you can't!" Julie yelled. Until then the sweetest woman in the world, she jumped over the coffee table and slapped him, hard. "Oh no you don't!" She pounded on his chest and swiped at his face. "I know you! You already carry so much shame! Don't do something that will make it worse! I know what these episodes in your life have done to you! This will kill you! You will end up dead! If you do this, you are as good as dead!"

Andrew tried to get the chair between them. Julie did not relent. She attacked him. "I am *not* going to let you do this to yourself!" Not *do this to me,* but *do this to yourself.* "If anybody can get through this, *we* can!" She kept hitting him, but she was crying now. "You're not going to do this! *It will destroy you!* I am not giving up! Everyone else has left you. Your mother left you, your father left you, your grandfather left you! You have been suffering ever since. SO I AM NOT GOING TO LEAVE YOU! You can't push me away! You can't make me quit! We are going to counseling! I am going to find someone and make an appointment, and we are going to hang on, because I know you, and if you do this, you are as good as dead."

Cowering from the voraciousness of his wife's attack, shocked by the integrity of her words, and blown away by her tenacity, Andrew agreed to see a counselor.

This is the story of how Andrew and Julie Ervin Bennett repaired their marriage and rescued Andrew from self-destruction.

Repairing a marriage is disorienting. At any one time, either spouse can feel regret, anger, and hope simultaneously. I have special admiration for the Ervin Bennetts and the ten other couples I interviewed who pulled it off. Their stories provoke essential questions that are applicable not only to couples in trouble.

The Ervin Bennetts' journey probes the question *What kind of love should we be looking for, aiming for, and giving?* Over the next year, everything Andrew went through challenged the way he had long answered this question. Changing what you want and expect from love is extremely hard, because those imprints are burned in during childhood and by adulthood have become so instinctive they literally define us. Those urges are inseparable from the rest of us; they're not a part that can be removed and replaced. Andrew was guided by a desire to save himself, to be healthy, and to be a better man. He had help from friends and clinical professionals, but he credits Julie more than anyone for demonstrating a kind of love he had never considered before.

His reeducation began with Julie's initial reaction on that night in late July. Andrew credits his eventual transformation to her astonishing response. That moment shocked him.

"It was so *selfless,*" he recalled. "I went in there worrying how much I was going to hurt her. I expected tears and tragedy and *How could you!* And while she *was* hurt, her first instinct was not to protect herself, but to protect *me.*" He recited her words: " *'I'm not going to let you do this to yourself.'* She knew that the times I had done this same thing in the past made me hate myself unforgivably, and made me consider taking my grandfather's means of escape. Her reaction really blew me away. I had never been loved like that before. Nobody had ever allowed that I might make mistakes and he or she would still love me. It was an altogether different kind of love than I was familiar with. *Sincere,* and *giving.* By this definition, I had never actually loved anyone before. I thought I had, but my love was *always* selfish. It was always *about me,* about the feelings *I* was getting from the relationship."

I turned to Julie. "And how was it that you gave him this, right away no less? Had you planned what to say?"

"Not all. It was instinctive and impulsive."

"Didn't you want to just throw the scum out, let him rot in the hell of his own creation? That's usually the first reaction—fury over being lied to, of your trust being violated. The willingness to work on it usually comes later."

"I just saw him as I would a friend in need. I didn't take it personally. Not for a second did I believe the issue here was whether some other woman was better than me. I wasn't even really trying to save our marriage. If we ended up only friends, that was okay. I was genuinely worried for him."

I asked Julie, "Had *you* ever been given this kind of unconditional love? Is it through having received it yourself that you were able to give it to him?"

"No, that was not the kind of love I saw modeled growing up. If anything, I learned to deny problems and smooth things over. I really think it was the situation, it was what *he needed* in the crisis point. I just felt it."

"He needed to know that someone was not going to leave him?"

"Yes. Those who were supposed to give him that kind of love had all left him."

I turned back to Andrew. "Does the story of the tree fit in here?"

"I think about the tree a lot. I've always expected its metaphor to have an application in my life. And it does now. Maybe the purpose of my scar is to remind me that my life is already vulnerable and precious, and I shouldn't throw it away, I shouldn't act on a whim. I shouldn't uproot the tree just because I don't want to risk it dying on me."

Surely Andrew's compulsion to leave women after many happy years together is tied to his childhood. But the connection can be interpreted in many ways. Andrew's therapists focused on the fact that he always seemed to leave women right when a significant uptick in responsibility arose, such as him and Julie deciding to become parents. So they labeled Andrew with *abandonment theory*. "The boy abandons because he was abandoned," they told him. In the primitive way that a boy who is hurt turns around and hurts someone else, the boy in Andrew had stored up his hurt for years, and despite his best intentions, he had an overriding impulse to hurt those who loved him, to leave them just as he had been left.

Now, that theory might be descriptive, but it certainly never helped Andrew change his behavior. It never disarmed the attraction of starting over with another woman.

Shortly after that night in July, Andrew and his therapist rewrote that script. This new interpretation only became clear when Andrew tried, and failed, to tell the other woman it was over.

Andrew had agreed to see a marital counselor with Julie, but neither of them was ready for Andrew to move home. So that night he went back to his friend's lake house. He was excited to work on his marriage with Julie. But what of this other woman, whom, only hours before, he'd considered his soul mate? Andrew had to break it off, and in meeting her to break it off, he ended up confused again. Andrew and Julie's first appointment was on the calendar. The morning of that appointment, Andrew chased down his personal therapist in a panic, brought her up to speed, and told her he was having an impossible time telling this woman it was over. He wanted to. He did not want to be throwing his life away. He was miserable.

She said to him, "Andrew, do you know what this sounds like? Do you know what you seem to be describing?"

He had no idea.

"You're describing an addiction. You're unable to give up this relationship, despite it destroying your marriage, your career, and your savings. You want to stop, you have every intention of stopping, but you cannot control yourself."

"Wow. An addiction. That really does seem to describe what I feel."

The metaphor of addiction gave Andrew a new lens through which to view his behavior. It stripped the luster off his liaison. It was going to drag him down as surely as alcohol. To continue was sadistic. It also put a new label on what he got from the affair—*a high*. He was addicted to the romantic rush, the electric charge of being with someone novel.

And as with any other addiction, he was using the high to escape, to numb the pain, to fill the hole that had been dug in childhood.

Andrew felt like this got at a truth that abandonment theory never had. He did not *want* to leave Julie for any other woman. What he wanted was the *newness,* the incredible spell—glorious love!—that made his sorrow magically vanish.

Meanwhile, Julie had become suspicious. That very day—literally, during the hour he was in his breakthrough therapy session—Julie called his best friend and asked him point-blank if Andrew was still conducting the affair. His friend did not lie. Julie learned who the other woman was, *called her,* and threatened to tell this woman's husband and children if she did not stay away from Andrew. It worked. The woman sent Andrew a text message: "Julie knows, and it's over."

That afternoon Julie showed up at their first counseling session, unsure whether she wanted to continue. She was furious. Andrew came to her in the waiting room. She glared at him. "You are unbelievable," she said scornfully. He got on his knee and apologized, and then proceeded to plead for another chance on the grounds that he had just had a significant breakthrough, and for the first time in a long time, he felt hope.

Here's why she believed him, and was able, eventually, to forgive him: because she agreed with his new interpretation. In fact, it was very similar to her own views, which were based on neuroscience: When you touch someone new, a hit of the hormone oxytocin is released into your bloodstream, and it is, literally, a high. Andrew had misinterpreted the high as love and had assumed the activator of that high was his soul mate. Julie never believed in soul mates or even understood their appeal. To Julie, real love was something else entirely, something much harder to learn, not this primitive biological response that any schoolboy can have.

"That he had the affair was just not as shocking to me as it would be to a romantic," she explained. "I knew that, underneath it all, he is a good man and a special man. There was no one like him. He had been good to me for nine years. To some, the longer you've been together, the *more* it's a betrayal, the more it's a shock. The years prior become tainted. But not to me. Those were good years, without struggle. Our turn had come."

On the advice of their counselor, they did not rush back into married life. They spoke by phone every afternoon for fifteen minutes to check in and voice their feelings. They practiced listening without finding blame in what the other was saying. The counselor recommended they begin dating.

Their first date, they went to their favorite sandwich shop and ate outside at sidewalk tables, then got ice cream. There was a lot of tension, in the way there is with any first date—wanting to come across well, and hoping the chemistry will spark. They were more honest than they had been in years, which was a thrill. Both knew that they had a tendency to sweep issues under the rug to avoid conflict. If they could maintain this level of honesty—without being unnecessarily hurtful— they had a chance.

At the end of the night, they were allowed one kiss. They had been apart ten weeks (since their separation in June), so there was more *newness* in that kiss than either expected. On their second date, they made out in the car. The night ended with both wanting more. Andrew's therapist had insisted that if he was going to treat his compulsion as an addiction, he should go cold turkey for a couple of months—no sex, period. In a way, this directive liberated Julie; she didn't have to be as protective of herself. She was free to want her husband without worrying that they'd end up in bed too soon.

Rather quickly, the Ervin Bennetts reached an important milestone: the realization that a marriage can still feel *new,* despite years of routine and the big scar of infidelity. When couples tap back into this wellspring, it is then (and often, *only* then) that they really commit to the rebuilding effort. They see it might be worth bothering, after all. There's actually some hope. As with the old elm, the sign of life in a marriage is its marvelous capacity to renew itself.

However, the levity of newness did not last for the Ervin Bennetts. A couple of days after their second date, Andrew had planned a camping trip up near his childhood farm, at Sleeping Bear Dunes on Lake

Michigan. Julie did not like camping. Or at least, she didn't think she did—the truth was, she had never tried it. She wanted Andrew to stay; he wanted her to come with him. He went anyway, and once he was gone they both were dismayed. They had quickly landed right back in one of their old arguments. They called each other, and Julie decided that she would get in her car and drive across Michigan to meet him after her morning shift at work. This was great. They were trying something new together.

While the weather had been beautiful that morning, a big storm hit Michigan right as Julie was leaving Ann Arbor. Julie was tired—she normally took a nap after her early-morning shift—but she jumped in her car despite fatigue, and despite the inclement weather.

So she was not in bed when lightning struck their condominium.

The Ervin Bennetts' apartment was on the top floor of a twenty-unit dwelling. The lightning hit the roof right above their bedroom, which exploded into flames that could be seen three miles away—where the 911 call came from.

PHOTO: © ANN ARBOR FIRE DEPARTMENT

The Ervin Bennetts made it home four hours later. Two of their four cats were never found. Much of the building was saved, but their home was destroyed. This was especially painful because it was the second home they had lost—eighteen months before, they had built a new home, only to have it quickly condemned for the presence of mold.

They were still in a lawsuit with that builder. Now they would have to fight their insurance company over the fire, too. The only glimmer of hope they had—the only thing they could point to—was that Julie's life was probably saved by not being in that bed. If they had wanted a sign that good would come from finding new solutions to old arguments, here it was. On the other hand, their home had been torched by the heavens. How should they interpret that?

What it meant from a practical point of view was that they had to fight side-by-side, rather than against each other. This was both good and bad. The fire forced them to find friends to stay with, and then find an apartment. They were thrown right back into living together. For the first month, they were just grateful to be alive and have each other. Yet being in survival mode prevented them from continuing the delicate, discerning work on their relationship that they had started before the fire. If that work was not continued, their problems were sure to resurface.

Sure enough, in a month the shock of the fire wore off, and to Andrew this was like coming down from a high.

The old urge stalked him. He did absolutely nothing to inflame it—he went to his therapy and counseling dutifully—but it dogged him. In the back of his mind was a remnant from the affair, this idea that the other woman might be a better match for him—primarily because she emphasized her career more than Julie did. (New research shows that most spouses cheat not with someone who is more attractive than their spouse, but with someone they consider *more interesting* than their spouse.) Julie worked, but she never considered her work to be part of her identity, and she never valued her work as she did her relationships.

This was treacherous ground. To Julie, it was infuriating and humiliating. Had she not proven herself already? After all she had put up with, why was the blame being put on her again?

"I had a prejudice against people who didn't try to fulfill themselves through work," Andrew admitted to me. He knows exactly what it was about. "My own career was in a shambles, and I wanted someone to energize and inspire me. I wanted someone on my arm that made *me* look good."

Julie fought to make Andrew recognize that the real culprit here was his unrealistic expectation. He longed for a single woman to meet all his needs. He wanted one woman to be his emotional savior, his sexual provocateur, his intellectual collaborator, and his career peer. (She also had to like camping.)

In throwing out the old notion that work is the domain of men and home the domain of women, many of us have, like Andrew, gone a little overboard, and made it undesirable to have separate domains of any sort. We have a tendency to confuse similarity with equality. We want our partners to be our equals, but we think this means we need to be able to share *everything*. We go looking for someone who likes everything we like and wants everything we want. In this way, we will never be held back. We can be committed and yet never be slowed down. It sounds like a neat loophole, but it sets a standard that guarantees disappointment, because there is no such person. Even if there were—do any of us really want to marry our twin?

In other words, learning to be comfortable with the fact that we'll have differences is like learning to expect problems—it's the only way to last. Needs should be met by a package of people, except in the bedroom. Andrew needed to enjoy his wife's strengths and, if necessary, go camping with the guys.

"It was a very different way of thinking for me," Andrew recalled. "I struggled to accept it, because it seemed unromantic.

"But then I realized that in the name of romance, I was asking other people to make up for my own deficiencies. My weaknesses are my own problem. I was projecting them on Julie. I pretended she was holding me back, when I was holding myself back. For the first time, I took responsibility for my own life."

For a decade, Andrew had assumed that in order to heal himself, he had to reunite with his father. Twice before, he had attempted to rekindle their relationship. At one point Andrew confronted him, demanding to know why he had brought Andrew's brother into his new marriage but not Andrew. Andrew found the answers to be unsatisfying. He left every encounter with his father feeling unresolved. The truth was, if not for the genetic link, there was nothing connecting them.

That fall Andrew finally admitted this. He wrote his father a letter, part declaration and part apology. He told his father that he recognized that they really did not have a bond at all—never really did. And he was not going to chase it anymore. He was no longer going to expect their relationship to be something it was not.

"I was learning to let it be, not try to fix it."

"And did he write back?"

"He did. He really agreed. Most of his life, he had felt the same way, that he was supposed to have a relationship with me, but one never took root. He, too, was going to let that expectation go."

"How did you feel? Let down?"

"No. Relieved. I don't miss him, I miss the idea of him."

Andrew stopped looking to others to fill the hole in his heart.

He was really tested when the other woman started calling him again at home. He could see it was her. Her name showed up on caller ID.

It served as an invitation.

One day Andrew answered it. They talked. She was unhappy in her marriage and wanted to see him again. He told her that he considered her dangerous and destructive if she was willing to jeopardize both her family and his. But he said this nicely, so the next day she called again. Weren't they soul mates? she asked. He told her that was an illusion, an escape. He loved Julie. He asked her not to call again. She continued to anyway. She never left a message. After a week Andrew told Julie. She felt very threatened. She thought they were over this. They got a new phone number.

Julie fell into a depression. It was understandable. She had given her husband so much. She had lost her cats and her home. She wanted children, but her job did not provide health insurance and they had canceled Andrew's to save money. It was a depression they simply had to wait out. Andrew did not try to push her to feel better. She appreciated this. He started working again. This helped his confidence a lot.

But the other woman had succeeded in getting back inside Andrew's head. Once she was in there, it was hard to get her out. It tempted him. Putting his marriage and his career back together was so hard, so complex—how great it would be just to take a little break!

One day, he was fighting an incredible urge to show up at the other woman's office. So he went driving on the interstate. Scenes from their afternoons played in his mind. They were such havens, those hours. A complete escape. It would sure take the edge off. If he could do it just this once . . .

No! That's exactly how an addict thinks! he told himself.

The words of his therapist came to him: *Slow it down. Notice what you are really feeling.*

I am aware of the feeling of wanting to go be with her, he thought, with a little less frenzy.

Slow it down even more. What are you really *feeling, Andrew?*

I miss her, he thought, calmer still.

Do you?

No. Something snapped. "I miss my *mom,*" he admitted. And in that moment, he burst into tears. He sobbed so hard he had to pull the car over on the interstate. He sat there for ten minutes, bawling. It was true. He missed his mom. He missed Grandpa. He had never let himself just say this. His whole childhood, what he had lost was never spoken of. He had been taught to deny it. Ever since, if he had ever come near this feeling, he found something to cover it up.

For the first time, he did not try to escape his true feelings.

"I miss my mom," he repeated. "I miss my mom."

This chapter began with an anecdote that sounded like a fairy tale. It was frustrating for me, as the teller of that gem, to have to let go of the fairy-tale quality and descend into the complicated mess of a marriage in trouble. How charming it would have been if I had stopped the story right there, after the photo of the elm!

Yet that is life.

As we mature, we all have to make this transition. Like Andrew, we all have to let go of some of our fairy-tale expectations for love, and learn to embrace a kind of love that can survive a few hard winters.

Doing this can be a formidable challenge, because those romantic notions are often rooted in our very deepest wishes to be swept away. Nobody wants to give that desire up. We all want to feel special, we all want love to be transcendent. Besides, what is being offered in exchange? It's difficult to see the romance in hard work.

True, true. But which of these, ultimately, is a better story?

1. A boy meets a girl, and they live happily ever after.
2. A man falls in love with a woman. They suffer. They lose one house to mold, another to fire. They run out of money. Out of weakness, he cheats, but he learns from it, and she guides him back to health. She fights depression, but he waits for her to work through it. His mom left him, his dad left him, his grandfather left him, but she refuses to leave him. They last. They still love each other.

Love that has been tested is far more awe inspiring than love that has never known anything but bliss.

Don't look for a partner with whom you have no problems, but one you are good at overcoming problems with.

Just remember: The story of the old elm tree is no fairy tale.

It has a scar, and it is real.

What makes family

still necessary?

Boxes

Uma Thangaraj

At one point or another most of us have asked the exigent question *Is the bond of family inherent in our human nature, or is it an intellectual construct that once served a useful purpose but is no longer really necessary?*

Much has changed in the last forty years. Birth control has minimized the consequences of having sex, so sexual attraction doesn't have to lead to marriage. Women have become economically empowered and don't depend on men to provide for them. The elderly are less dependent on their children to house them. Young children have been granted rights by the courts and can even emancipate themselves. We need one another, but not like we used to. In general, participating in family has become more of a choice and less of an imperative. We've got options. For some, family has become a vestigial organ. It's there, hanging around like an appendix or a tonsil, but it is of little real use anymore.

Uma Thangaraj is one person who views family this way. She is unsure what the purpose of family is, and she is skeptical about whether a valid purpose will emerge, at least in her life. But her life story is revealing; like a sample of rock pulled from a mountainside, her life has layers that correspond to the different eras of family over the last few centuries. By studying these layers, we can understand how families today stack up against families of old. Are we better off? Is being able to choose whether to participate in family a good thing? Or is it allowing people to give up on family too easily?

Uma and I were walking from her van down to Lake Superior. It was mid-February, during a winter that dumped three hundred inches of snow. This was near the northern tip of Michigan's Upper Peninsula—a titanic spit of land that, if pointed out on a map, most Americans would presume is part of Canada. It's the kind of place where snowmobiles drive right up to gas stations. A church and a bar compete on every opposing street corner. There is a ski hill in the center of town. Uma's two children, Siddhartha and Samya, spent most of the weekends of their childhood on its slopes. Sid is now a freshman in college, Samya, a junior in high school. Uma works at the hospital in the marketing department. The name of the town is Houghton—proud home to Michigan Tech University and a winter that lasts into May.

"This may be a third or fourth life for me," Uma said, her feet punching through the snow. "So much has passed that there are days in which India feels like an exotic, faraway land."

Life One: Uma grew up in a neighborhood of Madras that is only a quarter mile from great beaches on the Bay of Bengal. She woke to spectacular sunrises and the salty smell of the ocean. The River Adyar flooded in monsoon season. Those are her earliest memories, plus this: In the living area of their home sat a large particleboard box, as big as a footlocker and kept under lock and key. This held her dowry. Now and then Uma's mother would add to it—some silver dinnerware, or jewelry, or even pots and pans. As Uma understood it, this dowry box was meant to give her and her future husband a head start in making their own home someday. It was not to be given to her husband's family as compensation, like traditional dowries—no, her family was supposedly past that, because her mother and her father were a love match. At a time in the mid-1960s when it was unheard of to seek out one's own partner, Mom and Dad met at college, fell in love, and defied their families. Both became professionals—Uma's mother was a doctor, her father an engineer and college professor. They were trendsetters. Uma expected a very modern life.

But Uma's father did not love her mother for very long. While they remained married, he secretly married a second woman in a nearby city. Uma's family was not Muslim, which—in another country—might condone this practice. They were Tamil Hindus in India, and bigamy was completely illegal throughout the country. Uma's mother discovered this other marriage when Uma was young, but did not divorce her husband, for one reason and one reason only—to preserve her daughter's future. Divorce was so taboo that if Uma's parents legally split, Uma would be considered unfit for marriage. Uma's mother insisted on one condition—the second wife would bear no children.

Because her father's bigamy was so rarely spoken about, Uma grew up not knowing it was hurtful. She remembers going to visit this woman with her father when she was about six. Her "stepmother" was always very kind, and jealous of Uma's relationship with her real mother. When Uma was eight, her stepmother came to live with them in Madras. Two years later, Uma's mother managed to get away by finding employment in Libya. Nobody considered it odd that Uma's mother did this, because it was (and is) common to work in oil-producing countries, where pay is far higher than in India. At school, classmates asked Uma who this other woman was, so Uma invented the idea that she was her "aunt."

The lesson her parents drew from their situation was that when it comes to choosing a partner, no one should trust young passion. But this was never communicated to Uma. She figured her parents married for love, so she would, too. Uma was a romantic, trapped in a culture that doubted whether passion could be the basis for marriage.

When she was thirteen, Uma was sent to a Catholic boarding school. She was grateful for this, because her father was routinely drunk and violent, and Uma was defenseless without her mother to protect her. When Uma was fifteen, she came home on holiday and discovered a new family had moved in to the duplex next door, having come from Hyderabad for a fresh start after their youngest son was killed in a motorcycle accident. They spoke Telugu, not Tamil, and were meat eaters. Uma's family was from the Yadav caste, while this new family was from up north—they had different rituals and traditions. But they were friendly. When Uma knocked on the door, the father teased her playfully. Everyone in the neighborhood thought there was a dark cloud over that house, but Uma had been inside, where the mood was always so much warmer and welcoming than in her own house. The death of the youngest child had opened their hearts to strangers.

Uma began hanging around with the middle son, who was twenty-two. They spoke English together. He recorded mix tapes for her from his records. He introduced Uma to D. H. Lawrence through the poem "The Snake." When Uma went back to school, they wrote each other and fell in love. When together, they were not sexual but very intimate. After a year of this, Uma's mother came home on a vacation and took stock. She did not like this boy. He was in graduate school getting his master's in literature—it was unlikely he would be able to provide for her daughter. Uma didn't care. She was going to have her own career. She secretly continued the relationship. They envisioned a life together, and named their future children.

When Uma was seventeen, her father found some of her love letters. He beat her badly and insisted that the relationship stop.

Her father had been receiving marriage offers for Uma since she was fifteen. He had planned to wait until she was out of school to deal with his daughter's future, but he decided to take advantage of the crisis. So he called his old business partner—with whom he had split over a grudge long ago. (Having been forced to resign his professorship in a scandal when his college was tipped off about his second marriage, he wanted to get back into contracting, which had been his former business.) He invited this man and his son Raj to dinner. The son was twenty-six years old and close to finishing his engineering PhD in the United States. He was home on vacation, and ready to have a marriage arranged. In all ways, Raj was a perfectly fine candidate, from a traditional family who had invested years in his education so that he would be able to provide for a family. Uma was invited to the dining room, briefly. The next morning her father told her it was settled. He had traded Uma for a share in the construction business. He was going to call her mother in Libya.

Her mother went along with it. "My whole life, she had stayed in the marriage for one reason," Uma recalled. "Marrying me off was the payoff—it justified the humiliation she had endured for so long."

Later that week, Uma met her fiancé a second time.

Raj asked, "Do you remember me at all? From when our fathers were friends? You were a young girl."

"I remember your little brother a lot more. But I remember one time, when I might have been five. Some sort of commotion was going on in the alley behind our house, maybe it was a fire engine racing by—"

"It was a funeral procession."

"You lifted me up on your shoulders to look over the fence."

They smiled. It was a helpful image to have.

Their horoscopes were matched by an astrologer. The matching of horoscopes is meant to reveal compatibility and confirm a good marriage. (These horoscopes are etched into palm leaves by priests and made into booklets when children are born.) The matching process also defines certain details, such as the exact time of the day the marriage should occur. It is all based on numerology, using the birthdays of the betrothed and their parents. Uma and Raj had six of ten matches. Anytime you're taking the choice out of a situation—by locking yourself in, as with marriage—people naturally get mystical. Young American couples convince themselves they are destined to be together because of casual similarities—for instance, they both grew up on a Meadowbrook Street, or their favorite Tom Hanks movie is *Big,* or her shoulder tucks so perfectly under his arm, or they both visited Paris in grade school. In the Indian caste system, where only a few upper strata of society have control over their fate, individuals can't derive their sense of their life being "right" from choosing it willfully, so their sense of rightness is constructed through symbolism and notions of destiny. Insignificant similarities are ascribed meaning and taken as signs.

After a week in Madras, Raj returned to America to continue his schooling. The marriage was scheduled for a year later. Until then, they would write letters. In Uma's mind there was nothing wrong with Raj. He was just not the one she chose.

To the community, Uma's engagement to Raj appeared to be a rather straightforward arranged marriage, but in fact it was more like a *forced marriage,* conducted against her will. It is an important distinction. Forced marriages are considered a violation of international laws that define basic human rights, while arranged marriages are common in half the world today, and were accepted in Europe as recently as one hundred years ago. Most of Uma's classmates would have their marriages arranged by the time they left college—but their parents just arranged introductions, then allowed the potential partners a chance to click. If they did not click, they went back on the market.

Not being given a chance to click was part of Uma's objection. What truly angered her, though, was that her father was using her for his own financial gain. Indian families work on the notion that parents know best and will make wiser decisions than hormonally juiced seventeen-year-olds. But parents are supposed to do what is best *for their children,* not what is best for their bank account.

"I was torn whether protesting would do any good," Uma reflected. "I was afraid of my father's rage, so most of my complaints were directed at my mother and aunts. In front of Raj and his family, I submitted. And then I hatched a secret plan."

She and her lover planned to run away. He arranged for train tickets to the north. They had it all worked out. But then a week before they were to make their escape, a maid in Uma's home stole some food. Uma's father dragged the maid into the street and beat her terribly in front of the neighbors, then called the police. When he got off the phone, he turned to Uma. "I hope that sets an example of what I would do to you if you crossed my word."

Uma got very scared. She was a minor, while her lover was not. This made their escape a crime, kidnapping. She was less worried for herself—she could take a beating—than for her lover, who would go to jail if they were caught. She told him she could not go, and cut off communication. A year later, she and Raj were married in front of a thousand people. Then she went to live with Raj's family while he went back to America to apply for her visa. Raj's mother ran the household, with Uma in an inferior and junior position. The contents of the dowry box were quickly distributed through her mother-in-law's home.

Uma swallowed her complaints and learned to accept it. She was very good at this—her mother had been quite a role model. The Hindu faith also encouraged her attitude, with its philosophy that learning to accept fate is a fulfillment of the dharma.

At least she was away from her father.

I asked her, "What was it like on your wedding night, to have sex with a guy who was basically a complete stranger?"

"The first night was a little awkward, but after that it was fine. You have to understand—neither of our homes was very loving, but everyone told us we were going to love being married, that it was this great thing. And so there we were, two naked people, and things started happening. So we concluded, *Okay, this is what love is.* This must be what it feels like."

Was it love?

Uma laughed gently. "I know better now. But I was glad to at least feel something."

A year later, Uma was allowed to visit America on a tourist visa for three months. When she returned to Madras, she was pregnant. She was thrilled. Another year later, when Sid was three months old, American immigration allowed her to join Raj, who had moved to Houghton to teach at Michigan Tech. When she arrived with her life in two suitcases, she was nineteen years old. While she had been pledged to her husband for three years, she had been in his physical presence only slightly more than three months. She barely knew him. Yet she was curiously optimistic. The premise of arranged marriages is that love will emerge over time, and the tradition defines *real love* as the kind built through decades of union. Uma was looking forward to that.

"I was ready to play house. I was in love with the idea of being a domestic goddess, right up to the point where I finally experienced it."

Life Two: Some 150 Indian families had been drawn to Houghton by the university. None spoke Tamil, and only a few were from Madras, but they made Uma and Raj feel welcome. The young couple bought a house, then a dog, then a little house for the dog. Uma made Raj laugh heartily. They held their baby boy and marveled.

All too quickly, the charm wore off. The young couple's differences emerged. Uma was led by her feelings, while Raj was unemotional and analytical. He had no expectation that he and his wife would share their inner lives—to him, it was a practical arrangement: He would provide, and in return he wanted his kids cared for. At the dinner table, Raj was accustomed to silence and the deference of women who spoke only when spoken to. Uma was accustomed to chaos, argument, and drama, everyone speaking at once. Raj was not used to a woman asking about his work, for that was *his* domain. His mother *never* asked his father about work. All day long Uma waited for her husband to come home, to bring word from the outside world—to stimulate her with conversation—but he was a man of few words, unsure how to share, and each night Uma's disappointment grew. Back in India she had received emotional support and conversation from Raj's entire family. Here she had only her husband to rely on. He did not want to be bothered. Neither had a clue how to make it work. *Love can be made,* they had been taught—but they had not been taught how.

Winter came early, leaving her profoundly isolated. "When my son was born in India, all he had to do was whimper and someone would be there to pick him up—an aunt, an uncle, a cousin, *someone.* In Houghton I was stripped of my support system. I was worn out quickly."

As a Hindu, Uma had been taught that the self does not exist apart from its connections with others. The Western emphasis on the individual is considered both immoral and futile. Her entire culture was predicated on this philosophy, and children were not taught to make choices or be self-reliant. Thus, Uma had never had any practice at being alone or learning to play by herself. In order to acclimate to this frozen slice of America, she withdrew from her past. At first she and Raj had maintained a prayer area in a closet with an oil lamp and incense, but late that winter they both stopped praying.

"When we start life over in a new country, we come without the photographs and mementos that constantly reinforce history," Uma said. "When I walk into the homes of American friends, there are stories everywhere—a quilt sewn by a grandmother, an armoire, a ring, photographs of the parents as children—while everything in my house was new."

When Uma's daughter, Samya, was born, Uma's mother came to help care for the baby. She could tell Uma's spirit was broken, and so she encouraged Uma to go back to school and get a college degree. Uma did not see how this was possible with two young children until her mother offered to quit her job and live with them. By then Uma's mother had divorced her father. She had converted to Islam, because under Islamic law it was very easy to get divorced. Uma had also written her father severing all ties. This freed them to be mother and daughter again.

Raj was at first offended that Uma wanted a degree and a job—"I make enough to support this family!"—but then he realized school might hush his wife and give her something to do.

To Raj, she was just taking classes. But to her, she was *getting an education*. It gave her a shot of confidence. It unlocked the soul that had been trained to be compliant. She liked the way other men looked at her. Raj did not like the person his wife was becoming. When he came home and there was no dinner on the table, he criticized her. "Why should I be inconvenienced for such a frivolous thing as your education?"

Uma hid her troubles with Raj from her mother. Then one day Uma confessed to the abuse she had taken as a teen while her mother was in Libya. Uma had never blamed her mother, because she'd assumed her mother hadn't known. But now Uma's mother admitted that she *had* known, or at least suspected it, which devastated Uma. The rest of that week, Uma fought openly with both Raj and her mother. Then she withdrew, spending the late evenings online, chatting with her classmates. Raj became suspicious about what she was telling them. He attempted to log on to her account to read her e-mail, but Uma caught him and accused him of violating her privacy. In that moment she surged with a hatred built up from twenty years of being treated as property, with nobody acknowledging her individuality, nobody listening to her, nobody caring what she thought, nobody ever putting her needs first. She bolted like a skittish horse. Uma left her kids with her mother, saying that she was going to class. Instead, she threw some jewelry into Raj's car, drove down to the local pawnshop, and traded the jewelry for three hundred dollars. With this, she bought a one-way ticket on the next bus south. Six hours later she arrived in Green Bay, Wisconsin. It was not her style to think things through in advance.

Next to the bus station in Green Bay was a Motel 6. Uma paid for a room. The next morning, when Uma looked out the window she saw a Sears and a Kentucky Fried Chicken. So she went over and applied for jobs at both places. Within a day she had been hired by both. In this, you can really see how amazingly untrained Uma was to think freely: The bus got her to Green Bay, but once she stepped off she only made it a few feet. For all intents and purposes, her rebellion was over. If she had walked a few blocks, she would've had several decent hotels to choose from, where people didn't argue all night and police cruisers didn't trawl the parking lot. She could have secured a better job. Instead, she stepped into what was right in front of her, accepting it.

"I wanted to run away, but I had no place to go," she said.

"What were you thinking of accomplishing?" I asked.

"My heart was trying to lead me from my marriage, but I wasn't mature enough to do it the right way."

"Did you call home?"

"No."

"What about your kids?"

"I had their portraits in my wallet, which I couldn't bear to look at. In my purse was a roll of film that I'd taken at Samya's first birthday party. On my seventh day in Green Bay, I had the roll developed. The minute I began looking at the prints, I broke down and called my husband. He drove down to get me."

When they got home, Uma could not bear to talk to her mother about her marital problems, because she knew her mother would insist she stick it out. Still devastated from the news that her mother had failed to protect her as a teen, Uma told her it was time for her to leave. She pushed her mother away and stopped speaking to her.

"I did not talk to her for three years," Uma said. "Mom never stopped trying to call me. But I didn't know how to come back from that faraway place."

Uma continued to demand more of a partnership from Raj, more intimacy. Every time they fought, he came home the next day with roses. But his behavior never changed. Soon the roses came to symbolize his unwillingness to change. To this day, she hates roses.

Uma and Raj went to a counselor. Their sessions only revealed how different they were. Raj was afraid of the shame of divorce. He fought for the *idea* of marriage, but didn't fight for the *quality* of their marriage. It was okay with him if their marriage remained loveless. To Uma, who had longed for romance her whole life, this plan sounded like death. To break the stalemate, Uma offered to move out. Raj gasped with relief. After an eight-year marriage, they tried a six-month separation. Raj kept expecting Uma to come back. She knew it was forever.

At the time, Uma believed she was fleeing her marriage to Raj. Now, with the benefit of hindsight, she can see she was really fleeing the box forced on her by her parents. She had no sense of her identity, no clue who she was. Many live happily this way. Not Uma. She had to break out of the box, no matter what kind of man Raj was.

Uma and the children moved into a two-bedroom shoe box in the basement of a three-story apartment building on the highway. Her daughter was inconsolable. Samya lay facedown on the carpet, screaming and begging for the familiarity of the family home. What could Uma tell her children that might deflect the blame? She did not want to say bad things about their father. Uma hooked the VCR up to the television and put in a video. Thank God for Walt Disney.

For the first time in three years, she called her mother.

To Uma's surprise, her mother said she was doing the right thing.

———

Life Three: In a fair world, Uma and Raj would have split the responsibility of caring for Sid and Samya. Raj would have provided Uma with enough income to make her rent. The financial aid department at Michigan Tech would have increased her student loans because she was now a single mother of two.

But Uma Thangaraj had never known a fair world, and so she did not know enough to demand she be treated justly.

She has a very hard time talking about those first years alone. It makes her anxious to remember that period. She says only that it was "rock-bottom poverty" and "absolute bare minimum." Raj helped only when they were penniless. They never agreed on child support. He was fighting the divorce by starving her out.

The Indian community in Houghton treated her as if she were in India and had initiated a divorce. Her friends refused to see her. Men in these families averted their eyes and wouldn't speak to her when they saw her on the street or in the grocery store. She became an outcast and a threat.

On the rare nights that Raj spent with his children, Uma went out to bars to look for love. She was a twenty-six-year-old with the hormones and good judgment of a fifteen-year-old. She was an exotic target for single men, and an easy one. She had no training in what to look for, no sense of how to sniff out a promise made only to deceive. Was this love, the empty feeling she had when sneaking home at two A.M.?

She remembers a depression, a sense of spending a winter in a dark hole. Finally a vision came to her—a hand, reaching into her dark hole, offering to pull her out. It was the closest she had ever come to a direct religious experience. Her mood improved.

After two years Raj gave Uma another chance. She did not want it. He moved to Cleveland, where he married again. For the next five years he was not involved in the children's life. Uma raised them by herself.

When Uma graduated, her next step was akin to that day she got off the bus in Green Bay. She walked a few feet, over to another university department, which hired her to teach English to foreign students.

Eventually she spread her wings, getting as far as the local hospital. She was finally earning a decent living. She bought a small house up the hill from downtown, with a view of the ski hill across the canal. Owning property was a major milestone. Like the other milestones, it was both gratifying and terrifying.

One day she woke up and realized she was at last truly free. She had a home. She had money to travel. Her children were turning out great. She had found new friends. In her thirty years it seemed she had lived three hundred years of history. And here she was, a modern woman who did not need a man to care for her, or help her raise her children, or help her solve her problems. If she needed a man, it was for one thing and one thing only: companionship.

In this same situation, many women falter. Not knowing love, and never having been loved, they seek out the familiar—the one kind of love they *do* know—and end up in a bad relationship again. In Uma's case, the psychiatry textbooks warn that she would choose men who would trap her, men like her father or her husband. This compulsion would be hardwired into her brain's neurons. But Uma did not follow the pattern. If anything, she gravitated in the opposite direction.

She chose safely. The first two men she fell in love with were guaranteed to never trap her, for they were loners, explorers, modern-day Jack Londons who never wanted to be trapped, either. They lived in other states, so these were long-distance relationships, which was fine with Uma, because she was comfortable writing love letters. Sometimes the feeling she got writing a letter was sweeter than anything a weekend together could provide. Neither of these men was the type to make a commitment, but that was okay with Uma as well. She was taking it slow, absorbing what she learned in order to choose better next time.

Three years ago she fell in love with Frank, who lived in San Diego. They met in Michigan or California four times a year, spending a very intense week together. The premise of their relationship was that they were lovers of life, free spirits who could not be chained. It was the kind of hungry passion she had always desired. She began to think he was the one she had always been destined to meet. This love was the payoff for her past. That first Christmas, he gave her a present wrapped in a Russell Stover candy box. Uma kept the candy box in her bedroom, and over the next two years she would add to it—photographs from their trips, two ticket stubs from an aerial tram ride over the San Diego Zoo, cards that read "I love you just the way you are." Just as a dowry box symbolized love in her childhood, this keepsake box would symbolize love in her adulthood. The purpose of the first box was to *provide;* the purpose of this one was to *treasure.* When home alone, Uma would sift through the box, and each memento—a square of wrapping paper, a note—stirred her longing.

After two years, Uma began to crave more closeness and structure. This was a good thing. It's natural. How great it was that adversity had not stolen her desire for a real relationship! But Frank didn't share her yearnings. Eventually he broke up with her.

At first Uma experimented with being callous and uncaring. She had been through too much to cry over this. She gave herself a month to get over it. On the last day of July, she and a girlfriend took an early-evening walk down to Lake Superior. They found the beach of "stamp sand," small brick-colored pebbles brought in from quarries. On this beach Uma lit a small fire. She and her friend drank a bottle of wine as the sun fell into the lake, bringing back Uma's memories of her childhood's ocean sunrises. Then Uma dropped the keepsake candy box into the fire.

"Closure is a beautiful thing," she wrote me late that night. "The letting go has taken place."

But the loss proved heavier than she expected. While the symbol of their love had been scattered into nature, the love itself endured. One week she would assert she was over it. The next week she would admit she was not even close.

Six months later she was still grieving.

"I wish I was not so vulnerable," she said, stepping up onto the berm that contained Lake Superior.

I had never seen this lake in winter. I knew it was much colder than the other Great Lakes, but I was surprised that it was frozen over as far as the eye could see. I thought of Uma's heart, and how easy it would be for it to get locked in ice. I had only admiration for her vulnerability.

I think of Uma as a young mountain. There are old mountain ranges, like the Appalachians, and there are young ones, like the Andes. The earth's young mountains are tall, steep, and rocky—they shot up fast when tectonic plates collided, leaving a lot of clues as to how this happened. In this same way, Uma is a young mountain. We all struggle to balance romantic ideals with pragmatic needs when building relationships. It is rare to find someone like Uma who has shot up so quickly, and whose life has left so many clues as to why she loves the way she does. Like Uma, our society is infatuated with romantic ideals in this current era. Maybe we've been on the rebound, just like her. But we're learning better balance.

"I'm not sure why you are here," Uma said.

"What do you mean?" I asked, stepping onto the lake.

"I don't have a story. I have no happy ending. I have been in love, but I'm afraid I would not recognize real love if it was right in front of me. I don't know where my home is. I love being a mother, but I have put the rest of my family from my mind. Until my children have babies, I have no clear purpose. So while I enjoy talking to you, and I am happy you are here, I really do not know why you chose to come."

"Uma, how can you say you have no story?"

"But it is so unresolved."

"Uma, look how much progress you have made in less than half a lifetime. Your story is the story of all womankind. Like women of Europe three centuries ago, you were considered the property of your father and treated as an asset in a business deal that enriched him. Like the women of America in the twentieth century, you were an isolated and undereducated homemaker longing for her husband to show emotion. Now you are the most modern of archetypes, the economically empowered single mom. Your legacy is our collective legacy. Just as your choices today are affected by your prior lives, our choices and views of love are affected by the lives of our ancestors. The things that come out of your mouth—that you don't know where your home is, that you don't know how to recognize the One, that family is not very important—I hear those very same phrases everywhere, routinely. I'm here because you represent a *lot* of people."

"And what do you make of us?"

"Is it any wonder people are confused? The definition of family and marriage has changed radically. In just a few generations, we've decided that intimacy should be the basis for marriage. We've determined that children should be nurtured and hugged, not just provided for. Just a century ago, there were masses of children working in factories throughout the United States and Great Britain. It's inevitable—when change happens that fast, and the expectation for marriage and family rise so fast—it's no surprise so many families haven't been able to adapt on cue. In fact, I would say it's amazing how many families *have* managed to adapt and meet these ever-new needs."

"Wait—isn't family life going to hell? That's what everyone says. Nobody values family anymore, et cetera."

"Quite the opposite. Don't you think the modern family aspires to a greater purpose than ever before? I sure wouldn't want to go back in time. I'm sure you would never want your daughter to have to live your childhood. Isn't that why you and Raj never moved back to India?"

Uma nodded. I was hinting at the question we had never addressed directly: Was she really better off today than with the life she was born into? She had lost her culture and her extended family. Her kids had keys to the house way too young; when they came home from school, there was nobody there to greet them. If her mother and father had not gambled on passion forty years ago, might none of this have unfolded? Maybe so, if Uma had been born to a father who did not beat her, and did not humiliate her mother, and did not govern his family like a tyrant. But that was an *if* she did not have the luxury of enjoying. So she fought for the quality of her life. She has demonstrated remarkable resilience, and sometimes resilience takes the form of courage to go at it alone. Yes, she lost something along the way. But she would never go back.

Uma said, "My regret is that I have never been able to show my children a successful relationship. I have never been able to model that for them. I worry they won't know what one looks like."

"I've seen you with your kids. Haven't you provided them with more love and autonomy and respect than you ever dreamed of? How is that not a great thing?"

We arrived at the spot where she had burned her candy box last summer.

"Is there a reason you wanted to see this?" she asked, because there was nothing there but stamp sand and snow.

"I guess I just wanted to be able to say I stood at the place where your next life began."

Sure, families have changed. Maybe extended families are spread out over three continents. Maybe our children have keys to their houses too young. Maybe we have lost most of our cultural roots. But the biggest change to the family in the last two hundred years is the gradual recognition that everyone in a family has rights, not just the father. Most of the changes we are seeing stem from this indispensable and fundamental enlightenment. Going backward is no answer.

They say you can't choose your family, but increasingly, people do. People build families out of whatever they've got that works, Swiss Family Robinson style. They build with friends and in-laws, with adoptions and second or third marriages. Uncles replace fathers while cousins replace sisters. They build with grandparents they're not really related to. They build new traditions, and they pass these on to their children and friends, spreading a simple value—that we are stronger together than alone.

Being able to choose a family is on a trajectory similar to being able to choose a spouse. Once unheard of, it will eventually be routine. This does make it harder to stick together, because it's so easy to leave. But if you look into almost every family's history, you see a similar story somewhere in the last hundred years—the family has had to make a huge transition, from being a family ruled by force and autocracy to one held together by desire and kinship.

We imagine that family used to be stable and pristine, that it was untouched, like nature, for generation after generation, right up until the last forty years, when we started tearing it apart. But this is an illusion, created by how briefly we have been here.

I only knew one of my great-grandmothers, though all of their stories are similar. Nana lost her mother in birth, then ran away from a cruel stepmother at age twelve by working as a nurse. The man who married her did not want children, so a century ago, in an era when women simply did not initiate divorce, she did so anyway. She went looking for love. The man she found had been banished from his family at sixteen for getting a girl pregnant—they never spoke to him again. These two outcasts discovered each other, loved each other until they died; and some of what they learned made its way to me. There are times I wish I could bring her back and show her the scene in my living room. *Look, Nana. Look at what has shot up since you passed. Look at all the love. Look at the life women have.*

Uma is young, only thirty-seven. One day her grandchildren or great-grandchildren will invite her to their house. *Look, Uma.*

Look at what you helped create.

Is it harder for

them to accept you

or for you

to accept them?

The Palace

Brian Olowude as a boy,
sitting on a swing beside one of his sisters.

Did you ever use a fantasy, or your imagination, to get through a very hard time?

In Brian Olowude's case, what he invented was a fantasy that his father wasn't dead after all. He was just in hiding, because his life was in danger. But he was a great man, the most polite and respectful man his mother had ever known. He would never forget about his son out there. He would emerge soon and come to the rescue. He would turn out to be fabulously rich, and he would buy a house in the Carmel Valley—a palace—where they would have maids and servants and drivers. Mom wouldn't have to work. This fantasy always ended with his family at Disneyland.

As Brian grew up, the fantasy took the form of conjecture. Okay, his father was dead—but what if, hypothetically speaking, he had lived? How much would be different? Would he pay for Brian's school? Would he get Brian a cool job? Would he take Brian away from this mess of a family? Working out the scenarios in his mind always soothed Brian. He never gave up his daydreams.

Brian was the youngest of six siblings. The two oldest had one father, who was mostly absent. The next three had another father, also mostly absent. Brian, who was the baby, had a separate father. After him, their mother, Sandra, never loved another man. They grew up on the central coast of California, in a town called Seaside. Sandra was on welfare and disability. A Section 8 stipend kept them out of the housing projects, which were just down the hill. They were poor but Brian was never hungry, and all his boyhood memories are happy ones. He revered his siblings. He worshiped his mother. She was in the PTA and made sure her kids were treated well by their teachers. She put Brian beside her on the couch to watch PBS, and when *Masterpiece Theatre* came on, everything in the house stopped.

Their family had been in Monterey County for generations. Back in the Cannery Row era, Brian's great-grandmother had cleaned houses for the wealthiest white families. They did not have money, but they had class. A great-uncle was the first black pharmacist in California. Another uncle had received a PhD at University of California at Davis. Around the house, every child completed his chores before being allowed to watch television. When they went shopping, the children were perfectly behaved.

"I really had two childhoods," Brian explained. "During that first part, it did not make a difference that we did not have our fathers around. But then my brothers became teenagers, at which point the lack of a father figure showed itself."

His brothers started going "down the hill," into the housing projects. All the bad stuff their mother had warned them against was down the hill. The good habits Sandra had taught her children were no match for the tempting mischief of teenage peers. Brian's brothers got into low-rider culture and drugs, and were soon operating just to the left of the law. His oldest brother was twelve years his senior, so Brian was still a boy when he moved out. Two of his three brothers got shot. Both survived. Brian remembers going to visit his third brother at places like the juvenile hall and the boys' ranch, then the California Youth Authority and state prison—steadily progressing upward, as if through junior high to high school to college to graduate school. "Those were not bad places in my mind," Brian swears. "They were just the places my brothers went. I liked going to visit them on Sundays. Sometimes we would have a picnic or get to visit my aunt on the same trip."

His sisters followed their brothers down the hill. Sandra simply couldn't control them.

As Sandra watched her children go bad, she would cry herself to sleep while listening to Billie Holiday. When Brian's sisters became teens, Brian moved out of their room and into his mother's, and so he heard these tears across the room. "Promise me, Brian," she would plead. "Promise me you will not turn out like your brothers and sisters."

Brian was determined to be the normal one, to be the one who did not make his mother cry.

He refused to go down the hill. He refused to get into trouble. He was still just a boy when his brothers decided they needed to toughen their little brother up. So they would beat him up, repeatedly, almost every time Brian was not in his mother's shadow. Sometimes they would bring friends over to help administer Brian's daily lesson. They all recognized that Brian was different. He was a geeky kid, and sensitive, and would never last on the streets unless he learned to defend himself. But Brian absolutely refused to do so. Like a nonviolent protester, he never—not once—swung back. He loved his brothers. He held a conviction that he was not supposed to hit his brothers, regardless of what they said or did. He doesn't know where this came from. It was just in him. *You do not hit your brothers.*

"C'mon, hit me!"

"No!" he cried.

"Hit back!"

"No!"

His sister chimed in. "Brian, if you hit them back they'll leave you alone!"

"No!" he sobbed.

Eventually they climbed off him and went their way, muttering, "There's something wrong with that boy."

That was how it played out during the day. But at night Brian was taken over by persistent and violent nightmares in which it would all play out differently. His mother would hear him cursing and saying the most vile things during his sleep. He would toss and turn and sometimes punch the wall, injuring his hand, waking up screaming. All day long he would hold his anger in, and all night long the anger would pour out. By seventh grade Brian had developed an ulcer. He would also sleepwalk, and sometimes in his dreams he would be required to jump across chasms, and so he would do so, landing on the floor, injuring his legs.

His mother's solution was a bit of a Band-Aid. She urged Brian to picture happy thoughts as he fell asleep.

"Think happy thoughts!" she said and smiled cheerfully.

That was when Brian constructed his fantasy, and he elaborated on it every night. It worked fairly well, surprisingly. It seemed to quell his nightmares.

The vision that Brian imagined was built around the tiny fragments he had been told about his father, who had been a Nigerian graduate student at the University of California at Davis. By the time Sandra found out she was pregnant, Brian's father had already gone home to Nigeria to fight in the civil war. When she tried to contact him through his old friends at UC Davis, she learned he had been killed in that war. His name was Bisi Olowude. She had one picture of him, torn at the corner, which she kept on Brian's page in the family photo album. She told her son that Bisi had been very polite, the most respectful man she'd ever met. Bisi's father had been a village chief somewhere in Nigeria.

This was a fairly glamorous nugget to a young boy. That he had been a graduate student and the son of a chief made Brian picture a tall, royal man—very different from the street toughs who walked the hills of Seaside. To Brian, his African roots helped explain why he was so different, and made it *okay* to be different. They helped him be less ashamed that he was dull and awkward while his siblings were flashy and funny. They gave him an honorable reason for being darker, and for having a broader nose. *It's not that I'm weird,* he reminded himself. *It's that I'm half Nigerian.*

Only once did Brian's fantasy have to confront reality. It happened when he was thirteen and went to Chicago with two uncles for a political conference. He was really looking forward to one of the speakers, a man who had fought in the Nigerian civil war, known as the Biafran Wars. Prior to that point, Brian had had a naïve notion of civil wars, all

Clark Gable antebellum propriety. Instead, the speaker told of horrible torture and brutality. In three years more than two million people from the Igbo tribe had been slaughtered. Brian left the room on the verge of tears, and he cried to his mother when he got back to his hotel room. It destroyed him to picture his father dying this way. He tried to drive everything he had heard from his mind. He needed to imagine his father dying slowly in a hospital, cared for by pretty nurses. He knew it was a lie, but he couldn't help himself.

In a curious way, having a dead father seemed better than having fathers who had gone missing, as was the case for Brian's siblings. Abandonment issues can work on people beneath the surface, pulling invisible strings, but there was nothing invisible about his siblings' yearnings. One of his sisters wrote long letters to her father, noting her various achievements. She would assert, "I'm the kind of girl a Daddy would be proud of!" But she never heard it from him. To this day, she still drops everything for a man. When Brian's oldest brothers were young, one of them had been kidnapped by his father for a year. So the other brother always wondered *Why did Daddy take you and not me?* As a teen, he would blame his mother for driving his father away. And recently, he has taken his father in to live, despite years of desertion, because he had such a longing for the man.

Today Brian has one brother serving a life sentence. Both of his other brothers have survived being shot. One refuses to take his medication for schizophrenia. One of his sisters is into drugs whenever she is not in prison. Meanwhile, Brian took his mom's advice. He tried to be the opposite of his brothers. Slowly he grew into the life she wanted for him. Brian went to community college, and from there to college, where he met his wife, Annie. He received a full scholarship to graduate school, and when he had completed his courses there, he came back to California to study for his PhD. In what field? Psychology, of course. Though his family didn't pay attention to the details. "Are you a lawyer yet?" they kept asking Brian.

Through that whole journey, Brian never stopped daydreaming about the story of his father. The day he left for college, his mother gave him the one photo of his father to keep. One year he called UC Davis. Though their student records were private, he was able to learn that his father's full name was Samuel Bisi Olowude. Another year, he met a Nigerian man who told him that his family name, Olowude, was not a name among the Igbo tribe as Brian had always thought, which made Brian want to learn more. So his daydreaming took the form of occasionally surfing the website Nigeria.com, reading about the culture. He once posted a message asking if anyone knew about the Olowude family. With so many people looking for old school friends online, just maybe one of those people could tell him something about his father's family. He never heard back, though. It didn't matter. Foraging for scraps online was its own reward. It kept his imagination going on a slow, gentle burner.

For twenty-five years he had imagined a better life and, lo and behold, a better life had indeed come to him. It was not exactly the life he'd imagined, but that is not the point. He found a way to keep his head up. His imagination had pulled him through some very hard years. Looking for his father, he had found himself.

In the official manual to coping with your family, you are not likely to find much reference to using your imagination. There is a lot about healthy ways to argue, and about managing household finances, and tips on conducting family meetings. There are exercises in the back that can teach you how to listen without feeling impugned. There are referrals to counselors and therapists, and if you can afford them, that phone call will indeed be worth it.

But the official manual is not going to encourage you to live an hour of every day in a fantasy of your own making. No therapist is going to instruct you to invent a castle in the sky to soothe your stress.

Even Sandra's advice to Brian sounds laughable: "Think happy thoughts, Brian!"

Yet we all do it. We hope for things we know are virtually impossible, not because we are deluded, but because the state of being hopeful is a nice state of existence. It creates a tiny calm amid a swirl of confusion. We often do not really want this vision to come true as much as we want the fantasy to always be there, comforting us, like a child's blanket. No matter the torrent going on here on earth; that moon we wish upon is safe. As we grow up and get older, that moon comes closer, and the fantasy matures into something a little less absurd, a little more plausible. A daydream.

It does have its dangers. Once you learn to cope this way, it can be hard to turn it off. Escaping into your imagination is easier than dealing with reality. In addition, ramped-up fantasies can turn us wanton. It's easy to start thinking you are impoverished when you are not. It's easy to overlook that your life is already bountiful with good people. It's easy to become ungrateful when you have so much to be thankful for.

Our imagination is the most powerful coping skill we have, and the challenge is to move away from it as we gain the ability to affect the course of our lives. But we must never give it up completely. It points us in a direction. It steadies us with hope.

We are all in search of a family to which we feel we belong. On the verge of turning thirty, Brian started to feel like he had found a sense of belonging, in an alternative, improvised way. The center of that family was Annie, his wife, five years going on forever. It included his friends and their children—people who meant as much to Brian as anybody they were related to. It included his nephews, for whom he felt great responsibility. It only somewhat included his siblings; he helped them occasionally, but he did not overextend himself. Of course, it included his mother, whom he remained close to, and his grandmother and aunts. This loose association of disparate pieces represented the people he belonged with. Sometimes, in his imagination, he placed them all at that big house in the Carmel Valley.

He was never going to be rescued by anyone but himself.

He still felt different, an outsider—not quite black, because he was part African, and not quite American, because he was black. He and Annie were living in Fresno. He was close to finishing his PhD, and when he did he would buy a house. Kids would probably come, eventually. He felt a little guilt at times over his life turning out so well, but he knew he would have felt a lot more guilt if it hadn't. He never made his mother cry. When she listened to Billie Holiday, it was not for him that she wept. He still had the occasional nightmare, and Annie told him that he still cursed in his sleep. He was a quiet man who kept many of his thoughts private. He treated everyone with kindness, and those who knew him adored him.

He thought his search for a family was done. Until something happened that opened up a whole new lung of yearning.

The picture Brian kept of his father.

One day the phone rang in Fresno. Annie answered it. A man, in a very formal tone, asked for "Bree-Anne Olowude." Annie called Brian to the phone.

"Hello?"

"Hello. This is Bree-Anne?"

"Brian."

"Ah, I see. You are a man. I mistook your gender. My apologies."

"That's okay."

"You are the one who posted a message on Nigeria.com?"

"Yeah, that was me." It had been at least six months, and Brian had forgotten all about it.

"I have contacted the Olowudes for you. I have forwarded your posting to them."

"You know them?"

"Brian, if the information you provided about your father is factual, then your father is the uncle of a good friend of mine whom I worked with at Chevron in Nigeria. My friend would be your cousin. And if it is true, then you belong to a very good family, a very strong family. My friend would like to speak to you. He will call you tonight at eleven P.M."

"Okay."

"Brian, your father is not dead. He is very much alive, and living in Rome."

Your father is not dead. The news was so shocking that Brian did not think to ask a single question for clarification. Nor did he doubt it for a second. When he came out of the study, he told Annie and then burst into tears. "I gotta call Mom," he sobbed.

Late that night Brian's cousin Tunde Olowude called. Brian was still too shocked to think of questions, such as how his father had escaped the war or why he was living in Rome rather than Nigeria. But Tunde asked Brian a lot of questions to make sure his story was true. Brian explained how his mother had met Samuel when he was a graduate student.

"That does sound like my uncle," Tunde affirmed. Brian also learned that he had two younger half sisters. One was in England, at boarding school; the other was in Nigeria. Their mother was in Rome with Samuel, who worked with the United Nations.

Tunde asked Brian to send all the identifying information he possessed to his friend, including the photograph of his father and one of his mother, Sandra, and copies of his driver's license and birth certificate. His friend would forward it to Tunde through the Chevron parcel system, which was trustworthy.

Brian did this, but he did not hear anything for a week. Then some photographs arrived from Tunde, which were mostly of his children—only one included Brian's father. Tunde continued to e-mail, apologizing for the delay and assuring Brian that all was fine, he just had to wait for his brother Remi to get back from London before telling him about

Brian. *Tell his brother? Why not my dad?* He wondered if he was being stonewalled. He should have been consumed with the question of how different his life would be now. But the lack of communication made Brian obsess about one thing: *Why isn't anybody letting me speak to my Dad?*

What Brian was beginning to confront was that Nigerian families have a particularly rigorous hierarchy. In a Nigerian patriarchy, the younger brothers do not leave the family to seek their own fortune; instead, they serve their older brothers—sometimes literally, as personal assistants. So even though Tunde was the head of the insurance department at Chevron, he could not simply call his uncle Samuel Olowude himself. He needed to present the information to his immediate senior brother, who would approve his taking the story up the chain to his first senior brother, Remi. Remi then needed to tell Samuel, and once he did, Samuel took two weeks to get up the courage to tell his wife. Brian's impatience grew. He began to think he should just call information in Rome and ask for Samuel Olowude. He feared that the brothers might encourage him to go away, even though Tunde's e-mails were cheerful. Brian could only imagine how the Olowudes might look upon the existence of an unknown son, and he feared they would think he was illegitimate. *I have always been an Olowude,* Brian found himself thinking. *They don't need to give me the right to be one.* In his e-mails to Tunde, he expressed hope that they would make their decision soon and let him reunite with his father.

But even Brian's doubts betrayed how American he was, how little he understood. A younger Nigerian brother jumps at the chance to do something that will make his older brother happy. Brian's existence was great news, and Brian's cousin was thrilled to be able to tell his senior brothers. Even though children are rarely born out of wedlock in Nigeria, two factors made the shame of it negligible. First, Samuel was not to blame, since he never knew Brian existed. The only person at fault was the student at UC Davis who told Brian's mother that Samuel had died in the war. (Apparently he'd made the story up without knowing the seriousness of the matter, because Sandra had guarded the secret that she was pregnant.) Second, the Olowude family is extremely proud of its heritage, and their name is unique to their family—no other family in Nigeria has that name. So there are no Olowudes in the world who are unaccounted for, and none who have broken away as strays. When Brian surfaced, they were not about to let him become the first Olowude to depart from that tradition. There was no question that they would accept him, at least in formality if not emotionally.

You might wonder how it's possible that every single Olowude is accounted for. It is because the name is only five generations old. In Nigeria there is a system for continuing the patriarchy even when there is no male heir; Brian's great-great-grandfather was chosen to begin a new line. *Olowu* is a Yoruba word for the tool used in goldsmithing, which was the family trade. As a grown man, Brian's ancestor brought Baptist fundamentalism to his village, Inisa, and he brought trade, turning their village into a regional trading center that benefited many. (Inisa is still a sleepy and rustic community, but it is the home to more than ninety thousand people.) Ever since, the Olowudes have been taught that they were chosen to do great things. Today every child of Brian's generation has at least a master's degree, and they have been educated at schools throughout Europe and the United States. So they were not surprised to learn that Brian had risen above his poor background to get an education. To them, Brian's success was proof of the Olowude mettle.

Brian had to wait a full month after learning that his father was alive before talking to him.

"After thirty years, waiting for a whole month was interminable," Brian described. The process made him feel rejected, despite their encouragement. Now he laughs at his American impatience.

Finally Samuel called Sandra to ask for her permission to call Brian. It was early in the morning. He was a formal man, and he followed formal lines of introduction. Sandra called Annie to warn Brian the call was coming. She was worried for her son. She didn't want him to be hurt.

Annie woke Brian up. "Brian! Your dad is going to call here in one hour!"

Brian jumped out of bed. He paced around the house. Rather than making a list of all the questions he wanted answered, he began to panic about how to answer all the questions his father would have for him. He froze up, as with stage fright. Brian was also worried about coming across like an impatient American, disrespectful of other cultures.

"Hello?"

"Hello. This is Samuel Olowude. Is this my son?"

"Yes."

"It is good to be talking to you."

No crying, no emotion. No *This is your daddy!* Brian was not exactly disappointed. It was more like they were having a conversation and leaving much unsaid. Brian assumed that his father was as confused by what their biological connection meant as he was. But it was a good conversation, and it lasted about fifteen minutes. It was very formal. Samuel asked a lot about Brian's work, and the main point he made to Brian was that he never knew Brian had been born until two weeks before. He really wanted Brian to know he had not been neglected intentionally. But he did not offer the emotion Brian really wanted to hear, like *I missed you so much.* To Samuel, these were not matters one discussed over the phone.

"The next thing we must do, you must come to Rome."

I can't afford to fly to Rome, Brian was thinking.

"We will send you a ticket," Samuel added.

"Okay."

"You will come alone this time." Meaning, *not with Annie.*

"Okay."

"We will be talking again very soon."

Then Samuel put his wife on. Brian's stepmother seemed to intuit Brian's anxiety about whether he would be accepted, and she expressed more enthusiasm. "We must make up for lost time," she cooed.

When Brian hung up, he realized he had not asked his father a single question. It had felt like he was interviewing for a job, not a reconciliation after thirty years. He did not know how to process it. He had not even remembered to get his father's phone number.

In his fantasies, it had *never* played out this way.

Brian now knew for sure that his father was indeed alive, but except for those tears on that first day, it was not cathartic. The mystery of his father's existence had been replaced, instantly, by an even tougher enigma, one even harder to sort out: What did it mean that he had a family on the other side of the planet? Who were these people? Of course he wanted some facts, but was he supposed to care for them deeply? Did the facts and the biology mean anything, really? Brian had a lot of friends whose family did not mean much to them at all. A Christmas card, an occasional trip, a phone call now and then. *What did it mean to have a family?*

When he got on that plane to Rome a month later, he knew he was going to trade away his daydreams for the truth. He was okay with that. He could handle it. His life was grounded. It would have been different had this happened ten years earlier. When the plane took off, Brian found himself overcome with a sense of belonging to his mother and siblings—a sense he had not had since childhood. It would be okay if this did not go well.

The trip to Rome made a small dent in the riddle of what it all meant. His father and stepmother met him at the airport, and they brought him a big stuffed panda bear, as if they were picking a boy up at the hospital. His stepmother smothered Brian with a big hug, but his father's hug was brief, more of a pat on the back. He was quiet and reserved. "Okay, let's get the bags," he said. When they got to the apartment in Rome, Brian was shown his room. He was excited to be in Rome, but it was dawning on him that he didn't really know these people. He also couldn't tell how well off they were. He was ashamed that this question mattered to him, but it's hard to fault a man who grew up poor for wondering what having money might be like.

Brian spent the next ten days sightseeing in Rome, mostly in the company of his stepmother. Brian grasped that socializing was a woman's job, and she was great at it—every day, friends came by for a visit. But his father did not take time off, and Brian could not tell whether that was a clue to his father's feelings or not. They went to his office to have lunch on most days. One day they went on an excursion to the seaside.

Brian was unsure what to call his father. In the family, everyone called him "Daddy." Brian was not quite ready for that; it seemed inappropriately intimate. He did not want to insult his father, though, so he simply avoided calling him anything.

Most of what Brian learned on that trip came from his stepmother. The scar on his father's forehead was a tribal marking. They were from the Yoruba tribe, one of the four major ethnicities in Nigeria. Samuel had left the United States because all the student visas had been recalled during the Biafran Wars. Though Samuel did begin his mandatory government service upon his return, a man of his stature never would have seen the war firsthand. Samuel's work was in the trade of agricultural commodities, such as cotton. His degree had been in agricultural biology. Probably the biggest piece that came into Brian's possession was a philosophical understanding of how his family viewed "family." Family was something sacred, and any individual's deeds reflected upon the whole. They were proud of one another, and showered one another with praise.

One day Brian found himself walking in a mall with his dad. They got a soda and sat down at a little plastic table. Samuel was telling Brian some things about the Olowudes, like "always respect your mother" and "always respect your wife, never hit your wife," when Brian suddenly realized: This was their big talk! His dad was imparting the family wisdom! The setting had thrown him off. He began to listen harder. He learned that there had never been a divorce in the Olowude family. He also learned that everyone in the family had spent at least one night sleeping in their ancestral village, Inisa. It was about a four-hour drive from Lagos. Brian would be expected to visit. The whole village would want to meet him and his wife.

"I always wanted to go to Africa," Brian responded.

Then his father gave him an envelope with two thousand dollars in it. "To help with school tuition," he said. Brian had never held so much money. He was grateful, and he could not help but feel that the gift was pretty cool, even though he wasn't sure what to make of it. Was this a lot of money to his father? Was it pocket change?

Brian started to feel more accepted. One thing that really helped was that his cousin Remi flew in from Lagos for a night. *If he flew all this way to meet me,* Brian realized, *then this family is taking me seriously.* They had a small party. Brian learned to call his cousin "Uncle," because all elders are given titles of respect.

Brian gradually understood that his father was not being quiet and withdrawn *just toward him.* He was that way with everybody. When he came home from work, he did not wrap his arms around his wife. The hug he gave Uncle Remi was the same hug he gave Brian at the airport. He was just a quiet, reserved man. He treated everyone amicably. In this way, he was more like Brian than Brian wanted him to be.

"So for how long will you be coming to Nigeria?" his stepmother asked.

"I was thinking a couple of weeks," Brian tried.

"No. That will not do. You cannot visit for such a short time, not on your first visit. You must stay for one month, two months, or three months."

He would have to wait until the next summer to get that much time off. "I guess a month, then?"

When Brian left Rome, he realized that in ten days he had not seen a single argument, and not one unkind word had been directed at another family member, least of all him. He thought back to the friend of Tunde's who had first called him out of the blue, and how he kept praising the Olowudes as "a great family." The truth of that was just beginning to sink in. It really wasn't a question of whether they would accept him; the real issue was whether he was prepared to fully accept *them*.

If going to Rome was to meet his father, then going to Nigeria was to meet his whole extended family. Brian's stories of his trips there are laced with the yearning of too little time with Dad amid the deluge of relatives. There is little one-on-one time in Nigerian families. This was the first thing he had to adjust to. In America we have this idea that we make our strongest connections to people individually, sort of as secret compacts, away from the hubbub. We demand our heart-to-hearts. To an American, the hubbub is just noise. But to a Nigerian, the hubbub *is* the genuine and telling part. An individual simply cannot be known out of context; to know a man, you have to know his family. You have to see where he comes from.

Brian has now been to Nigeria three times. The first, for his introduction to the extended family. The second, for his sister's wedding. The third, for the funeral of his father's brother. His family has come to the United States once, for his cousin's graduation in Pittsburgh, and his sister has visited him in Fresno twice. Gradually, the answer to what it all means has come into focus.

To start, when he and Annie got to Nigeria, he discovered that his family is richer than in his boyhood dreams. While Brian's father is highly respected and certainly very well off, Brian's "uncle" Remi is a Nigerian mogul. Remi is mostly known for being the CEO of the big insurance company in Nigeria, but he also operates a television station and a mobile phone network, among other companies. Brian understood his family was wealthy from the minute he arrived in Lagos—

they were being driven around in Range Rovers and Mercedeses, as a caravan. Plus, security police flanked the caravan. The first night, they were taken to a hotel. A personal assistant had been assigned to Brian and Annie. Rather than checking them in at the hotel, the assistant insisted on seeing their room, and when he deemed that it was not on a high enough floor, he drove them to two other hotels until he found the highest available room over Lagos. When they went to Remi's house in Lagos, there were maids and servants. Remi's house has been rebuilt recently, and it is as if the designer was able to read the floor plan right from Brian's boyhood fantasies. There are plasma-screen televisions in every room, a gymnasium, a solarium, a huge pool, gold fixtures, a dining table that seats twenty-two guests, an elevator, a six-car garage, and a ten-man team of security guards.

Imagine Brian walking into that palace of his uncle's. His whole life, Brian had wondered how many of his family's problems might disappear if only they had money. It was impossible not to be giddy. It was impossible not to feel as if his dreams had magically connected him to these people. The similarity of his fantasy and his new reality spoke to him; it danced in his mind, and titillated him with the possibility that his life was not all random.

In the eyes of the Nigerian populace, Samuel and Remi were not famous men simply because they were rich; they were rich because they were men of great character and tradition—men who had walked out of a small village and transformed their lives and yet never forgot their origins. So wherever they went, people were desperate to be near them. Crowds followed their caravan. As soon as Remi left his house, word spread. And whenever he entered his house, the phone began ringing with callers desperate to make a connection. The hierarchy of brothers screened every invitation, bringing only the important issues to the attention of their first senior brother.

What strange kind of brothers were these? They did not hit one another. They did not haze one another. They did not torture the youngest to toughen him up. Brian thought back to those incredibly strong feelings from his childhood: how he revered his older brothers, and how he would never hit back. Among his African brothers, he felt like Cinderella sticking her foot into that glass slipper. Was this in his nature? Had it come to him in his genes? As a psychologist, Brian did not really want to believe that biology trumped formative experiences. But he had to admit, it was another eerie correlation.

At one point, in a restaurant, Brian thought he was talking to one more of the family employees when the man identified himself as Brian's cousin—a cousin who served as the personal assistant to an elder brother. Brian apologized profusely. That moment said a lot about how strongly the family maintained its shape even though they were wealthy. In most rich families, it goes to people's heads, and everyone feels entitled to their stake. That was not at all true among the Olowudes. People accepted their roles with humility. They trusted the patriarchs to look out for them.

This was most apparent when Samuel's brother, Remi's father, died. He passed away in June, but they kept his body on ice until December in order to properly prepare for his funeral, which would be held in their village of Inisa. Brian had been to this village on his first trip, but he marveled at all that had been built to handle the crowds that would attend the funeral. A thirty-two-suite resort compound was constructed just for the occasion. Then a new church was erected. The funeral was not a mourning, but a celebration of Daddy Ife's life. He had been a librarian, but he was buried like an emperor. The memorial lasted three days. More than five thousand people attended. When it was over, Remi handed the keys to the new church to the deacons, and to the village elders he handed the keys to the resort compound, to be used as a community center.

So what *did* it all mean? As far as money was concerned, Brian learned to be more like his cousins: Don't ask, but know you will be cared for. "Knowing my family has money helps me sleep at night," Brian told me. "It is their money, not one bit mine, but I feel like if I needed help, or my mother needed help, they would be there for me. That's reassuring." When Brian went to buy a house in Fresno, he got up the courage to ask his father for help with the down payment. His father wired the money right away. "That meant a great deal to me," Brian explained. "I'm not in it all alone. I've got backup now."

His Nigerian family's strong connection to their roots and traditions has been equally interesting to sort out.

When Brian went to Nigeria, there were some customs he could pick up easily—such as the slight bowing when greeting and the frequent blessing of every house they entered. There were also some onetime customs that were quite fun; for instance, Brian's family wanted to reenact his courtship of Annie, and because Annie had brought her father, Arturo, to Nigeria as well, all the Olowude men prostrated themselves on the carpet in front of Arturo to ask for his daughter's hand on behalf of Brian. Then they gave Arturo several thousand dollars as a bride price. At that point, Annie was whisked away by the mothers and instructed on a woman's role in the family—principally bearing and nurturing children, but also socializing and maintaining the family history. And even though Brian and Annie have a traditional division of responsibility at home—Brian provides, while Annie maintains their home—it was weird to see how outwardly explicit the gender roles are for Olowudes. His trips to Nigeria have made Brian recognize just how American he really is—that he's not such an outsider after all.

But those enchanting Nigerian customs do not really challenge his worldview. He can pick them up when he visits, and he can leave them behind when he gets on the plane home. The tradition that does really challenge him is the supreme importance the Olowudes put on family life. To them, it's the bedrock of their existence. Could he accept this? Would family ever mean as much to him as it does to them?

His answer is still a work in progress. The way they treasure family is uplifting. It has strengthened the bond he has with all his families, including his mother's family and Annie's family. They've taught him not to forget where he comes from, and that includes Seaside and all the people there. They always ask after his mother, whom they call "Big Mommy." However, Brian is comfortable with his space—they are not part of his everyday life. When Brian talks about this dynamic, I develop a mental image of a man with a broken leg that has just barely healed, and the cast has just been removed. It's scary to put weight on that leg. You have to learn to trust that it really can support you again. Brian's been doing that. But he is a mature man; his ways are fairly set. It'll be some time before he runs on the new leg, if ever.

What light does Brian's one-in-a-million story shed on our struggles over family? His experience reminded me of the stories I'd heard of adopted children finding their birth parents. Reconciliation between children and their birth parents can be a great thrill and lead to a long, caring relationship, or it can be utterly odd and detached—surprisingly meaningless. It can also be devastating—I interviewed a husband whose wife committed suicide after she found her birth parents. The big reason it has worked so well for Brian is that there is no guilt or shame on either side. Brian thought his father was dead, while his father never knew Brian was born. They don't have to forgive each other.

Another comparable paradigm is marrying into a family. Already an adult, set in his ways, Brian began his relationship with the Olowudes at age thirty. After the initial shock of acclimation, their effect on him will be gradual, and it will play out as they share family moments over the coming years.

No family can live up to a fantasy, as Brian has realized. The first glitch came when his sister was married in Ibadan, and his stepmother's family was not as accepting of Brian as the Olowudes were. When he got back to Fresno, he didn't call for a while—he just got busy—but the Olowudes feared that Brian had cut off relations.

Also, Brian and Annie are unsure if they will have children—there are some health concerns that make doing so a challenge. It is very hard for the Olowudes to understand somebody *choosing* not to have children, since in their view the entire point of marriage is to raise offspring. So Brian is starting to feel like their acceptance of him is not as unconditional as it once seemed. Would they have been so accepting of him at first had he not been so educated?

"The more time I spend with them, the more I see that they are indeed a great family, but they are still a typical family, and by no means perfect."

"Has that been a letdown?"

"Not really. It's been better. They went from being the living embodiment of 'family' to being a real family complete with issues and problems. It sort of makes it easier for me to fit in, because I'm by no means perfect, either."

"So what *do* they mean to you, if they're not in your everyday life?"

"They *are* in my thoughts every single day! Let me put it this way. I have two families. One is the family of my childhood, the other is the family of my adulthood. As the family of my childhood has fallen below a line where I can really help them, it's been nice that this other family has emerged for me to belong to. It's more important to me than my daily routine would ever indicate."

"How do they compare with the family you always imagined?"

"You never get exactly what you imagine, do you? The Olowudes walked into my life, but they *are* my family, and like all families, you're constantly getting used to them."

He added, "I think of my life like this: It's as if I found an old painting in my attic. I love this painting so much, I hang it on my wall. Thirty years later someone comes along and informs me my painting is a Picasso. Well, that's exciting. It's fun. But I don't love it *because* it's a Picasso. I already loved it."

I could tell Brian was hedging a bit. He was protective of his mother's legacy, and he did not want the excitement of finding his father to drown out all she did for him growing up.

"Was there any one-on-one time with your father in Nigeria at all?"

Brian thought about it, and then he remembered. "We did not have times to just sit and talk, no. But most mornings, after breakfast, my dad would retire to the porch to read the newspapers. He reads three or four, and ponders them very carefully. This is usually his private time. But I would join him, and he would hand me a paper to read. It might not sound like much, but I felt very close to him. I never got to be a boy, watching my dad shave or putting on his clothes, mirroring him, wanting to be like him someday. Those mornings on the porch came close, though. It would all hit me. I couldn't believe I was in Africa, sitting on a patio with my father, getting to share a part of his life he does not normally share."

Annie says his father's family means more to Brian than he can put into words. "It has answered questions I didn't even know he had," she told me. "You should have seen Brian when we went to their village, Inisa. All these people came out of their tin-roofed shacks in their best dresses, and a big crowd formed. They were there to see Brian, but really, they were there to see his father. They considered being in his presence a big honor. They revered him. What son would not relish seeing that his father is considered a great man of the people? Brian has always felt a little guilty for turning out less troubled than his siblings. And finally, his dad was showing him, it's okay that you are who you are. You are not all alone anymore."

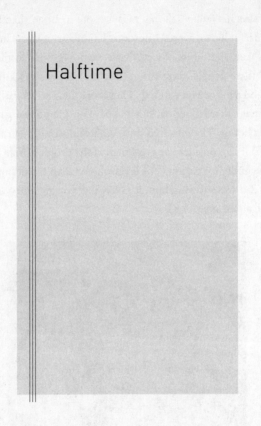

Halftime

When I visited families, I was quickly caught up in their drama and their hopes. Soaking up so much information was intense. Their stories spiraled in every direction, usually incoherently. I overloaded, almost every time. My quiet plane rides home were welcome respites. When I got back to my office, I needed to sit, think, and unwind.

I'm guessing you could use the same. Let's pause and distill.

Though every week I flew off to meet new people, the feeling I got from hearing their stories was reassuringly consistent. I began to believe it is possible to overcome problems that we have long assumed are intractable. In every story there came a point where our protagonist had to decide whether it was wise to move forward with his or her life despite what had happened in the past. Their experiences proved to me that the past's grip can be broken. Not that every problem with your family can be worked out, but that more can be worked out than I ever thought. If it can't, then a better experience is still possible—with someone else or a new family.

I know it's hard. I know in real life it doesn't work out in a mere twenty-five pages. I never thought it was going to work out for me. I never thought I would feel comfortable around my parents. My family liked to argue, and growing up there were times our arguments came to blows—usually over the most innocuous things. The biggest fight I ever had with my dad was over a bottle of Clairol Herbal Essence shampoo. In my twenties, I don't know if I was deadened or just bored, but when I visited home it was a chore—a duty and a responsibility, not something I ever looked forward to. It got worse when my marriage fell apart—I thought I would never choose to get married again, because in my experience marriages were only good for getting people hurt. I ended up renting a room in a boardinghouse, with the shower across the hall, and I couldn't bear to answer the phone for four months. Every night it rang with people reaching out to me, and the guy in the room next door was pounding on the wall, and all I could do was pretend I wasn't there. I certainly assumed I never was going to be a parent—the idea of having a kid scared the heck out of me. It was too easy to screw a kid up, I believed. And the financial responsibility seemed overwhelming.

I was okay with all this—it actually didn't bother me. I just wasn't a family person. I had stopped trying. It was like I'd had a bad experience with shellfish, and so I was staying off the cracked crab.

But it did work out. For me, the transition from feeling indifference to feeling good took about six years. We worked on it, persistently—me, my brothers, my parents, and my girlfriend (now my wife). We decided that making it better was important, and we learned to give one another what we needed. If there was a turning point, it was the moment I found my hope and willingness to try harder. The story of that moment is at the end of this book.

So much of our disappointment and frustration with family is a function of our expectation. We have a tendency to idealize certain notions of family. This by itself isn't bad, because it's good to aspire. But when we come to *expect* the ideal, and we assume the ideal is prevalent, we're quickly let down by our reality. We feel cheated and resentful—and often give up—when our experience is actually fairly representative.

In the same way, we generate excessive tension by worrying about whether our experience is abnormal. We beat ourselves up because we worry we're falling short of the ideal, or we fear we've lost something essential that prior generations had. I'm not talking about the public-debate angle here—how one television pundit beats up some other pundit's vision of family. I'm talking about how we do it to ourselves—how we load ourselves up with guilt and consternation to the point of being frazzled, *so much so that we are unable to enjoy our experience*.

Let's consider some of the fears that come from comparing ourselves to *presumed* sociological norms:

- That stepfamilies and "alternative" families are a new phenomenon to deal with.
- That we have lost the traditional nuclear family.
- That we have lost stability in general.
- That divorces are so common.
- That the elderly are neglected.
- That we don't spend as much time with our kids.
- That children are exposed to too much these days.

These are real issues in some families, but as a society we are doing much better on these counts than we give ourselves credit for.

For instance, a much higher percentage of children lived in stepfamilies during the colonial period of the United States than do today. Parents died young and remarried repeatedly. In late-seventeenth-century Virginia, fully half of all children would lose at least one parent by the time they were thirteen. Almost half of those would lose the other parent as well and be orphaned. Households have always been mixed and complicated affairs. Throughout the eighteenth and nineteenth centuries it was common to take in orphans as wards and to share the house with boarders. Sharing a house with another family was common a hundred years ago. Living with Mom and Grandma was routine in the late 1800s for African Americans and Mexican Americans because adult male mortality was so high. Today we're prone to thinking adoptions are the new way to build a family. Actually, the number of adoptions is not rising—it has only held steady, during some decades when the overall family population has surged. The result: the percentage of U.S. families who adopt has dropped almost by half since 1973. In the United Kingdom adoptions were *four times* more popular just thirty years ago. Alternative family arrangements are indeed common today—but they're not new. They have always been prevalent.*

In fact, the so-called traditional family may never have been a ma-

---

*For more information on the statistics in this chapter and their underlying arguments, please visit my website, www.pobronson.com.

jority, even in the 1950s and 1960s, the supposed golden age for family. If you define a "traditional" family as father-breadwinner/mother-homemaker, then even in the peak year of 1960, more than 40 percent of all U.S. children were being raised in "nontraditional" families. If you add to that definition the standard that the children were from both parents' first (and only) marriage, then *never* have a majority of children lived in a traditional family. In fact, when young families starting moving to the suburbs in the 1950s, it was controversial. Many sociologists decried that it was breaking the extended family apart as the older generations were left behind in the cities. It was considered unwise to be having so many babies, reversing a three-hundred-year-long trend to bear fewer children. In other words, the golden age for family was not considered so golden at the time.

Now for the commonality of divorce. Never has a single statistic been so overly relied upon to indicate what is going on. Marital disintegration is traumatic to children and families, but divorce is only one measure of disintegration. So are death and desertion. Desertion was a huge problem a hundred years ago. Men simply left their families. They didn't bother to get a divorce, or they couldn't. Separation also didn't show up in the divorce statistics. In the late 1940s, for instance, the divorce rate spiked. There was one divorce for every four marriages—unheard of. But for every divorced family there were 1.5 separated families. So actual marital disintegration was much higher than the divorce rate captured. Marriages were never as stable as we imagine they used to be. Just because divorce was uncommon doesn't mean kids didn't have to endure instability. A hundred years ago, a third of all U.S. children lived in a single-parent family by their mid-teens, whether the missing parent had died, or deserted them, or separated.

The laws on divorce have changed so significantly that any measure of the historical divorce rate is just not apples to apples. Divorces were uncommon because they were hard to get. The sudden rise in divorce in the 1970s stemmed from a change in its legal availability, not a sudden and drastic change in the level of marital unhappiness.

Then, divorce is often criticized for being the easy way out. For many women, that's a blatantly unfair smear. Consider that in the United Kingdom it is estimated that one in every three divorces involves domestic violence. In Canada half of divorced women have been victims of abuse. Is that just poor people? Even in middle-class marriages in the United States, violence is cited in more than 20 percent of divorces. If you were to add to that all the divorces due to chronic infidelity and alcohol abuse, you'd have a huge chunk of divorces that should be cheered, not criticized. For many, divorce is not the problem, it's the solution that brings a better day. Thankfully, people have the right today to leave terrible marriages. Shaming them is misguided.

Do we want stability? Of course. Do we want long, happy marriages? Absolutely. But good marriages are not measured by the divorce statistics. Just because people stayed married didn't mean the marriage was any good or that it was a healthy environment for children.

Kids are not being shortchanged today to the extent we fear. Yes, far more children are in child care as both parents work—and the work hours are longer. But sociologists conduct time-use studies in which parents keep diaries recording how they spent their day. They've been doing these studies since 1915. It turns out that while moms used to supervise their children all day, they weren't necessarily interacting with their children. They were doing chores or cooking while little Timmy ran around with his siblings or played next door. Here's the kicker: Parents spend slightly *more hours directly interacting with their children today than in any other decade that's been studied.* This is true in the United States and the United Kingdom and just about everywhere. You might wonder how this is possible. Well, we sleep less, and we do less housework. And, I suppose, we don't just let kids run around. We engage them.

Certainly children are exposed to a lot of potentially bad influences. But if you are prone to panic over this, you have simply joined a club that has existed for hundreds of years. People have always panicked over this. I found an article in an 1875 *New York Times* decrying the inability to protect children from the perilous circumstances by which they were constantly surrounded. I have magazine cover stories from every decade in between wailing over this same concern.

The true history of childhood is brutal and unmerciful. Kiss the ground on which your children live today. In 1851 there were four million children in England under the age of twelve. According to the census, one in five lived on the streets as an urchin. Then a place was found for them: factories. In 1873 there were 120,000 children working in factories around New York. Twenty percent of a working-class family's income was earned by children under the age of fifteen. At the turn of the century, the New York City branch of the Society for the Prevention of Cruelty to Children took in 15,000 children—in one year alone. The farther back in history you look, the worse it gets.

In 1920 only 16 percent of children graduated from high school. Today 84 percent of children do. The legal notion that children have emotional and developmental needs is not that old. In the mid-1800s legal briefs argued that children were not merely chattel. In 1925 the phrase *the best interests of the child* was coined by a judge in the New York courts. But the full meaning of that idea was not accepted by the Supreme Court until 1968.

There are two schools of thought over what role a family plays in preparing a child for the world. They are similar to the old arguments over the nature of humankind (before civilization) between the seventeenth-century English philosopher Thomas Hobbes and the eighteenth-century French philosopher Jean-Jacques Rousseau. Rousseau believed that early humans' experience was idyllic before it became corrupted by modern stresses. Hobbes believed that early humans' experience was nasty, brutish, and short. Thus, a family adhering to the Rousseau philosophy prepares its children for the outside world by creating a safe haven from judgment and antagonism. A family adhering to the Hobbes philosophy prepares its children for the outside world by being a representative microcosm of what is to come. You can expose your children to too much, but you can also shield them too much.

Ever since the Victorian era, families have wanted to create Rousseau-style childhoods. But they kept turning darkly Hobbesian.

In fact, most of the statistics that make our society look so bad are actually indicators of good things emerging—that women and children have rights, that we value some privacy and independence, and that we hold the quality of marriages to a higher standard.

We've got it pretty good. The golden era for family is not in our past, it's in our future.

We need to appreciate how the radically changing world has forced families to adapt. People used to respect their elders, but it wasn't just for their sage philosophy about life. Elders used to have very valuable practical know-how. They could tell you when to plant your crops and how to build a cabin and how to sew a sweater. You listened to them because you needed to. For the last 150 years, every generation has grown up in a newly minted world. My grandmother can't fix the wireless card in my laptop. We've had to find new reasons to hang on to our relationships, and largely, we have. It's a miracle how well we've held together, considering all the changes thrown at us.

I'm generally not a believer in statistics because they can be so easily manipulated. For instance, we hear that children are terribly over-scheduled, that they are rushed from their tutor to soccer practice to their violin lesson. But we also hear that children watch way too much television, slumped on the couch. So which is it? It can't be both. We also hear that more and more African American babies are born out of wedlock. Well, the chance that an unmarried black woman under the age of twenty-four would have a baby is no higher today than in the late 1960s. What's happened is that African American married couples are having fewer children, so the out-of-wedlock babies are a higher proportion of the total—a problem, but not a *bigger* problem.

Then there's the dire news about marriage, the general conclusion being that today's generation has delayed marriage so long, many will never marry. Is that true? Consider the group of women who will turn forty in 2006. About 71 percent of them had married by age thirty. Somewhere around 83 percent of them had married by age thirty-five. And two years ago, a census report projected that 92 percent would marry at some point in their lives. Even if the actual results fall short of that projection, it hardly sounds like doom and gloom for the family.

Why am I bothering to clarify all these numbers? Well, because the "our-families-are-in-trouble" spin is destroying our confidence that we can have decent families. We are letting myths destroy hope. When I talk to young adults in their twenties, it's amazing how many of them are scared of starting a family. It's not just those who had a bad experience with the shellfish. A remarkable proportion of those who don't want to have children are educated, soon to be successful, and their own parents are still married. They hear the doomsday reportage and they believe it. "Why bring another child into this world?" they ask.

Instead, they declare that their friends are their family. By this they really mean that their friends are their *extended* family. As everyone knows, having family a mile away is a lot different from having them in the next room. In my research, I found that when people try to take it to the next level of commitment—for instance, buying a house with friends—the relationship changes under that constant pressure and close contact. Or maybe *curdles* is a better word for what happens. The great thing about friendship is its fluidity and nonexclusiveness. You can float among your friends as you see fit, and you can always be supportive. When you move in together there's a tendency to be more demanding and to start controlling each other—*Hey, you gotta wash your dishes!* You start acting like capital-F Family again, with the peculiar set of problems resident to interdependence and sharing a bathroom. It's a bit like weeding dandelions. *I thought I got rid of my family! Now my problems are back!* Just because you are not biologically related doesn't make family dynamics go away. In fact, the biological/nonbiological distinction we draw is absurd. I'm not biologically related to my wife. She was a complete stranger the day I met her at a baseball game. Then she became a friend. Marrying her hasn't made our problems go away.

Should we all rush to create families? Please, no! But we shouldn't be so terrified of making that leap. It's easy to fall into the trap of wondering if we're fully ready. Most changes in life happen without waiting for anyone to be ready. Life is asking us to rise to the occasion.

In other words, if you think of yourself as even close to ready, that's more of a head start than most get.

I'm lucky that both my kids are healthy and that my wife hasn't kicked me out yet. But I'm also just glad that the Fear of Family no longer looms over my life. In holding Family at a distance, avoiding those challenges, I was letting that fear define me, even control me.

So, we proceed.

These are the questions that drive the second half of the book:

- How long should we keep trying with family members who continuously give us pain? How do we decide when it is time to give up?
- What about marital boredom and monogamy? A lot of young people are scared of this, and it makes them nervous about a lifelong commitment. What should we tell them?
- As parents, how much should we let our children figure out for themselves, versus protecting and shielding them?
- Do we need to forgive those who have hurt us? Or should we demand an apology first?
- Should we end our silence and tell the truth, even if doing so will throw the family into disruption?
- How do we move on if we really have a tremendously deep pain that still haunts us?
- If we've been idealizing the wrong thing, then what is it that we *should* idealize?
- How tough should our love be? Should we be firm with our family, or should we be accepting of their weaknesses and faults?
- Where do we start? What's the first step?

The stories will only probe these questions. There is not a right answer to any. These are hard dilemmas, worth reflection. You may not find your answers, but you might find your philosophy.

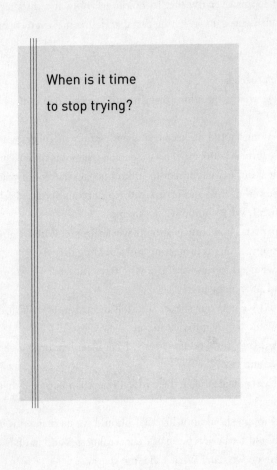

When is it time
to stop trying?

Jamaica?

Yvonne Witter

This is the story of a woman who finally learned that it's okay, sometimes, to say *No more.*

Two years ago Yvonne Witter decided that it was hurting her too much to reach out to her family. It was simply no longer worth it. The trigger—the final straw—was a Christmas morning when no presents arrived for her son. It was a quiet closure to a wound that had been bleeding for forty years. The final-straw moment was not a very big deal, really. It was all about the history.

Yvonne was one of nine Afro-Caribbean women I interviewed in South London. A businesswoman who works avidly for her community, she recently left a position at Lambeth College to form her own consulting practice, assisting microbusinesses and nonprofits on strategy. She is a connector, an inspirer, and a role model. She sits on the board of many admirable organizations. She dresses handsomely and professionally, and she has a grand presence. She takes every question under careful consideration—no answers come out rehearsed. She does not laugh at jokes, but she laughs easily in the face of futility, those things she cannot change. "Sometimes all you can do is laugh," she smiled. She confesses she is still a vulnerable woman. She might look like a strong survivor, but inside she is fragile. For a long time, old echoes rattled in her ears, the whispers of a ghost who fed off unrequited love.

She began our first interview doubting that she had anything to offer me. I had directed her to a web page I had set up that described my research. She had perused this page the night before.

"It made me question whether my situation would be useful to you," she said tentatively. "I got the impression that there is an undercurrent to your work, a message, that regardless of how you might think family is not important, it really is kind of crucial after all. So if that's what you're looking for, I'm not sure I qualify, because I'm not in touch with them, really."

She was right. At that point in my research, I was focused on finding great stories of people who had repaired their relationships. But her question made me rethink: Was that the only way to a happy ending? Might, in some cases, letting the relationship die off be another way to get healthy? I had avoided those stories because I feared they would be sad and depressing—and I figured, *We already know those stories. Is the world not already littered with them?*

When I'm confused about what a book ought to be, I go back to a simple rule I have: All people count. The Yvonne Witters of the world *count*. Her experience is as legitimate as anyone else's. I had something to learn from Yvonne—whatever it might be. Now I was afraid I would lose her before we had started. So I confessed this to her, and I asked for her help.

I said, "I'm interested in how you might counsel others who are considering pulling away from their family. At what point does it become fair to do so? When is too soon, and when isn't it?"

"That is a cutting question. But I'm not sure I am fit to counsel others."

"Well, I'd be interested in how you worked through that very question. I might learn something, and it would be a fit beginning to the conversation I hope to start with readers."

On these terms, we began.

Every child can remember the point at which it occurred to her for the first time that she was different—that maybe she did not belong to that very reassuring flock we call "normal."

In Yvonne Witter's case, this moment did not occur in her childhood. It did not occur until ten years ago. Until then, she was not a contemplative woman. She admits she was an angry woman, and untrusting. But she never pieced together how her past had shaped her personality. In her community, her story was not all *that* different. Lots of Afro-Caribbeans were raised by aunts and uncles. It was common to have moved back and forth between London and Jamaica.

In her mid-thirties, she took a workshop meant to bolster her self-esteem. The instructor gave everyone a homework assignment—to write a page or two on their parents. It was a simple exercise. The next day Yvonne came to class with nothing written in her workbook. The blank page had intimidated her, as had the pressure to speak in class about what she would have written had she actually written it. But she was really stuck on one question: "Which parents was I supposed to write about?"

"What do you mean?" the instructor queried.

"I have two sets of parents," she explained. "I'd need to write about all four of them."

"No," he insisted. "Just write about your real parents."

"I can't say which ones are real," she admitted.

"The ones you were born to. The ones who first raised you."

"But see—that's *two* sets."

She never turned anything in for class. But she did go home and write about her four parents. Having to explain it on paper was like going before an auditing board. It opened the door to so many questions, and she couldn't decide in what order to answer these questions, and she could not reconcile some of her answers with prior answers. Finally she admitted, *You know, Yvonne, it really* never *made sense that you had four parents.*

Yvonne was given away at birth to an aunt and uncle who were childless and willing to take her. This happened despite the fact that Yvonne's mother was married and soon had three other children. But here's what was so unusual for Yvonne—her birth parents lived just down the block. Yvonne called both sets "Mommy and Daddy." Her birth mother was somewhat cold to her, or maybe uninterested. At least once a week Yvonne came face-to-face with the mother who had rejected her. This was in Balland, in South London. Her mother had come from

Jamaica only the year before, at eighteen. Yvonne believes her mother was forced to marry her father and resented Yvonne for this. By contrast, her aunt and uncle had immigrated ten years earlier. They were older, and they were well established in the restaurant business. So there was a significant class difference between Yvonne's two sets of parents. Yvonne was never formally adopted or signed over. She understood that she belonged to her aunt and uncle, but there were times she was asked to pretend she belonged to her birth parents. A child just wants to know what the deal is. The deal was never spelled out to Yvonne. In school she was Yvonne Bailey, taking the name of her aunt and uncle. At church she was Yvonne Witter, employing the name of her birth parents. Yvonne thought it was funny when she was young. As she got older, she always wanted to ask her birth mother why she was given away. But this was never openly discussed, and the mystery took on the air of taboo. Yvonne couldn't summon the courage to demand an answer.

Even today, she has not figured out a terminology to distinguish which of her mothers she is talking about. She calls them both "my mother." It made our interviews confusing.

Discussing her past, she seemed to get weary—not annoyed, but heavy with the weight of it. As she descended, she would deflect with a quip, hoping to eclipse the need for elaboration. When I guided her year by year, she cried twice, although it was not dangerous terrain or volatile in a raw way. Her memories lacked specificity and vividness. She could not provide details where details ought to be. She said she did not contemplate or absorb the events when they occurred—she suffered them thoughtlessly. Not until her thirties did she contemplate her life.

Yvonne has been waiting her entire life for someone to love her consistently. When she was a girl, Yvonne accepted the love of her aunt and uncle. That was good enough for her. When she was nine, those parents took Yvonne and moved back to the Caribbean. The money they had saved went a lot further in Jamaica than in London.

Once there, Yvonne turned into a happy girl. It was no longer confusing, whom she belonged to. She had a close group of friends with whom she attended Sunday school and who were all in the choir. When she was a teen, one of the boys in this group became her boyfriend. Her parents became very strict when they heard about it. They warned her of what her life would become if she gave in to this boy. But Yvonne could not get them to understand. *We are not doing that. We love each other.* She held back the rest: *He loves me like nobody ever has.* She continued to sneak off to the beach to see him.

One day she came back from the beach and found that her father had completely trashed her bedroom, upturning the bed and emptying every drawer on the floor. Many of her personal belongings were broken. Yvonne was already afraid of her father, and now she was terrified. So she ran off to another aunt's house.

The word came that Yvonne was naughty and uncontrollable.

Without a discussion, her parents cut her off.

Seventeen years of love drained out of the barrel in a matter of days.

They telephoned Yvonne's birth mother and said, "We're not taking her anymore. We're sending her back."

They arranged for a one-way plane ticket. At the last minute Yvonne's uncle-father came over to the aunt's house where she was staying and implied she did not have to go. Another child might have taken the uncle's offer. But there was this voice in her ear, that old voice: *See, girl? You* do *this to people.* Yvonne was so sensitive to being unwanted, she could not turn herself around. She got on the plane.

"How did you feel?" I asked, expecting that she would say *hurt* or *rejected*.

Instead, she said, "Terribly guilty."

"Guilty? What for?"

"I believed them. I thought I was a naughty teen, and that I deserved it for being so ungrateful. They had taken me in, provided for me, and I hadn't respected their rules."

"You internalized it?"

"Yes, completely. I took their explanation as gospel. I blamed myself."

Although she'd been disinherited and discarded like an undersized fish, so strong was Yvonne's guilt that she returned to Jamaica twice a year to care for her parents as they aged, occasionally for as long as three months at a time. She continued to do so even when she married and had a husband to care for and a child to nurture without much money to do so. As she grew older Yvonne began to see it differently—not through the lens of guilt, but rather through the conviction that she did not want to abandon them as they had her. She wanted to prove them wrong. She kept going back for more than ten years, right up until she buried them.

I asked, "Always trying to earn their love back, to make up for having gone off with your boyfriend to the beach?"

"Yes. That's right."

"They never forgave you? You never got back to that good feeling you had as a young teen?"

"Maybe the way to say it is I never got over the hurt."

My head was spinning. In my mind, I had identified Yvonne as "the woman who decided to cut off her family." But when I drilled down into her story, I found the opposite. *She* had been cut off. And despite it, she kept going back, for ten years.

At eighteen, Yvonne returned to the mother who had once rejected her. By then her birth mother had moved up to Yorkshire—a far cry from metropolitan London. So Yvonne was not able to pick up the pieces she had left behind at age nine—her old friends were several hours away. For companionship she turned to her sister and two brothers. Her brothers fancied having an older sister all of a sudden. But Yvonne had been an only child until then, and she found sharing difficult. And her little sister seemed to resent her presence.

Yvonne and her birth mother managed okay. Yet Yvonne had just been tossed away by her parents, and in the process had been ripped away from the boyfriend she considered the love of her life. She wanted her birth mother to embrace her. Yvonne was desperate for an emotional connection, but that was something her mother couldn't give.

To top it off, Yvonne had been admitted to a university in Trinidad; attending was now out of the question. Her mom had no clue about higher education. So Yvonne went to the agencies to apply for a job. They offered her a position at the local Woolworth's. She told them she wanted to be a journalist—wasn't there something in that direction?

She was told, "As a black person, you should consider it an honor you're given a job in a shop and not in a factory."

She never forgot that line. Thereafter, every time a co-worker won a promotion she was seeking, she suspected her race was the cause. "It made me romanticize my adolescence in Jamaica. I wanted to go back. I just didn't accept being in England."

The notion of a promised land across the Atlantic worked on her mind like a distraction. She was never fully there in England.

Yvonne did not yet give up. She could have cut her family off then, but she did not. She needed to prove to her parents in Jamaica that they were wrong about her—that she was not a bad girl, and that she would not end up as another uneducated single mother on welfare as they had predicted. She wanted to avenge her past by getting married and creating a family of her own. She admits now that the man she chose was a good man, a very marriageable man, but that their connection was not emotionally intimate. She married Dennis when she was twenty-four, and they had Duane when she was twenty-six. Dennis was one of five brothers. Yvonne adored Dennis's family and wanted to adopt them as her own. But his family was from Grenada, and though dark-skinned themselves, they harbored prejudice toward Jamaicans. There was no chance of winning them over. "Caribbean rubbish," his mother would say when Yvonne left the room. Dennis's family refused to open the Christmas presents Yvonne bought them. They refused to wear the clothes Yvonne gave them as birthday presents. One Christmas, Yvonne invited them over. She cooked all day to prepare a feast. Her mother-in-law was not appreciative. "Are you trying to show me up?" she said.

"You couldn't just ignore her?" I asked.

"I couldn't. Rejection has always been my bogey. My skin was not thick enough to withstand their suspicion of me. And I *so* wanted to be part of this family."

Dennis was torn between the family he loved and the wife they didn't accept. He was unable to stand up to his mother. It was too hard on him, and after eight years Yvonne felt ground down by the pressure.

"I really wanted to be married and create a family thing," she said. "I tried to be the best wife I could. But his family was not cooperative."

"Was it a quick ending?"

"Not at all. Dennis and I made many attempts at getting back together."

"Did you and Dennis continue to raise Duane together?"

"Oh yes, we were very amicable and good friends, despite it all, for many years."

Yvonne was determined to make the marriage work, and when she couldn't, she became determined to stay on friendly terms with her husband. She was fighting her instincts. Encoded in her nerves was the impulse to run, to punish, to throw him away. There were times all she could think of doing was taking Duane and disappearing. The thought of doing this took over her mind, but did not appear in her actions. It was like an untouched obsession. She would not give in to it. She did not want to teach Duane, *This is how you handle your problems.*

So Yvonne did not run from Dennis or his family. But eventually she did decide to leave England and go back to Jamaica. "I wanted to be in a society where I would not be rejected for being Jamaican."

By then her birth mother had moved back to Jamaica and was living with extended family in St. Thomas parish, on the eastern tip of the island. The idea of following her mother and moving back to Jamaica became Yvonne's muse. Her aunt-mother had died by then, but Yvonne still had friends there, and her old boyfriend even wrote to her. So one day she sold her house and shipped all of her belongings across the Atlantic. She and Duane moved to St. Thomas, expecting never to see England again.

"Were you expecting to bond with your birth mother?"

"No. I was expecting to be embraced by old friends. I still had no real awareness of who my mother really was. I thought that she would have been supportive of my decision to come."

"She wasn't?"

"She did not understand. In her mind, as long as my husband was not beating me, he qualified as a good man, and one I should hang on to at all costs. If the marriage had broken down, it was my fault. She insisted I should go back to England and fix it."

"She blamed you?"

"Completely."

"So she didn't even say *I'm sorry for you* or *You must be going through a hard time*? She made no effort to comfort you?"

"That's right," Yvonne answered.

Yvonne was not able to avoid her mother, either. Yvonne had moved into a big house with one of her other aunts. This house had a small apartment on the side, which is where her mother lived. Yvonne's aunt was wonderful. But whenever the aunt was not present, Yvonne's mother manipulated the situation. "You came in too late last night. Your aunt's not happy." Yvonne considered renting her own place—she had money from the sale of her house—but she was going to use that money as start-up capital to get a fried-chicken-and-chips restaurant going. When Yvonne asked an uncle to use his building to house her restaurant, her mother undermined the deal—she wanted Yvonne to get a job and give her the money to build a house.

"My mom was never comfortable around me," Yvonne said.

One day her mother started to tell an old story to Yvonne. "Do you remember that guy who used to come around, ____? Oh, right, you *wouldn't* remember him, because *you weren't there then*." And she delivered this cut as if it were Yvonne's fault that she was raised by her aunt and uncle. Yvonne was so hurt that she finally blurted out the question she had never asked.

"Why *was* I given away, Mommy?"

And her mother went ballistic! "I didn't give you away!" she insisted. "Mommy—"

"You were not *given away*! You were not with *strangers*! You were with an aunt and uncle! We always knew where you were! You're being a troublemaker for saying that!" Her mother completely denied Yvonne's experience—as if Yvonne had never spent eighteen years calling another woman "Mommy."

Yvonne had a theory, one of the only things that could explain it: Maybe she was not her father's child. Maybe she was given away because he did not want to raise another man's child?

"Is that what happened, Mommy?"

"Why do you always create trouble!"

"Is it, Mommy? Is that what happened?"

"Don't you ever repeat that!"

For so long, Yvonne had saved this question, hoping to find the right moment to get a straight answer. For equally long, she had romanticized what life back in Jamaica would be like. She felt crushed. It was one thing to cope with hard reality. It was far more painful to lose her fantasy, because for a long time that fantasy was the only thing that had kept her going.

Yvonne's friends provided no escape. The old choirboy lover she longed for turned out to be in a relationship with a girl who was pregnant, and he was under pressure to marry her. Yvonne felt deceived by his letters. He apologized. She was devastated. Then her best girlfriend made a comment when Yvonne went looking for work. "Oh, you *Brits,* coming home to take all our jobs." It was just one remark, but it stung hard. Yvonne did not feel Jamaican or British. She belonged nowhere.

She intended to spend the rest of her life in Jamaica. She lasted only eight months.

"Now I think I should have stuck it out and reintegrated," she said. "But it was too painful. Every bad experience magnified my pain."

For the second time in her life, Yvonne returned to England. The first time it was not her choice, and her time in England was undermined by the big "what if"—what if I still lived in Jamaica? *I wouldn't be in this housing estate. I would be middle class and be able to get a middle-class job. I would be the same color as everyone else. I would still be with my high school sweetheart.*

This time it was her choice. The "what ifs" had all played out. That seemed to make a tremendous difference.

"I had never truly settled here the first time. The second time, I admitted this was what I could count on: myself and my son. This was what I got. I finally accepted this society as my own."

The miracle of Yvonne is that she did not mirror the crude methods used on her. Time and again, life handed her a nice transition point, at which it would have been quite natural to say, *I'm done with you all, it's not worth the bother.* She could have pushed her family away, and nobody would have blamed her. But she didn't want to treat others the way she had been treated.

When she was a baby, she was given away. When she was a teen, she was sent away. When she married, her husband's mother scorned her. When she returned to her birth mother after many years, she was blamed for making trouble. Finally, it was time to save herself.

Back in London, Yvonne began sharing the parenting with her ex-husband, and it went well. She took part-time work with a temp agency so she could enroll at university full-time, earning a degree in communications studies. She rolled right in to a master's program, adding degrees in business and finance. For the first time, she had her own source of confidence. At work she received the promotions she had always seen go to others. Her anger faded, and her judgment became clearer. She slowly freed herself of her guilt over the way her mothers had treated her.

Every couple of years her birth mother would visit and treat Yvonne like a sister. "That didn't work for me," Yvonne said. "I have spent my entire life trying to get my mother to love me. I'm done waiting." On the last visit, she asked her mother to stay at Yvonne's sister's house. She corresponded with her mother for a few years after that, but her mother continued to deny Yvonne's version of her childhood experience.

While Yvonne's most meaningful relationships (outside that with her son) are with her friends, she would never assert that her friends are her true family. Yvonne has an uncle whom she adores who lives several hours to the north, and if he were nearer she would be in his kitchen every day. She wishes she could provide a warm extended family for Duane, especially now that his father recently moved to America. The final straw was two years ago. Duane bought all his cousins presents. It was okay that they sent none that year, but he hoped they would remember him the following year. They didn't. Duane says, "Why bother, Mom? They don't."

And that was it. She could take all the blame, and she could take all the pain, but she couldn't take watching her son be hurt. For the longest time, Yvonne did not want to repeat her parents' mistakes. But maybe this time it wouldn't be a mistake. She decided to no longer put her son's feelings at risk. There was no ceremony. There was no discussion. It was the quietest door slamming ever heard. She did not rejoice, but we should rejoice for her, because it has paid off.

"I feel positive about my life these days," she told me. "I'm proud of my achievements and I have a new level of enthusiasm. My anxieties about parenting have all but gone. I have so much more love now to give to my son. We are building a strong, close family of two."

So, to make up or break up? The answer is not one or the other. Some relationships can be salvaged, and some are not going to get repaired, no matter what you try.

I used to think Yvonne's story was so different from the others I recorded because it didn't work out with her moms. It seemed melancholy to me. And yet she is in a better place, like the others, and she is happier now. Like the others we have met, Yvonne had nearly unlimited tolerance for pain, and nearly unlimited ability to forgive. So is her story all that different? Reconsider the prior chapters for a moment. In the *foreground* of those chapters we have seen reunion, but in the *background,* story lines like Yvonne's were playing out. James Louie does not share much with his siblings. Rosa Gonzalez divorced her first husband, quickly. Doug Haynes never sees his stepfather. Andrew Ervin Bennett no longer tries to bond with his father. Uma Thangaraj cut all ties to hers. Steve Murphy believes he will have no contact with his mom's family after she passes. In each case making this decision was necessary—but hardly easy. Those people, though cut off, still hang around—like phantom limbs, still sending messages to the brain. Even dead nerves feel.

All of which frames the question *When do you cut someone off?* Not cut them off as a form of protest, when you simply want them to know how hurt you are and you're hoping they will come back after they have absorbed your point. Rather, when do you really stop trying to make it work? Should you stick with it as long as Yvonne did? She went unrewarded for so long. Few would put up with that.

It's important to recognize that how hard you try is taught to you—it's taught by your family and your peers, and it's built into your culture. On one end of the spectrum, the relationship is the priority: You try everything you can possibly try until there is no *try* left in you. Then you try again. At the other end of the spectrum, your own health is the priority: Stop trying when the pain of this unrequited trying is keeping you from healing. I don't have an answer as to where on that spectrum we should be. But *I* never tried as hard as Yvonne. I'm prepared to try harder.

Yvonne summed it up this way. "The journey in a life like mine is about finding a place where you can exist at a level of peace—whatever it takes to find it. Every negative experience with my family reopens wounds. I had to stop putting myself in situations where I was vulnerable to my mother. I had to stop trusting her and confiding in her. I have to stop giving her the chance to hurt me. My mother was a hardworking woman who had a grocery shop in London and now has a business and a six-bedroom house in Jamaica. She has succeeded in her dreams. My uncle—her brother—says, 'Why can't she just acknowledge she gave you away?' He doesn't know why she can't admit it. But I need to get away from that. Leaving it alone allows me to manage my emotional self. I have not abdicated 'family.' It's just if someone is causing you pain, it might be time to abdicate that particular relationship. It might be time, when trying to get them to love you is always ill-fated. I can say this, and there's not a lump in my throat anymore. And that's how I know it's time. There's not a lump in my throat anymore."

Interestingly, Yvonne is thinking of writing her mother regularly again. Not to reach out—the opposite. She wants to write meaningless, vacuous letters. Because she feels that *not writing* gives her mother some power, as if they are still locked together in silence—as if this is a grudge, and both are waiting for one side to break. It is *not* a grudge, and it is *not* a protest. Yvonne is not waiting for her mother to apologize. She is not waiting at all.

At Christmas she sometimes goes over to friends' homes. Last year, she was unsure whether to accept an offer to a friend's house in North London.

"What do *you* want to do on Christmas, Duane?"

"Spend it with you, Mom."

"Do you want to go anywhere?"

"Can't we just have dinner and be together?"

"It's okay that it's just you and me?"

"That's what makes me happiest, Mom."

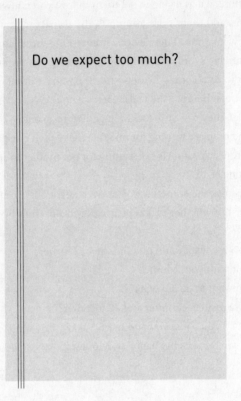

Do we expect too much?

A Cautionary Tale

Anne Jacobsen, on her porch.

Before Anne Jacobsen had her affair, she went to her husband, Jerome, and tried something shocking: She asked his permission.

"I want us to start seeing other people. On the side," she said.

Anne and Jerome were a traditional couple on whom ten years of marriage had taken their toll. They were great at running a family together, but those constant negotiations had desexualized their relationship. They loved the family, but their love for each other was a houseplant stuck in the corner, unwatered. Anne's proposal to have sex with others came out of the blue—by which I mean they had not worked up to this. It was not the next level of stunt in a progression of tricks meant to keep their love life exciting. Until that moment, their ten years had been plain-vanilla, missionary-style monogamy.

Anne had just returned to their home in Blacksburg, Virginia, from a vacation in Belize with her sister. Down there, she had felt totally free of responsibility. In the sparkling aquamarine scuba water and in the shadowy green jungles, Anne was overwhelmed with absolutely irrepressible *lust.* She was drooling over the men, particularly guys who lived the opposite way from her—guys who called no place home, guys who roamed the earth. She met one guy who was biking from Seattle to Argentina. Oh, to join him! Anne had recently started bicycling herself. Her envy was overpowering. She didn't do anything inappropriate, but she wanted to. She was coming unglued. She came home knowing *something* had to change.

Anne was a homemaker and mother of two who tried to spice that up by running a day care program in her basement rumpus room for her younger child—a two-year-old girl—and three other toddlers. Anne had been a Montessori teacher before becoming a mom, so she figured running a school in her basement would be the perfect way to have a bit of careerlike stimulation at the same time. Instead, she was going stir-crazy. In a real school, there are other adult teachers to interact with. In your basement, there is nobody but you and the two-year-olds. She gave so much to the kids that she lost her sense of uniqueness. She lost her sense of being *special*.

"I started falling apart. I disliked the work I was doing, I hated the idea that I had about sixteen more years of responsibility raising my kids before any personal freedom, and I felt completely unconnected to my husband." What got to Anne was a problem that people with real problems would love to have: monotony. She's lucky that this is her only concern. But there are a lot of lucky people in our society just like Anne.

Anne never imagined monotony would become her problem. "When I was young, I vowed I would never become a boring person," she explained. "I've tried to fight mediocrity. I've always wanted things to be meaningful." She thought she had made interesting choices along the way. How, then, had it come to this? She wished she knew.

Lobbying for this loophole made it interesting again, and fast. Needless to say, most people do not ask for permission to have their affairs. Why'd she do it? Not to get a free pass. Anne never thought that just because she asked, it was somehow okay. She knew it was wrong, but in her tortured mind it seemed the least of the evils before her. She wished she could just make this longing go away. She wished it had not come to this. She wished she could have the last five years back to do right. But they had waited too long, and the itch had become an obsession.

Why is it so easy to imagine having an affair, and yet so unimaginable to admit to your spouse that you want to? Most of us cope with monotony with one eye open, one eye closed—letting our minds go places we rarely admit. Having an affair isn't what scares us. Having to ask scares us, and being found out scares us. The *truth* scares us. In a way, *Anne* scares us. She's provocative.

Anne is not scared of the truth, and this is why she was able to ask. She doesn't have that innate fear of revelation, as most people do. As if she lacks the *lying* gene that in so many of us is triggered by stressful situations. She does not react to uncomfortable dilemmas by lying, fibbing, ignoring, or demurring.

Jerome had always been aware of this trait in his wife, and when they were twenty-one it was incredibly refreshing—here was a woman who was willing to live with both eyes wide-open. They would make conscious choices, not robotic ones. The autopilot would never take over. Anne was always more interested in getting to the root of her dilemma—truly understanding it—than in protecting the squeamish.

So she was not going to be dishonest with Jerome. She wanted them to try a different arrangement. She could have said the "right" thing—*Let's go see a counselor!*—but that would have been a bit of a lie, because it wasn't what she truly wanted. What she wanted was for a man to take her in his arms and remind her what it was like to feel sexy.

"I don't have any interest in seeing other people," Jerome answered cautiously.

"I do," Anne said quietly.

"Are you asking my *permission*?" he said, confused.

Yes, she was.

Seven thoughts ran through Jerome's mind all at once.

1. He knew he should say no—he should insist they work on it. But they'd said that before and done nothing.
2. After ten years of marriage, maybe this would finally be a catalyst for change.
3. He felt beaten down. Anne was so stubborn she would do what she wanted anyway.
4. Some part of him had spent so long trying to make her happy, and he wanted her to be happy.
5. Saying no to her just made him out as her oppressor. Tactically, he figured if he gave her the permission she wanted, she wouldn't actually go through with it, but she would realize her husband was an open-minded man.
6. Even if she did try it, she'd realize she didn't like it and would quickly stop.

7. He was scared of her honesty, but she was right. It had been five years since he thought of his wife as a sexual being. This would instantly change that. There would be no more denying his wife's sexuality.

"Okay," he said. "You do what you want."
Jerome did not know Anne already had someone in mind.

Most women fall in love when they have an affair, and as a result, the marriage breaks up. Anne knew this and struggled to avoid it. She did not want to lose her family. The important thing to note about the man Anne recruited was that Anne chose him specifically because she could never fall in love with him. Let's call him "T." T. was not remotely interested in having a family or children. He was not ambitious nor particularly thoughtful. And he was an avowed nonmonogamist—so he was not going to fall in love with her. The sex was terrific, but Anne was never remotely tempted to leave her husband for T. In a perverse and Machiavellian way, she got her rocks off under the guise of protecting her family. She was trying to find a workable, if unconventional, solution—to get her needs met without breaking up the family. She knew it was an awfully delicate construct.

Did it work?

Of course not. But what's surprising is how close it did come to working. Anne slept with T. three times over the next four months. She came away feeling like a woman. Empowered and sexual. Unfortunately, it did not make her ready to give more to Jerome—which confused her. She was honest with him, though. A week after her first rendezvous with T., she told Jerome she had slept with someone. She conveyed this with very appropriate discretion.

But Jerome wanted details. He did not want to know *who* she had slept with, or when, or where. But he wanted to know if she liked it—yes!—and then he wanted to know *why* she liked it. In asking, he was hoping he might honestly learn something. He didn't want to be asexual any more than Anne did. He wanted to be able to please his wife. Jerome had had very few sexual partners. He did not like how Anne had learned it, but if she had learned something that might help them, Jerome wanted to know what it was.

Oh, how excruciating!

Only because he insisted, Anne gave him the block-and-tackle details. The X's and O's. Plus some of the textural spirit—how she and T. kept their eyes open, staring into each other's souls.

It hurt Jerome to hear it—he was crushed—but he had signed up for this marriage, and he had long ago given up his fantasy that it would be easy. So he tried his best. The next time Jerome and Anne had sex—him feeling far more vulnerable and judged than she could ever imagine—he tried a few of the X's and O's. He kept his eyes open and tried to get her to look right back. This is where it all broke down. Because Anne did not like it. *It did not turn her on.* It was okay if T. touched her that way, but it was just too weird for her husband to touch her that way—as if he was copying T., rather than loving her uniquely in his own forceful way.

Oh, the rejection! Poor Jerome suddenly realized that this door to his wife's heart was open to every strange chap but him. And why? For no other reason than that he was the guy who'd put out the trash and paid the bills and assembled the kids' toys and sat across from Anne every night at the dinner table for ten years. He was too familiar. He was the guy with whom she had made ten thousand little everyday compromises—like ten thousand mosquito bites that had poisoned her, turned her against him. She no longer saw him as a strong man with a mind of his own. Jerome had tried so hard to be Anne's full and equal partner that he had given up all his dark mystery—the very thing that had attracted her to him twelve years before.

What a bum deal!

Both Jerome and Anne were convinced that if they did not have children, their marriage would be over. But they did, and so Jerome kept trying. He was training to run a marathon, and he put in mile after mile to exhaust himself—to exhaust his anger and pain. Over those four months, Jerome knew Anne's affair with her mystery man was continuing in some fashion. If it worked for her—if she was getting something out of it—he would try to be open-minded. But shouldn't he be getting something in return? Shouldn't his wife seem happier around the house? Shouldn't she have a skip in her step? Shouldn't she *at least* be more enjoyable company? Instead, Anne seemed as frustrated with Jerome as ever.

Were it not for that, Anne's contrived solution might have actually worked for some time.

That summer, two of Jerome's close friends came to Blacksburg to run a race with Jerome. Afterward they walked around the Virginia Tech campus. Jerome opened up to them.

One kept asking, "Why did you say yes to begin with?"

And the other asked, "If it's bothering you, why not tell her to stop?"

A few nights later, Anne and Jerome were in bed. She had encouraged him to be open with his friends (she wanted a husband who was open with others).

"What did you guys talk about?" Anne asked.

Jerome told her and repeated their questions.

Anne got quiet.

"I want you to stop," Jerome then added.

"Okay," Anne said. "I will."

The next six months were marred by a complete lack of direction. Anne did stop seeing T., but she didn't stop thinking about whether she would be happier outside this marriage. She refused to be contrite. She regretted hurting Jerome, but she wouldn't say she regretted it ever happening. "I don't feel guilty," she said, "though I feel guilty about *not* feeling guilty." She and Jerome found a marriage counselor. They went six times, but from the first visit they could tell this counselor was not the right one for them. The couple completed every exercise in books like *Divorce Busting* and *Divorce Remedy*—such as swapping lists of what they wanted and needed—but no doors of insight opened. They went through the routine, but without any commitment. Why did they lack commitment? Because they were not at all convinced any process could work. Anne was convinced her husband was too introverted for her—unemotional. Jerome was convinced his wife could never be happy. No matter how good a life she had, she would always want *more*. Both were right; both *knew* the other was right. Neither denied it. Both believed they could change, but neither believed they could change *enough*.

Jerome moved down into the basement to protect himself. It was a no-win situation, because even though he was feeling more than he had ever let himself feel, to Anne he was coming across more emotionally withdrawn than ever. He stopped caring about what she thought. At Christmas, Anne asked him to move back upstairs. He did, but he went to sleep at nine o'clock and woke at five-thirty to avoid face-to-face time.

They set one principle—don't argue in front of the children, now ages three and five. To this they stuck, and both Anne and Jerome gave each other credit for doing so.

They had darn near quit, but they did not leave. In a curious way, the undertone of animosity between Anne and Jerome served a purpose—it scared them from leaving. They knew if they divorced under these circumstances, they would not be able to co-parent their children without making a resentful mess of it. So they stayed—if for no other reason than to get to a place where they could divorce amicably.

When I visited in April—exactly one year after Anne's trip to Belize—neither Anne nor Jerome could commit to making it work. However, the stalemate had budged, and here's how: Both had privately come to the realization that even if they married somebody else, they would be in the same situation.

Jerome realized his tendency to withdraw would destroy any relationship he was in. Anne realized her insistence that life be endlessly stimulating would always cause her to act out selfishly.

Until then, their attitude was *Show me you can change. Convince me it's possible you can be different. Then I'll try.* They each considered changing to be a concession in order to win the other back. Unsure they even wanted to win the other back, neither would concede.

Now both wanted to change—not for the other's benefit, but for their own. Pushing aside the question of the fate of their marriage, Anne and Jerome had been pursuing their own inquiries for two months.

Another good thing: A friend recommended a marriage counselor, calling him "a miracle worker." They went to this Miracle Worker, and he astutely recognized that Anne and Jerome needed to meet with him individually. The fate of their marriage, they agreed, would be an issue for later. By my visit, they had each seen him three times. Both trusted him.

Anne and Jerome's home was in a unique development called Shadowlake Village. There were thirty-three homes in the project—a mix of stand-alone homes, duplexes, and town houses. These buildings faced one another across a strip of grass and a walkway, creating a commons for kids to run about endlessly. The streets and driveways plugged in to the back of the houses, not the front. In addition, there was one communally owned common house, with a big kitchen, a cafeteria-style dining room, some couches, and a kids' playroom. Once a week, a potluck was held at the common house for whoever felt like coming.

The people who had moved into Shadowlake Village came there for community. In a wonderful way, they had turned back the clock. There were thirteen kids under age ten here, all welcome at one another's houses. The seniors and single people served as surrogate grandparents and uncles. At night the grown-ups were on their front porches, striking up conversations. The environment is particularly helpful for the half a dozen stay-at-home moms like Anne—it keeps them from feeling so isolated (or is supposed to). If the place sounds a bit idyllic, a bit utopian, it works because people are realistic, not idealistic. Some hippies bought in and quickly sold their place when solar power was voted down for being too expensive.

This idea—that it began in idealism, but it worked because of realism—provided a template for Anne, because her marriage to Jerome had begun with similar high-minded idealism. When they were twenty-one years old, Anne had been sure that Jerome was her soul mate, her destiny. This was a feeling unlike anything else she'd known. The world suddenly seemed like a magical place, brimming with sheer potential. Anne believed she had found the right guy, and because of that, she assumed they would live happily ever after. Twelve years later, she was learning that's not what makes a marriage work and last. The right attitude might be more important than the right person.

Anne's attitude had always been that just because you get married and have kids did not mean life should stop being exciting. Why not have it all? Why not have great kids, fulfilling work, and torrid sex, as well as traveling abroad twice a year? Anne didn't just aspire to this—she felt entitled to it. Anything less was a failure.

Anne did not get this idea from her mother. In fact, Anne outright rejected the model of her mother and father—she wanted *more*. Anne grew up at a time when young girls were being barraged by the message that a woman can have it all. She attended school with girls who also soaked up this message, so she never heard a contradictory opinion. But just because you can have it all over the course of a life doesn't mean you can have it all at once. Just because women finally had choices did not mean that women no longer had to make choices.

It's said that there are four basic fears inherent to the nature of existence—you can have some of these fears no matter how well you might have been raised. They are the Fear of Dying, the Fear of Having to Choose, the Fear of Ending Up Alone, and the Fear That the World Is Intrinsically Meaningless. Anne realized that she definitely had this Fear of Having to Choose. Because she had always assumed that having it all was possible, she had never really forced herself to make a choice. She had never recognized that making choices—and being okay with the fact that this means there are other choices you will never get to taste and experience—was essential to being at peace in the world. But once Anne had this idea in her head, it worked on her mind like a mysterious medicine—it made her feel peaceful.

Some of the other young moms in Shadowlake Village knew about her affair. Others at least knew that Anne was struggling with whether to remain married. Neither Anne nor Jerome found this embarrassing. In fact, once it was out, they found it quite helpful, because they were surrounded by real-life examples of other marriages. Shadowlake Village is small enough that you cannot miss seeing how other couples get by.

One night the sisterhood of Shadowlake Village came to Anne's rescue. They were all drinking wine and eating chocolate in the hot tub. This time Anne wanted the hush-hush. How'd they do it? What were the secrets that made their marriages work? Just how good were their sex lives? Anne got a few juicy details from the other young wives, but what surprised her were the tales of the older women. Anne learned that affairs and divorces and rough patches were in every woman's story. Those who made it last had a defining attitude: They weren't leaving their marriage just because they weren't getting *everything* they wanted. If most things were good, it was worth staying.

Anne had heard this idea before—from her mother. Hearing it from other women finally made it sink in.

Anne came to the conclusion that her expectations had been too high, and that she was punishing Jerome and constantly making him insecure by demanding so much. She vowed to be more realistic.

But Anne's plan was easier said than done. Anne admitted she worried about whether the right attitude would be enough.

Was she just sticking together for the kids? Not at all. She was sticking at it because she loved the family whole. She loved being part of this family, loved the way her kids adored their father.

"Maybe my kids are here to teach me how to make the best of a less-than-ideal situation," she said. "That's definitely something I need to learn."

She felt like things were headed in the right direction.

"It's funny," Anne said. "I compromise so easily with my kids, so why is it so hard for me to compromise with my husband? I have normal expectations for my children, so why do I have abnormal expectations for marriage?"

What did Jerome think of that?

"I hate it," he told me. "I don't want to feel like I'm someone to be *settled* for. I hate the idea of someone giving up and saying, *Okay, I guess you're good enough*. Not really *wanting* me. She hasn't made me feel desired, accepted, or loved."

"Can you commit to getting there?"

"No," he said. "Not now. Not yet." He was considering moving out.

If his emotional honesty with me was any indication, I felt like Jerome had already come a long way.

In the end, it came down to exactly what the sisterhood of Shadowlake Village said it should. Most things in Anne and Jerome Jacobsen's life were good. Neither Anne nor Jerome changed all that much, but they found that a little change goes a long way. Their troubles had brought them closer to other couples in the village, so they had better friendships than ever. With the other moms, Anne could have all the intimate conversations her heart desired. The kids were flourishing. At Jerome's job, which was at a computer company, he took flak for being the kind of employee who valued time with his kids more than overtime at work—but he never caved to their pressure. Anne had no regrets about Jerome as a father. He did his share. In fact, running the house, they were a great team. She'd always thought so. And it wasn't like they had *bad* sex.

Eighteen months after her first trip to Central America, Anne went back to Belize with Jerome and their two children. If it seemed ominous to return to the place where her anxiety and negativity first bubbled over, her kids shattered that overtone, because when you travel with two young kids there is simply no time for self-reflection. Kids put you in the moment. They went swimming with rays, played with spider monkeys, came close to a jaguar, and climbed on ancient temples. When she'd visited the first time, Anne had thought her senses were open—never had the blue water been so blue, never had the green jungle been so green. But you've never seen blue until you witness it through the wide-open gaga of your child. You never have greater awe for the sight of a jaguar than when you are holding your son's hand. "It has come around full circle," Anne wrote me. "Or about as much as I could expect. It feels good to be back here and this time be calm about where I am in my life." The ability to travel had always symbolized freedom to her. Anne was finding out that her kids travel just fine.

Did they ever find that spark again? Did the sight of Jerome ever light her loins like it used to? That may be an impossible and unfair test for these two. Rather, Anne has this to hang on to: The last two years sure have been interesting. She surprised me. When we first talked, Anne seemed too impulsive to ever last in their marriage. I'm sure Jerome felt the same way. But she stared her impulsiveness down, without turning a blind eye to it.

So is that it? Is that the moral of this story, that we need to accept that romantic love is like a wild animal—it's inevitably going to become tame in a domestic setting? That monotony is just to be endured? That to make a marriage last, you have to be able to enjoy the soft pitter-patter of everyday life?

That might be realistic, but it's not very inspiring!

Anne, with her typical honesty, is still torn. During the winter season when she was growing into the philosophy of having more modest expectations, her younger sister visited for a couple of months. Anne's sister is twenty-five, and hanging around Shadowlake Village was giving her a close-up view of married life. One day she said to Anne, "I'm less and less impressed by this whole marriage-and-kids thing." It really stung Anne to hear this, because her sister was saying the same thing Anne had once said to their mom—basically, *What you have isn't enough for me.*

Anne was glad to be destroying her sister's fantasies, because those fantasies would just cause problems if her sister got married. On the other hand, the odds that her sister would ever get married had dropped by half after she'd seen what marriage actually entailed.

That frames the dilemma of extracting meaning from this story. Sure, it's good for married couples—and those considering marriage—

to get realistic. But if that message is broadcast too loudly, it will just scare young people away from an institution they are already hesitant about.

So what should we be telling the twenty-five-year-olds?

I'm on my second marriage, so I've learned from my mistake. I think monotony is the easiest problem to ignore, and overlooking it is dangerous. It may not seem like a "real" problem, so couples go five or ten years, easily, doing nothing to fix it—when suddenly it's too late and they discover their problems are all too real. At that point, you might have no choice *but* to endure it. Until then, you *do* have a choice. Babysitters are cheaper than psychotherapists. Plane tickets are cheaper than divorce lawyers. Making your spouse feel loved and secure is a whole lot easier *before* you cheat. That your mind goes places doesn't mean the rest of you will follow. If you can communicate well enough to cut those daily mosquito bites in half, the good will outweigh the annoying, and the marriage won't feel poisoned. Marriages are not *hard* work—they are gratifying work. The tools of this work are diligence, awareness, and communication. Getting good at this line of work pays off.

It was a full two-year journey before Anne found herself liking and loving her husband all over again. "For a while there, I thought I had married the wrong person, but I see now that Jer was a great choice for me. I doubt anyone could have lasted through all the stuff that I put him through. He has listened to every single last detail, and that says a lot about his acceptance. He has accepted me in all my craziness. Jer is stronger than he lets on. I always wanted to be loved in a remarkable way, and I see now—I have been."

Is a child's nature
fragile or resilient?

The Orchid King

Andy Matsui

In Salinas, California, the sun is constant, but the summers are never too hot because cool air blows in from the coastline ten miles west. This makes ideal conditions for growing vegetables and flowers. Lettuce has always flourished in this soil. Flowers, though, have seen better days. Back in the 1970s and 1980s, Salinas Valley was known as the Flower Capital of the World. You can still see an occasional carnation field, but the families running those farms are losing money and wondering when to shut down. Their operations have been devastated by imported flowers from Latin America.

There is one exception, however: a Japanese maverick named Andy Matsui. He is growing orchids in greenhouses the size of football fields.

Andy is one of those rare successful men who remains amazed at all that has happened, as if Lady Luck stopped by just yesterday. He bursts with a tickled, gleeful laughter after almost every anecdote. Though seventy years old, he is spry and quick. Barely a hair is gray. He usually wears khakis and a boxy, button-front short-sleeved shirt. His forearms are muscled and his palms are broad.

Andy keeps four types of greenhouses: a Germination House, a Standing House, a Blooming House, and a Shipping House. All but the Standing House have tropical atmospheres. The cement floors are moist with recent sprinklings. Overhead fans beat at the air, but vainly—as if it is too thick to be moved. The fragrance from the orchids is bright and sweet, but just as present is the earthy aroma of the tree bark and moss that fill the orchid pots.

The Standing House, however, is different.

When we walk into the Standing House, goose pimples jump out on my arms and I cannot control the occasional shiver. It's twenty degrees colder, at least. The cold hardens the plants and gets rid of their tendency to droop lazily. This is something the commercial grower does that the home grower or hobbyist doesn't. In the care of a home grower, the orchid blooms on its own seasonal schedule, when it is good and ready. A commercial grower gives his plants a bit of a push to tell them *It's time to change.* Their feed and water are cut back, which forces them to shoot up straight and hunt for nourishment and sunshine. It's good for them, Andy Matsui believes. Makes them tough. They stay here until they begin to bloom. At that point they are moved into the balmy Blooming House.

For an orchid to stand tall, it must spend about half its childhood in the cold. This might be a surprise to those who think of orchids as fragile flowers.

Here is what it looks like in a Standing House. The woman in the foreground of this picture is one of Andy's four children, Kathy. She was visiting from Tokyo at the time of my first visit to Salinas, and she translated when Andy reverted to Japanese.

I was drawn to Andy for a reason that might seem out of the blue or disconnected. I went to see him during a time when I was reading a lot of research on how today's parents might be doing too much for their children. Academics who study this phenomenon call it "overparenting" or "the overscheduled child." Mothers call it trying to be perfect, or giving your child a head start. There's no doubt that parenting has changed from the days when my mother admonished us, "Go out and play!" and did not see us for hours. Kids' imaginations are coddled, and their esteem is built up like a sand castle, and when they play soccer, no team ever loses. In this modern parenting environment, the hardest thing might be *not* stepping in. The scariest part might be letting your child figure it out for herself.

Can a seventy-year-old orchid grower from Japan teach us the importance of giving kids a break from the eighty-degree hothouse that childhood has become?

Can he remind us of the virtues of some time in the cold?

Toshikiyo "Andy" Matsui was born in Japan in 1935. His family had a four-acre farm in Nara Prefecture, a hilly region outside Kyoto. It was a slightly larger-than-normal farm because it was so far out into the countryside, at the end of a thin dirt road. "Beyond it, the boars," was their saying—nothing but forest. Fewer than 150 people made up the village, called Gojo. They nicknamed themselves "Dead End People." Both of Andy's parents were born in Gojo. The farm was inherited from his mother's family—she was the eldest sister in a family without any sons. Three generations lived under the one roof.

It was tough country. They grew a little rice, vegetables, potatoes, and wheat. On the hillside, persimmon trees. They kept a chicken house, a few cows, a goat, and a dog and cat. A rooster was Andy's pet until one night it appeared in a curry.

They kept a cemetery plot. Usually this would have been on the farm itself, but the few families of Gojo kept a communal plot. Andy remembers that the gravestones went back. *Way* back. Not one or two generations—"At least ten generations, maybe more," he said. Can you imagine? Ten generations, buried right there! As the oldest son, Andy's fate was set. He would take over the farm from his father eventually, and he would be buried beside his ancestors.

A younger brother and three sisters followed; this was a fairly large family for the times. The dramatic reconstruction of Japan in 1945—in which polygamy was made illegal and a new constitution was adopted—had almost no effect on their remote village. However, there was a food shortage in Japan for some time, and so the government paid very high prices to farmers, making their lives quite comfortable.

At eighteen Toshikiyo was baptized as "Andy"—something he still doesn't quite understand, because his family was Buddhist. Andy was restless and ambitious. College was out of the question—there was no loan program back then for those who couldn't afford it. But his father was only forty when Andy graduated from high school. It would be *at least* twenty years before Andy got to take over the farm. He met and married his wife, Yasuko, who was a teller at a bank in nearby Nara. They had a daughter, Megumi, and they lived with Andy's parents. His only access to the world outside Nara was the radio and the newspaper.

In 1961 Andy decided to leave the Dead End People. He was unwilling to wait twenty years for his turn to run the family's four acres. The newspapers told him that the future of farming was in California. He found a training program through the U.S. Farm Bureau that brought Japanese farmers to California for a year to learn American methods and then took them back to Japan.

His parents were opposed. In Japan, there was a deep tradition of honoring one's family specifically by maintaining the ancestral home. Their language makes a distinction between "temporary family," which includes only those around today, and the "real family," which includes the ancestors—meaning that just because you're alive doesn't mean you're more important. In addition, the conventions of patriarchy dominated. For an oldest son to refuse his position was, to say the least, controversial. Andy's parents told him that if he left, his brother would jump him in line to take over the farm. His mother was the strong and quiet type. She was a woman of few words. On his way out the door, she said with some anger, "Leave now, and you have no chance to come back to this house."

He restated this in Japanese for me, using the exact phrase his mother employed. It's a poignant memory.

Andy set his wife and his daughter up in a rented home in Nara. On March 24 he climbed aboard a ship sailing for California. He was one of three hundred men in a single room in the ship's tail. The weather was rough; the Filipinos smoked cigars the whole way; everyone got sick. The ship stopped in Honolulu for a day—"the best day of my life," Andy recalled. A Japanese gentleman from the University of Hawaii invited the farming interns to his research station, where they ate ripe pineapples, which Andy had never seen before. The ship arrived in San Francisco on April 2. Andy had ten thousand yen in his pocket, which he exchanged at the currency window for $30.85. He expected a Japanese man with whom he would intern to pick him up at immigration. His life was governed by a single rule: He could not go back. He had to figure this out for himself.

Andy Matsui's first passport.

When he passed customs, Andy was met by his "foster farmer," a Japanese landscape contractor who had been in the United States for twenty years. Andy climbed into the back of his pickup truck, and the guy drove seventy miles an hour to his business in Hayward. Andy spent the next months cleaning yards and pruning hedges and building gardens. He wasn't learning anything; the trainee program felt like a bit of a sham. But he was making eighty cents an hour, and every week he earned more than a Japanese salaried man made in a month. He was soon able to send home two hundred dollars, which was enough for his Yasuko and Megumi to live on for the year.

Andy began scouting for a farming business where he might actually learn something. His instincts took him to flowers, and in August he found a nursery in Mountain View that was growing chrysanthemums, which are the national flower of Japan. Rather than planting the mums in a field, as was done in Japan, this nursery was growing them in small pots in greenhouses. Andy asked the workers if he might learn their techniques and then take this wisdom back to Japan. They agreed (without asking their boss). Every Sunday, Andy would ride twenty miles around the San Francisco Bay on his bicycle to spend the day learning about potted mums. The techniques are quite different. Mums in fields bloom off new shoots growing up from old roots, and they bloom with the seasons. Potted mums are propagated from cuttings. Their blooming is triggered by manipulating the length of their days with blackout cloth.

In April 1962 Andy returned to Nara. His eyes had grown accustomed to the vast expanses in California, so Nara was a different world than he remembered. "Everything was so tiny bitty," he laughed. "I was surprised by how tiny the place I was born in was. It was a shock. The rooms were small, the people were small, the stores were small, and the roads were so thin."

He formed an association to teach farmers the secrets of potted mums. He quickly created a cooperative of 160 farms and even published a small book, *Potted Mums,* which revolutionized how mums were grown in Japan. He gave speeches and showed slides. He tried to get his father to join the association, but his father was uninterested. That said, Andy was not treated coldly by his family. They saw he was a success. But he did not want to stay.

To him, Japan was too traditional, too mired in its ancient ways. He'd had a taste of what could happen if you dared to challenge how things were always done.

He found another sponsor. His training visa lasted a year; at that point, he brought his wife and daughter over and applied for a green card. His daughter took on her christened name, Teresa, and his wife hers, Mary. Together, Andy and Mary worked two acres in East Palo Alto on behalf of a Japanese man who was aging and wanted some rest. They saved every penny they earned. Two more children were born, Kathy and Bill. Andy bought a trailer, and during the day the children stayed in the trailer, looking after one another, while the parents looked after the flowers.

Andy had a way with chrysanthemums. His were simply better than everyone else's; Andy's blooms were the size of cantaloupes, while everyone else's were the size of oranges. How'd he do it? With nothing but common sense. He gave his plants precise amounts of food and water and spray, at a time when most farming was done very imprecisely. The truth was, most immigrant farmers in America didn't know a thing about horticulture. They got into farming because it didn't require knowing English. By contrast, Andy was a real farmer.

In 1969 Andy purchased fifty acres in Salinas, with a loan from the Bank of Tokyo, for $165,000. When the greenhouses went up, there was no money left for a home. They moved the trailer to Salinas and crammed bunk beds inside. It was there that their fourth child, Paul, was born. About 550 Japanese families were already in Salinas, 65 of which were farmers; there was a Buddhist temple and a Japanese-language school the children could attend on Saturdays.

In Salinas, Andy became a successful flower farmer, first with mums and then with roses. He was able to build a small home on the land, and five years later he built a house in Pebble Beach. He surprised his wife, Mary, by building a traditional teahouse as an addition. When he first met her, Mary had been studying the Buddhist spiritual practice of *chado,* the "way of tea." She'd given it up when she began working the fields beside him. It was time for her to stop laboring and return to her calling. (Today she is a highly respected master teacher, and three days a week the teahouse is busy with students.)

Andy's fortune rose, then fell as imported flowers entered the U.S. market. Though he began to lose money, he had earned enough by then to provide his children with a comfortable eighty-degree existence. He could have hired them special coaches for their hobbies, and tutors for schoolwork. He could have nursed their esteem, made sure they fit in at junior high, made sure they had friends. He watched other Japanese farmers treat their kids this way, showering them with luxury. They gave their kids fancy cars and hosted parties and let them rack up charges at the pool club.

Instead, Andy put his children to work. He paid them thirty-five cents an hour to work in the afternoons and sometimes in the evenings. Their job was to pick the tips off the stems or to make newspaper pillows that protected the heads of the mums. Andy wanted them to know what real work was, and he also wanted them to hate it. He wanted them to long for jobs that used the mind, not the hands.

Even then, he felt his children had it too easy. Their eyes were glued to the television, they never learned Japanese, and though they spent their Sundays selling second-rate flowers at the farmer's market for spending money, they never saved any of it. He worried all they were being taught in school was how to smoke marijuana. Homework rarely was assigned.

So during high school, he pushed them to find more menial work elsewhere. Teresa and Kathy were cashiers at McDonald's. Then Teresa, who had gone to the public high school in Salinas, surprised her father by being admitted to Harvard. He did not know she had applied.

At the time, Andy was starting to wonder who would take over his farm when he got old. In his heart, he hoped that one of his children would come back to Salinas after college and be groomed to run the operation. But was there even a future in farming? By then half of the Japanese farmers in Salinas had failed or chosen to get out. He couldn't even sell his farm—as a money loser, it was worth nothing.

How could he ask his children to stay, when he himself had not stayed to run his own father's farm? He had given up that right.

So he told his children, "Those who can't go to Harvard have to take up their father's flower cultivation business." He left the door barely open. The way he said it, somewhat teasingly, with a denigrating tone, made it clear that staying in Salinas was like staying in Gojo, Nara Prefecture. Only for Dead End People.

The more he thought about it, the more he fretted that he was not giving them enough of a push. He worried that his money would inevitably attract his children back to Salinas and they would never know what he knew: the adventure of having his own life. He also felt that their chances of success would multiply if they got to pick their own trade. So he swallowed his desire to have a child stay and work with him, and he closed the door the rest of the way. He gave them a push the only way he knew how, the same way his mother had—by taking away their safety net. He began to tell all his children, "I will send you to college, but after that you should never expect another penny from me your entire life."

This would be his legacy. The cold Standing House atmosphere.

"Did you think he really meant it?" I asked both Kathy and Teresa, on different occasions.

"Absolutely," Kathy insisted. "We saw him work hard. We knew he was serious. We had to make our own life."

Teresa said, "The example he had set for us was very strong. He had left his family and made it on his own. We all knew that we would not have his respect unless we did the same."

All four got into Harvard.

He said, "Today parents always try to do the maximum to nurture their children along. It is a mistake. I tell my friends who have young children, 'Do the minimum, not the maximum.' Give them what they need, and let them figure out the rest for themselves."

Once you've given your kids a push, does it mean they will stay away forever?

When I interviewed Kathy and Teresa, I had the clear feeling that both felt they had to stay away from their father to maintain his respect. Kathy and her family live in Tokyo; her husband is German. Teresa and her husband live in Minnesota. The brothers both live on the East Coast.

Kathy, for her part, worries that her own children are spoiled and materialistic. They lead a high-rolling life in Tokyo. She considers sending her kids to live with their grandfather so they will know hard labor. When it comes to pushing her kids out of the nest, she doubts that she will be able to be as tough as her father was. And she knows that her father is aware of it. Andy does not question her parenting, but Kathy wonders what he thinks and whether he disapproves.

Rumbling in both daughters' minds is a question, almost unspeakable: Will their father ever be as proud of his children as he is of his own flowers?

Is this sad? Is this the dark side of the Andy Matsui legacy, that three generations of a family will never again live under one roof? Is this the classic American dilemma: that independence and the pressure to succeed inevitably push families apart?

Most of the world's families do not value independence. They do not foster the notion that you need to separate from your parents or that you need to be on your own for a while before you get married.

For instance, in Italy, only 7 percent of young Italians have left home by the age of twenty-five. You leave home when you get married, and sometimes later. Japan is near Italy's end of the spectrum. Sixty percent of young Japanese men in their twenties still live with their parents; the figure is 80 percent for the young women.*

We might naturally assume that whatever the percentage, it must be going down, everywhere. The changing economy has created what is called an "authority breakdown." Because children no longer work in the same trade as their fathers, they need their fathers' wisdom far less. In addition, there's an education gap: Children get more education than their parents ever did, and so children are less intellectually shaped

*For more information on the statistics in this chapter and their underlying arguments, please visit my website, www.pobronson.com.

by their parents. Lastly, all around the world, people are marrying later and later. They're not going to stick with their parents that whole waiting period, are they?

Well, actually, they do. Despite all these factors, *young adults are staying with their parents longer than ever.* This is true all around the world. Why? The most common reason given by young Italians is that they're happy with the living arrangement. They like it.

Only a small part of the world values independence: the United States, England, and the Nordic countries. And the extent of the difference is dramatic. In Denmark 75 percent of young people will leave home by the age of twenty-five. That's *ten times* the percentage of Italians.

America stands out as the land of individualism, as one huge ice-cold Standing House. Its cities are full of young professionals whose identity is defined far more by their job than by the family they rarely see.

Andy's life embodies this trade-off. His kids are all independently successful, but they're not around. For a long time I tried to see the tragedy in it, envisioning Andy as an isolated King Lear, but his personality is too sunny for the part. He loves all his children, and he has a relationship with each of them. So what if they live thousands of miles away? That's hardly a knock in today's world. They see one another.

Meanwhile, an interesting thing has happened in Japan. The economy has been in a sluggish recession for a decade and a half. The cause of this has been widely agreed upon: For two generations, the economy was structured to protect companies and salarymen from the brutality of the market. When this system was first created, it was populated with workers who came off the farms and were the first in their families to go to college. Those people knew hunger and the war's devastation. They had fight in them. They built the economic miracle known in the 1980s as "Japan, Inc." But the next generation that grew up in this economic hothouse did not have the same background. All they knew was the safety of lifelong employment. They were unwilling to take risks or break with tradition. They had no fight. As the closely held Japanese *keiretsu* business networks are unwound and the safety net is taken away, they are finding that very few of these older men are able to adapt to the colder, harsher climate of competition.

One of the most interesting trends in Japan is called the "vintage-year divorce." These are divorces among couples married more than twenty years. Nearly unheard of a quarter century ago, they now make up one-fourth of all divorces in Japan. Five out of six of these divorces are initiated by the wife, and they usually coincide with the husband being forced into early retirement.

For decades, it's been easy to point at America as a country with an economy that really takes its toll on families. But it's not just America anymore.

By the late 1990s all but four of the sixty Japanese farmers in Salinas had been pushed out of the business. Cut flowers now came into the United States from all over the world, at prices that U.S. farmers can't compete with. As Andy turned sixty-three, he realized he had been losing money for too long. It was time to quit and sell his land to the lettuce growers for nothing. This consideration weighed heavily upon him. He didn't want to be the man who gave up. He wanted to be successful in his business life until his very last day alive. That is what he came to America for. While it might be smart to cash out now, it seemed like quitting.

"It felt like dying," he said.

Is this what I want to teach my kids? To quit?

He asked himself what he would do were he a younger man. He believed that orchids would be the flower of the twenty-first century; they were far more exotic than roses, and grew in thousands of varieties.

Could a sixty-three-year-old man handle it?

Had he put out all his blooms?

Andy measured his resolve and said to himself, *Hah! The fight is not gone out of me! I have twenty or thirty years left to live.*

Cut orchids were already a commodity dominated by imports, but Andy wondered if he might do for orchids in the United States what he had done for mums in Japan—create a market for them in pots. If he could do this, he would be insulated against foreign competition, because there are strict rules against bringing potted soil into the United States, for fear of invasive microspecies in the soil. Back in 1998 almost no stores sold potted orchids. Florists sold cut orchids, and hobbyists grew their own. Andy would have to create the market from both ends. He would have to reinvest everything he had ever earned, grow his orchids (without a lick of experience), and hope he could find customers.

Friends said he was crazy. His nursery managers tried to talk him out of it. Nobody believed in the future of the California flower business.

"Their negativeness always encouraged me to jump one step higher," Andy recounted. He gained strength from their discouragement, just as he always kept his mother's words close to his chest: *Leave now, and you have no chance to come back to this house.*

Andy did not even tell Mary, for fear she would balk. Mary knew he was traveling around the world to learn from orchid growers, but she did not know he was revamping his entire nursery. She slowly realized what he was up to.

One day the following year, he came home from the nursery with some potted orchids.

"What's the matter?" she asked. "Is the market bad? You can't sell them?" She knew her husband. If he could sell them, he wouldn't have brought them home.

He promised her they were seconds—a lesser grade.

"This is a celebration," he said. "The stores love them."

Today you can buy potted orchids in every supermarket. You can buy them right out of the shipping boxes at discounters like Costco. They're inexpensive and they're gorgeous and they last for months. This is largely due to Andy Matsui. He is the world's largest potted orchid farmer, and he dominates the American market, with a market share of 35 percent. In 1998 his business was worthless. Today he is worth at least $150 million, and his fortune is growing fast. Last year he increased production 30 percent, and this year he will expand even more.

Kathy said, "When we were kids, we thought our dad was just like all the other farmers here. Now, finally—his gift is truly apparent."

The surprise success of Matsui Nursery has made Andy reconsider what he ought to do with it. Should he leave it to his children after all? But what do they know about farming? He discussed the possibility with Teresa, but he quickly realized that bringing someone without experience into the business would doom it. When he began to look into estate planning, he discovered that dying is more trouble than living. He didn't want to burden his children with the mess of selling off parts of the business to pay the taxes.

"Whom do I really owe?" he wondered. "To whom am I indebted?"

The answer was in his heart. He loved his company and the 160 people who worked for him, most of whom were Mexican immigrants in the very situation he was in forty years ago. He loved this country that gave a stranger a chance. He loved the valley and its community. He loved the fertile land.

All along his journey, there had been people to reach out and help him. He thought of the nursery school teacher in Palo Alto who did not charge him to let his young children attend her school. He thought of the banker at the Bank of Tokyo who loaned him ten grand without collateral. Complete strangers, really.

Andy makes decisions quickly and permanently. This was no exception. He decided to give his company to the employees and give his money back to society. He will set aside some for his wife. Over the last year he has created a not-for-profit, the Matsui Foundation, and a scholarship program to send the children of farm laborers to college. Last June he went to the high school that Teresa and Kathy graduated from and he asked the teachers to find a worthy child who could not afford college. A boy there was headed to San Jose State; his family had come from Mexico only three years before. He was a very good student. Andy gave his family forty thousand dollars.

By next year, a dozen families will receive such gifts from a complete stranger.

As for what his children might think, Andy does not worry. He has not really enforced his rule of never giving them a penny; he has reached out to help them many times. But almost all his money will be plowed back into the fertile soil of strangers with hope and fight.

Andy has visited his childhood home in Nara many times. His brother still runs the farm and has a nursery business. Both his son and daughter have joined him in the trade. Andy's mother passed away almost thirty years ago, but Andy's father is still strong at ninety-two, and he lives with Andy's brother as the patriarch—so the tradition of three generations under one roof has not been lost. Also, as was tradition, all of Andy's sisters married and moved to join their husband's families. The village of Gojo has annexed the surrounding villages to now be called a city with thirty thousand people. But that was just an accounting trick; nothing moved, nothing changed, and the village is still tiny and remote.

The ancestral grave site is still there, and well maintained. Soon Andy's father will leave the temporary family and join the permanent family. When that fateful day comes for Andy, he won't join his father beside his ancestors. He will be scattered over the blue water of Monterey Bay.

His mother never got to see his flowers. She and his father were going to visit in 1974; Andy had just built his little house beside the trailer. He paid to have the garage converted into a bedroom so his parents would have a proper place to stay. At the last minute, they learned Andy's mother had cancer.

Andy's father visited in 1978. It completely changed his attitude. It was clear that all the stories Andy had told were true—some of which were so outrageous that his father had been unsure. But to see three-thousand-acre lettuce fields with his own eyes, and then to see fifty greenhouses—each one the size of a Japanese farm—on his own son's land!

A few years back Andy's father decided he needed to leave something for his family. The ancestral home had come from his wife's family; he felt like he had not given anything. So he asked Andy for the money to build a new house, attached to the old house.

"I was very honored," Andy commented. "I appreciated being included. And I was grateful my father was not too proud to ask. That meant so much to me. I knew there was no resentment left when he asked me."

Andy sent the money immediately. The new home has been built. Andy's father has seen pictures of the orchids and the nursery. Recently his leg gave out, and he can no longer walk. But he is desperate to come back to California to see his son's operation. "I want to see your farm again!" he tells Andy. "I've got to come one more time before I die."

The idea of it excites him like nothing has in years.

He tells Andy, "I don't want to stay in your big place in Pebble Beach. You still have the old ranch house on the farm, don't you? I want to stay there. I like that simple house. Right on the farm. I'll stay there. Okay?"

Andy laughs, telling me this story, but I can tell it almost brings him to tears, tears of joy. "Once a farmer, always a farmer," he explains, conjuring the rest with a knowing nod: that time in the cold never leaves you. Once a man with a work ethic, always a man with a work ethic. Once a child who stands straight to reach for the sun, always a reacher. Once with fight, always with fight.

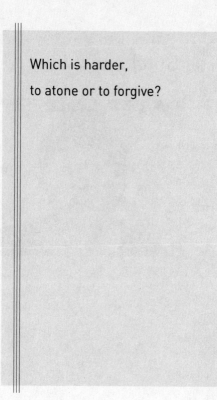

Which is harder,

to atone or to forgive?

The Butcher's Wife

Denise Hughes

There comes a time for many of us when we decide we're not going to pass the trouble on. No matter how bad it was for us, no matter how angry it still makes us, no matter what the mess we are in, we are clear on this: We will keep it from hurting our children. They will know a better day.

Denise Hughes, as she is now known, remembers the night she decided these would be the stakes that defined her life.

It was sixteen years ago, on a Friday night in Belfast. She sat on the couch cuddling her three-month-old baby, Gary, thinking of all the things she would do after he fell asleep. Finally, his breathing slowed, and his eyes rolled back under not-yet-shut eyelids, and Denise realized that if she moved he would wake up again. She was stuck on the couch a little longer. That was okay. Gary was a gorgeous baby. The center of her life. About all she could do was watch television. The news was on.

Her husband had left several hours before, carrying a bag. He said only that he would be back tomorrow. Denise had learned not to ask. She knew he had made his way up through the ranks of a Loyalist paramilitary group. She was accustomed to the police searching her house. She was accustomed to her husband being dragged off to the Gough Barracks for questioning whenever there was a murder. Like most in Belfast, Denise had grown up in this kind of environment, so she didn't think too much of it. She was raised to believe the IRA was murdering her people, trying to run them out of their country. Sixteen years ago she thought a little violence was an acceptable form of vengeance. But she was about to see the dark side of it, and come to hate it with a passion.

The television news cut to the scene of a murder out in the countryside. A gunman had broken through a family's living room window during dinner and shot the father. The man's eight-year-old boy held him as he bled to death.

Somehow, Denise just knew. A woman's intuition. *Her husband.*

The bag.

The overnight stay.

She just knew.

If he wasn't the gunman, he was part of it.

They say that when you have a baby, your way of looking at the world completely changes.

In that moment, holding her baby, Denise's perspective changed completely. Every son has a mother. That boy has a mother. How could anyone do this to a mother?

Denise looked at her life and realized that in eight years, that would be Gary holding his father. She knew her husband's life would be short. It was inevitable. Her little boy would grow up on the streets, where he would learn to throw bricks at Catholics just for the laugh. Waste hours collecting boney wood and tires for bonfires. Drinking to be one of the lads. Squat in empty flats, wait on riots. Soon mugging people and scamming the immigrants. He would end up inside. She knew how impossible it was to prevent, because she had soaked up those inclinations, too. She had spent many Friday nights during her teens down on Roden Street, in the Empire District. The road ended at what used to be the Blackie River but was then a huge construction site for the new Westlink Highway, which divides the Loyalist South Belfast from the Republican West Belfast. Fifty kids would be on either side of the gap, hurling rocks and rubble at one another, singing fight songs and screaming "No surrender!" Denise never felt hatred; she was just out for the *craic,* the good time. Wee lads, too—kids as young as six would be there. It starts young. In Belfast, by the time a child is two years old, he knows the orange shirts are the good guys and the green shirts are the bad guys, or vice versa. Nobody escapes it.

Would it be any different for her son? Was it possible to even dream he could end up different from his father? Was there any chance he would learn to value his education, rather than his hands—his mind, rather than his fists? Would he ever know there was a world out there to explore beyond the so-called peace walls that sliced Belfast into smaller and ever smaller camps?

What had happened? In the passing of a generation, Belfast had gone from being a great city, a world leader in shipbuilding, to a place tangled up in knots over what *your* people did to *my* people.

Denise looked at her son's face and made a promise that she would find a way. She was in no position to make this promise. She had been out of school since she was seventeen. She was twenty-one now. She did not know that she was already pregnant with her second child. She worked as an office girl in a factory. She didn't have a penny in the bank. The course of her life was set. But she would save Gary from it. Somehow, some way.

The next day her husband came home, and within twenty minutes the police were at the door to question him.

She could not have this man as her husband. A few weeks later she was able to drive him away. Not a week after that, he was shot by the police. He suffered brain damage, and he was jailed for seven years for murder.

A second boyfriend rescued Denise. He had some money and a semidetached three-bedroom outside Belfast in a quiet village called Moira. She couldn't believe her luck, until she found out he enjoyed hurting women when he was drunk. Her parents did not help her, and encouraged her to stick with it. (What's a little violence around the house when there's so much in the streets?) She was afraid to be on her own with her children, but when she found out her bully was seeing someone else, she decided that was it. She got a restraining order. One night he jumped the back fence, broke into the house through the back window, and tried to kill her. She broke two of his ribs with a chair and called him an ambulance.

She was no fool. She had been ready for him.

She did not want to move into the public housing estates and live off the government, but she had no choice. By then she had three children under five. She was afraid to let her kids onto her own front patio. The most Denise could manage to improve her lot was to sign up for a correspondence course. Working was out of the question—the kids took every ounce of her strength. Her middle child, Ashleigh, was diagnosed with Asperger's syndrome. Denise's mother lived several miles away and helped out only a little.

"That was my lowest point," she recalled. She became antsy at the memory, and her words came urgently, rushing, as if she needed to get out of this bad neighborhood before she was recognized by someone from the old days. "The only way was up. It couldn't have gotten worse. I was twenty-six, and I was like an old woman. I did not know happiness. I did not know how I had got into the mess that was my life. I resented my parents, and I resented my children. I was lost."

Lost she was, but it *could* have been worse. Unable to control her own fate, she could have whacked her kids around to establish control at home. She could have found her escape in a bottomless bottle of beer. She could have channeled her frustration, as so many do, by flying the Union Jack and complaining about the Taigs down the road. Hers was a stormy house, for sure, but even at her lowest point Denise was sound. She had a clear mind. There was no hate in her, no blame. She was willing to try another way. And if life gave her a chance, she would not look back.

It did, and she didn't.

The chance came when she walked her kids to school one day, and on the walk home stopped off at a butcher shop for some sausages. There was a new guy behind the counter, Brian Hughes. He caught her eye, then chatted her up. He was soft-spoken and had an amusing temperament. He had been laid off from a job selling textbooks and had fallen back on the family trade. Brian had learned to cut meat at the age of six, as soon as he could see over the counter at his father's shop in Portadown.

"Unlike my father, I'm not going to be doing this forever," he promised Denise.

Denise did the stupid thing girls often do with guys they like: She matched him up with her girlfriend. Luckily, their date was a disaster.

"He was so boring," her friend reported.

"Boring sounds pretty good to me," Denise said, thinking about the fathers of her children.

Soon after, Denise was out in her front garden when Brian drove by on the way to a friend's. He got out and said hello. They spent three hours sitting on the curb, chatting.

Brian was Catholic, but it didn't seem to matter—at least not at first, when their attraction was private. Brian had been to university. He was an open-minded man. What side he took on the Troubles was not high on her list of criteria. He had been married before as well, but he did not have kids. Like Denise, his priority was to find someone who did not resemble his previous spouse.

They kept their relationship secret for a year and a half. Not just because of the taboo of dating the enemy. They had both been burned before and did not want to endure another public retraction if it did not work out. And Denise did not want to expose her children to a man until she was sure about him. She was in no rush.

When I asked Brian why he fell in love with Denise, he said firmly, "I'm willing to see people for who they are." He loved that she was loud and brash and did not back down. He could always hear Denise walking toward the butcher shop, hollering after her kids. They bonded over films and philosophy. "The first time we kissed," he said, "It went through my bones and straight to my soul."

Still, you might wonder why an educated guy like Brian Hughes fell in love with an undereducated mother of three living in public housing. Well, Denise *was* all that, but not around Brian. The Denise he knew left her kids with a babysitter and met up with him late at night. The part-time relationship suited Denise perfectly. "It was all of the affection with none of the responsibility." On Brian's lunch hour, he walked up the hill a hundred yards from the butcher shop to a red phone box and called Denise.

They certainly did not have it easy, but their love was in a bubble. When bubbles pop, though, love becomes just a consideration.

Think of what Brian was facing. He wasn't even sure he wanted kids. Denise already had three! He was just a butcher, with a mind for a better life. Would he ever get there if he took on four mouths to feed? What if they needed expensive schools? Then, what about the politics? Brian liked to believe it didn't matter a bit to him, but politics are so pervasive in Northern Ireland that nobody can claim to be unbiased.

Brian was from Portadown. He drove me around his old neighborhood, pointing out the locations of every shop that had been bombed, and he took me down the parade streets that were currently the subject of protests and burnings. As a teen, he would be searched by the street police for no reason. Even if he could look past Denise's loyalties, could his family? Could his friends? Could the guys at work? Northern Ireland is not like America, where a couple can move to a new city for a clean start. Your past never leaves you. No matter where you are, everyone knows what side you are on.

Now imagine what Denise was facing. She thought Brian was great, but she had thought the last two guys were great, too. Could she trust her judgment? There was *no way* her family or friends would accept Brian. Denise was from South Belfast's The Sandy Row, an insular and tight-knit Loyalist stronghold. From the time she was six years old, she knew what to do when they got a bomb warning: crack the window sash so the window merely rattles and doesn't blow in. Then walk up to Library Hill or St. Aidan's and wait out the bombing. She did not meet a Catholic person until she was sixteen. When Denise took me to her old neighborhood, I quickly understood why she would be afraid to bring Brian here. The prejudice is not subtle.

Northern Ireland is no bigger than the state of Connecticut, and it has a population similar to Columbus, Ohio. Since 1969 there have been more than 37,000 shootings and 16,200 bombings. That last figure does not include the petrol bombs regularly hurled over the peace walls.

Note the masked gunman on the lower left of this mural.

It takes a special couple to not be intimidated by the social pressure to choose someone from your side of the wall. Then there are the interpersonal pressures.

Twice Brian moved in with Denise and the kids, to try it out. Neither time did he last more than three days. Denise was too territorial, too accustomed to being the only boss in the house. "You make me feel like an unwelcome lodger," Brian told her on the way out. He went to England for a few months to take a breather. Denise wrote him a Dear John letter breaking up with him. Brian wrote back with a wedding proposal and flowers. She said yes, right away. They courted properly for a year before marrying. When Denise's mother asked after his religion, Denise refused to answer. All the kids asked to take Brian's name. The two girls asked to call him "Dad." Gary called Brian by his name. They found a house in Lisburn, a few miles from Belfast, and hoped that nobody would come knocking on the door at night.

Denise had done well in her correspondence courses. Brian encouraged her to consider attending a proper university.

"It's the next step," he told her.

"I can't," she said. "Not with children."

"You would be surprised," he insisted.

He urged her to at least go with his younger brother to a recruiting fair at the University of Ulster in Jordanstown. There she learned that because she was older, she was eligible for a two-year fast-track degree.

"Great," Brian said.

"Who'll mind the children?"

"We'll figure it out," he assured her.

"But—"

"But what?"

It is hard to comprehend how controversial this notion of going back to school was. In the United States finding someone to look after her kids would be Denise's biggest obstacle. Not so in Northern Ireland. When Denise was seventeen, she had wanted to attend university. But her parents told her to get a proper job. Her father worked in the shipyards, while her mother was a nurse at Belfast City Hospital. The Protestant culture of Northern Ireland teaches that the only honest work is work done with the hands. Paper pushing is not the way decent folks make a living. For a century the Protestants had a monopoly on the jobs at the shipyards. Even today young men aspire to being plasterers or joiners or bricklayers, though the jobs are scarce. More likely they will join the army. It is an informal caste system, and people do not aspire to move up in class. This is who you are, this is where you belong. Their life is a noble life. Going to university was seen as a betrayal of their culture. Anyone who did so faced the accusation of being a haughty social climber. To reach for a different life was to insult the life of those you were leaving behind.

"When I told my mom I was going to university, she nearly had a coronary," Denise remembered. "She is now very proud of me, because she's seen I've done it. But back then, she said I needed to be home making dinner. She didn't think the education would help me any. She offered to get me a job mopping floors at night if I needed money."

The Catholics did not have this reservation. They had been oppressed and ruled for more than two hundred years in Ireland by the British, and in Northern Ireland they had been precluded by law from holding good jobs until the early 1960s. Education was their only way up. Thus, Brian was sent to university, while Denise was not. In Northern Ireland the creed that worships tradespeople is so strong that a simple shop owner, like a butcher, is not considered a tradesman. Shop owners are considered capitalists, as if they descended from lords and landowners. And in a way, that's a fair analysis, because Brian certainly had the entrepreneur's mind-set—with a bright mind, a little school, and some hard work, you can change your fate.

Change their fate they did. Brian started to learn computers, and he soon was working for himself installing and maintaining systems for small businesses. This gave him the flexibility to get through the day's various obligations. Money was tight, but they made it. Brian went from being unsure he wanted children to caring for three several hours a day. He found he liked it, and he wanted more. Denise went through two miscarriages. When she took her final exams, she was three months pregnant with her fourth child, Conor. Her GPA was 2.2. "I barely made it!" she laughed. "I got such satisfaction, though. I felt like a human being."

A human being with a head full of ideas about feminism and political tolerance—which made it hard to go over to girlfriends' houses to discuss window drapes and the new clothing on the racks at Marks & Spencer. Denise lost the last of her old friends in a short time. That was okay; she didn't fit into her old self anymore. She'd put on fifty pounds of mental muscle. She had grown up knowing who her *people* were. Now she was *an individual.* And she wondered where this new life was taking her. What was she going to *do* now that she had a mind of her own?

She made an astute judgment: She did not ask herself what her intellectual strengths were. She did not analyze which fields were growing and which were shrinking. Instead, she looked for her purpose in what made her angry: the sectarian divisiveness that she had come to hate. Then she looked for organizations where she might do some good. Brian was already the capitalist in the family. He was starting to bring in some money. That freed her, in a way, from feeling like she couldn't take a risk.

Her first job was with an organization that retrains former paramilitaries after they had served their time in prison. She turned them into productive workers again. She was good at it, because she had traveled a bit of this road herself. After two years she moved to another organization that helps train the police to understand the local communities. In Belfast the police are considered a third religion. They have had to deal with so much violence for three decades that they have closed ranks, in a way, and have created their own way of life separate from the neighborhoods they patrol. Denise runs seminars with police that are part healing sessions, part cultural education.

Denise does not live in the dangerous neighborhoods of Belfast anymore. But her work takes her back there, and she is known as a fair person. So she has unique access to both sides. She was able to drive me through some enclaves that only the locals get to enter, such as The Village in South Belfast, where UDA paramilitaries fly their flags over their bars, and Twinbrook in West Belfast, where unemployment is at 85 percent and one in three girls is pregnant by age fourteen.

I have great admiration for Denise. In trying to save her children's lives, she ended up saving her own. Not only had she and Brian changed their fate over the last ten years, but she was giving back, trying to fix what she could, one mind at a time.

Then Gary became a teenager.

——

Gary and Denise work each other constantly, pushing and negotiating. They do it with the furious pace of rap music, the longest sentence rarely more than a few words. On the way home from rugby practice, Gary convinced his mom to stop for some french fries from a Chinese takeout. Sensing a soft heart, he went for more:

"Chips *and* fish, Mum?"

"Chips."

"Two chips, then?"

"Okay." Pause. "Get two and share them with your siblings."

"One for me and one for them?"

"Nope."

"I'll just get one, then."

"No, Gary. Get two. And share them. And *that's it.*"

"But I don't get much food put out for me!"

"You'll share them, Gary!"

Which he did. Neither ever wins a negotiation free and clear. When he concedes he needs to take a shower, he tries to get something in return—such as a few quid for the next day's lunch. When Denise agrees to drive him to a match, he begs her to drive him in the new car. There's no quit in him. Or her. She keeps him just uncomfortable. They are two very strong-minded people.

A couple of years ago Denise started to realize she was no match for Gary's peers. She could take him out of Belfast, and thereby keep him from joining up with the gangs, but she couldn't keep him from soaking up the culture—and the culture was already soaked with prejudice.

One day he came home wearing a blue Rangers scarf. All the Protestant boys wore them, but if they wore one in the wrong neighborhood they could get shot. On the one hand, it just showed his support for a soccer team. On the other hand, it was a *statement,* a symbol of political affiliation. Usually the intent is to offend, to provoke.

"Did this not cross your mind?" Denise gasped.

"It's only football, Mom!"

"It labels you!"

"Lay off, Mom."

Brian came in, took one look at the scarf. "So you support Rangers, then?"

"I do."

"Who's their top striker, then?"

Flustered, Gary admitted he had no idea.

Denise could challenge any outright racist comments Gary learned, but the cultural references were too ingrained to avoid. He didn't yet have a job or a girlfriend or anything to stake himself to. In that vacuum he glommed on to the culture as a form of identity.

"I was asked what religion I was today at school," he said one night.

"How did you answer?"

"Protestant."

"Really? What church do you go to, then?"

"I don't."

"Then how are you Protestant? If you don't go to church?"

"My grandfather's Protestant."

"And Brian's father's Catholic."

"Brian's father doesn't take me to footballers, does he?"

"Gary, if you were in America, and your father was Mexican and your mother was Italian, you could say you were both, right?"

"Suppose."

"You're both, Gary. You are both and you are neither, because you don't go to church and neither do we."

"Both?"

"Yes!"

"Well."

When they are at a certain age, it feels like nothing you say to your children makes a damn bit of difference. They are simply not listening to you, not trying to impress you. Gary did not even seem to notice how radically his mother had changed her fate. Every time he walked out the door, she feared the world would take him away. There was simply nothing to occupy these kids, nothing to do *but* loiter. Her work took her down to Cluan Place and Clandyboye, where there were masses of youths milling about, bored out of their skulls, drinking, shooting heroin, and she wondered how long it would be before Gary ended up there.

"Going out?"

"Yeah."

"And where to?"

"The bonfires."

"Really? What do you want to go for?"

"It's good *craic*. Everyone's going."

"You want to watch grown men get drunk and throw up on each other? That your idea of a good time?"

"Just be with my friends, Mom."

"Women getting into catfights, women hitting each other with bottles, someone light up a pile of tires? Explain to me why that is an interesting evening and I will take you down myself."

"Sounds fun, actually."

"Kick everything Catholic while you're at it."

"You went to bonfires when you were a girl."

"And you could get a burger and an ice cream. It's sinister now. It's naked sectarianism."

"What do I tell my friends?"

"You tell them your mom took you to Pizza Hut and rented you two DVDs and we sat on the floor and watched them."

"Pizza Hut? Or Mexican?"

"All right. Mexican."

"The new car?"

Denise decided to look into the history being taught at Gary's school. They taught him about the kings and queens of England. They even taught him about the Mormon Church and the Native Americans. But regarding the history of Northern Ireland, they skimmed the Easter Rising and that was it. It was a typical British version of history, straight from the textbooks. Little effort was made to inform the students about the war dividing their own country. The school was doing nothing to counteract the prejudice picked up on the streets.

Denise realized her only tool to shape her son's horizons was to change his environment. She encouraged Gary to apply to better schools. Gary chose the school with the best rugby team, which also happened to have an esteemed academic reputation. The night he was accepted, Denise was over the moon, crying, so proud. Her friends and parents didn't understand why it was worth the money, but Denise never hesitated.

Soon after, she and Brian moved to the countryside, to an old farm-house forty minutes from Belfast. It is half a mile from the nearest shop. There's no way to get in trouble out there.

A funny thing happened to Denise and Brian when they moved to the countryside. There was practically never a moment to enjoy being in the country. They turned into a prototypical modern couple, stretched in all directions, constantly driving their children to their ac-tivities, and rarely eating as a family. Their entire lives became con-sumed by logistics. Their four children were in four different schools. One took the bus, one took a taxi, one rode with Dad, one walked a mile to a carpool pickup. Denise and Brian became ships passing in the night. Like most couples stretched thin, they managed to do all this by sleeping little. Denise had become a supermom, burdened by her am-bitions to do every part right. The sum was less than the parts.

In theory, a woman with a background like Denise's would be thrilled to have a modern mother's problems. In theory, she would have that elusive trait we all crave, *perspective*. She'd be amused that her only challenge is to get her five-year-old to eat two more bites of pasta before he gets his ice cream. Nothing a modern mother goes through would upset her. But so much for theory. Denise was not above all that. She was consumed by it, same as anyone.

And she found herself longing for the old days. Those days when it wasn't just you and your husband against the world. Those days when you had grandmothers and uncles around, and neighbors to help out. Her own mother had not watched the kids in four years. Denise found herself longing for the sense of community she had known growing up in The Sandy Row. The houses were tiny two-up/two-downs, and nobody had any money or sent their kids to special schools—*but they looked after one another.* Nobody bothered to lock their doors. As a little girl, when she walked down Abingdon Road, the people in every single row house knew her name. Her grandmother had worked as a nurse in the maternity ward of Belfast City Hospital, so Gran could honestly say to every single kid, "I held you when you were a baby." Gran took care of Denise every evening while her mother worked the night shift.

She was six years old back in 1974 when the Ulster Workers' Council Strike brought down the Stormont government. And though it was a time of strife, Denise had nothing but fond memories. In the eyes of a child, it was like a big carnival. For a while nobody had any food or electricity. The schools were closed. Denise wandered along the railway wall, where families propped up corrugated iron to make lean-tos, and they turned over oil drums to light fires to keep warm, and she would walk campfire to campfire, be handed soup and toast, sing songs. Everyone stuck together. Everyone shared.

Denise knew she had made a trade-off. She knew she had chosen to leave that way of life. But it hurt. She became desperate for a sign that it was worth it. Desperate to know all she had done in ten years actually made a difference. Would it ever pay off? Would she ever know a day that her children would think for themselves, with their own clear judgment?

If she saw Gary at home, it was to bookend his day, twenty minutes on either end. He seemed to change girlfriends more often than his underwear. He got a job at a restaurant busing tables, but who knew what he might get into there?

Then one February day Gary came home from school and announced he was going to America. Denise thought he was kidding.

"You are, are you?" she smiled.

"I am, Mom."

"California, I suppose?"

"Nope. Somewhere called Youngstown, Ohio."

"What are you getting on, Gary?"

"My school nominated me. Do you know what the Ulster Project is?"

"You're in the Ulster Project?"

"You know it, then?"

"Yeah, I do." Every year a dozen Catholic and Protestant teenagers from Northern Ireland participated in a two-week exchange with teens from Ohio, to broaden their minds. "Gary, you're in the Ulster Project!"

"Didn't I just say so?"

"But why you?"

"Dunno, Mom. Maybe because of all that charity work I did."

"What charity work?"

"For Make-A-Wish."

"The class project?"

"It wasn't a class project, Mom. Me and my friends, we did it on our own."

"Those candles you sold?" Denise couldn't believe it.

"Yeah, the candles, the doughnuts. And the T-shirts we made, and that cross-country run we held."

"Gary, I thought that was a class project!"

"No, Mom. You were always saying do something worthwhile."

"Gary! How much did you raise?"

"Three thousand."

"Three thousand!"

"More than anyone in Northern Ireland."

Denise's eyes filled with tears. She and Gary had been pushing each other for so long that she never really knew where he stood. Now she did. It had been worth it. Worth every moment.

"When do you go?"

"In July. But we start meeting at St. John's next week."

"With Catholic kids?"

"Yup. Mom?"

"What?"

"Good thing I told them I was Protestant when they were asking, huh?"

Gary went to Ohio last July. They met with the governor, and then the two dozen teens flew to Washington, D.C., where they took Mass at the Basilica of the National Shrine of Immaculate Conception, one of the largest Catholic churches in the United States. That afternoon Gary called his mom. She went to bed that night with two images that defined her life. Sixteen years ago, Gary's father had walked out the door to plot a murder. Sixteen years later, Gary sat for Mass in a Catholic church in America. There is no higher reward for a mother than knowing her child has turned into a fine human being.

I would like to ask you now to see Denise's story another way. Take it beyond the peace walls of Belfast, beyond the borders of Northern Ireland, and back over the ocean into your home. What's the connection? Belfast, to me, was like a big extended family locked in a grudge, unable to get over its anger, with a few siblings crying out, *Come on, get over it!*

The Hughes family was able to change its fate because Denise and Brian have been willing to see each other for who they are, not who they used to be. They were willing to believe that life did not always have to be that way. They were willing to change. This is a remarkably simple truth, and it's not even controversial—we need to be willing to change!—and yet how often are relationships ground down by people who are unwilling to give up the past? That day in the butcher shop, Denise did not see a meat cutter, and Brian did not see a woman who had forgotten what happiness felt like. Each saw a good person.

When I was in Belfast, I found myself thinking a lot about what's involved in forgiving someone. What do people in your life need to do to be forgiven by you? What must happen, if anything, before you are willing to see them for who they are today, rather than for what they did to you long ago? How do people redeem themselves, in your eyes? Do they need to admit what they did? Do they need to repent? Do they need to have changed their ways, and if so, for how many years before they have proven to you they are truly deserving?

The irony of Belfast is that despite the Protestant-Catholic street war of the last thirty-five years, it is hardly a religious place. Only 25 percent of people there go to church more than twice a year. It is *not* a religious war; it is a political war. That said, there are religious roots behind it, which have created two very different philosophies of forgiveness and redemption. The Protestant notion of redemption is different from the Catholic notion. Both have merit. These are ideas we all struggle with when we consider forgiving the people in our family.

One school of thought evolved from the Calvinist idea that good people are chosen by God before birth. Their souls are predestined, and they do not redeem themselves; God or Jesus did the redeeming. Character is fate, and someone who acted badly in the past will probably act badly again. It's that hard-liner mentality, very suspicious of anyone who argues, "Hey, but I'm nice now." People who hurt us in the past are to be regarded with great skepticism, and we must be wary that their cleansing ritual wasn't just an empty pantomime. Every time people screw up, it's proof they have not really changed. This is the guarded voice in our ear, the one that wants to lay out tests before forgiving. At heart, it's the voice of someone deeply hurt who wants to never be hurt again.

The other school of thought evolved from the Catholic notion that everyone since Adam and Eve has screwed up. We are all marked with stain and sin. Only through continual examination of our faults and repentance can we redeem ourselves. Not only *can* our fate be changed, but it *must* be changed to lead a good life. And what goes for me applies to everyone else, too. We are expected to believe that people can change. We are supposed to give them the benefit of the doubt. We *have* to forgive them, from the moment they confess or atone. In fact, in this school of thought, true atonement is a private examination—it does not have to happen in public, meaning there does not have to be a public confession. This moral examination must indeed happen, and it must be sincere, but those who wronged us are not required to show remorse or beg or admit everything they ever did wrong. Under the other school of thought, the burden of proof is definitely on the atoner. In this school of thought, the burden shifts to the forgiver. It is *hard* to forgive people when they simply tell us they've changed but they haven't really offered any proof. This is the voice in our ear that says we need to forgive people in order to move on—regardless of whether they have properly apologized. This is the voice that knows holding on to resentment is poisonous. This is the voice that wants to let go of that anger, wipe it clean, despite legitimate fear that we might be opening the door to being hurt all over again.

We all have these two voices in our heads. For some, one voice is dominant. Some people set themselves up to be hurt over and over. Some people live rigidly, accepting ever-fewer people into their kingdom.

No one can tell you that you need to be more forgiving, or that you need to let your guard down. No one can say that you need to accept everyone in your family for who they are today, ignoring what happened back then. But hatred serves no purpose, and there is no profit in hanging on to a grudge. The way you think about forgiveness is probably not the only way. There are many approaches to forgiveness that cultures have developed over thousands of years. These are taught and passed on, like languages. If your way is not getting you anywhere, you might consider others. Learning how to forgive is another rite of passage every family must figure out.

Forgiving your enemies is the easy part. The hard work is in forgiving those you trusted to care for you, those precious few you believed would keep your interests in mind, the one person you thought would never do that to you. Forgiving those you love is not something you do once, like a ceremony. It's required of you, in some form, every single day.

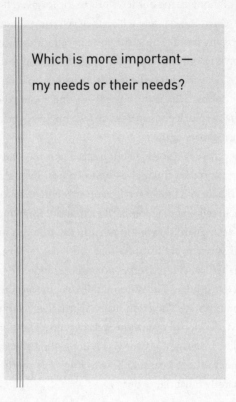

Which is more important—
my needs or their needs?

Silent Car Rides

Sarah Iverson

This is a story about a good divorce. It had all the positive traits you would want, if you were making a checklist. The parents waited until the kids were in college, or close. Reasonably quickly, they learned to stop bad-mouthing each other to the kids. The whole family attended counseling to manage the breakup. Custody did not become a battleground, and neither parent was plunged into poverty. Both parents remarried in one year's time.

And yet, despite all that, it was incredibly scary.

Especially for the middle child, Sarah Iverson, who was nineteen when she heard her parents were splitting up. She's twenty-one now.

Sarah Iverson shared her story in order to help some parents who are worried (or terrified) about what they are putting their kids through. She wants those parents to know it can work out, as it did for her.

At nineteen, Sarah seemed to have everything going for her. Her teens had not been rocked by rebellion or despair. Anyone who met her thought, *That young woman has a bright future.* Her voice was like a firm handshake. She stood rail-straight and took care of her appearance. Her grades were excellent, and she held down two jobs—a summer internship in organizational psychology plus three shifts a week at a clothing store, where she was the assistant manager. Her relationship with her longtime high school boyfriend Tony had some on-again, off-again drama, but to most observers the two acted like an old married couple. Their relationship was exceedingly domestic—they cooked together, did laundry together, attended church together, and took each other to the doctor. Sarah was nineteen going on thirty.

Her father, Norman, was an attorney. Her mother, Amelia, taught special education at an elementary school. The two had met in college at Fort Hays State, and had been married for twenty-six years. Sarah's brother, Max, was three years older; her sister, Leslie, was a year younger. They had lived at the same house in Hays, Kansas, for all of Sarah's life.

Sarah was a good example of a kid who had a near-perfect childhood. Nothing tragic had ever happened to her. She might have been set for college and a career, but Sarah was unprepared for seeing her super-stable parents suddenly become emotional wild cards.

"I wouldn't have expected myself to handle it so poorly," Sarah admitted. "I don't know why I was so surprised. There wasn't any visible conflict, but even I knew they weren't happy."

Sarah knew that her mother was often out late at night with a man named Cyrus who was a minor family acquaintance. Sarah and her sister joked about following their mother one night.

"We teasingly called Cyrus her 'boyfriend.' But we absolutely did not think she was in love with him, or suspect she was sleeping with him. We meant it as a joke. We thought she and Cyrus were friends."

Did they consider divorce a possibility?

"Well, I did, some. But I thought my parents were too conservative to even consider it. I thought there was *no way*. They would stick it out, I was sure."

She was half wrong. Her dad wanted to stick it out. Her mother had stuck it out for ten years already, and she was done.

When Sarah learned the news (from her sister), the first thing she did was go into shock and throw up a wall of denial. She was at the clothing store when her sister showed up in tears. Sarah took a stab: "Are our parents getting divorced?" She didn't want to hear the answer. She ran into the back and hid.

When she got home later, her father—her stern, emotionless father—cried so hard he had to leave and go to a clinic for emergency counseling, sleeping pills, and antidepressants. The sight was more than Sarah could process. She threw up uncontrollably.

Her future felt contaminated. "For the rest of my life, I would have to choose which parent to spend holidays with. I thought that future boyfriends would see I came from a 'split family' and have their reservations about me—they would assume I didn't know what love was, and that I wouldn't know how to fight as hard. My kids wouldn't be able to visit Grandma and Grandpa together. I couldn't imagine having to tell my future children why. How my parents had cheated on each other. I felt like nothing would be the same. I was so disappointed that my parents could do all these things to our family. I had lost my family as I knew it."

Shouldn't nineteen be old enough to roll with the news of her parents' split? Well, kids can take things very personally. Growing up can be pretty harrowing, even when we have everything going for us. It doesn't matter where we're from or what we've seen: When it happens to *our* family, it can be unnerving, and it can hurt like hell.

Nineteen is a vulnerable age. In Sarah's case, she was on the verge of separating from her family and testing her independence. Her family was her bedrock and her fallback if anything happened to her. When Sarah heard the word *divorce,* she didn't realize her family would live on, just without their marriage in the middle. She thought her family had ended. Not that it *would* fall apart, slowly, but that it was over already. As if the Family—the *connectedness*—had died, suddenly and unexpectedly.

A new era of honesty exploded in the house. Amelia could not bottle up the truth of what she was feeling anymore. The truth was, Norman had not hugged her for years, and he could never be honest or open about the family finances. The truth was, she loved Cyrus. Last year, she had gone to Colorado with him.

Norman, for his part, became hyperemotional and confessional. He got specific about what he was apologizing for. They heard details they didn't really want to hear, but Norman felt he owed his kids the facts, particularly regarding his own faults. He'd had an affair twenty years ago with his secretary. He had neglected his kids when they were young.

For a few weeks Sarah soaked up all these facts in a quest to establish the moral score. She was angry at both of her parents, but it seemed important to know which of the two she should be *most* angry at. Figuring out who to blame is a sneaky way of establishing the semblance of control, but the facts led only to screeching confusion. She felt betrayed that secrets had been kept from her for twenty years. She despised seeing her parents torn down into weak people. She hated that, in this moment of greatest need, she was not allowed to be the unstable, emotional child. Her parents took on that role. They left her to play the part of the arbitrator-parent, the referee.

Then there was the horror of her family being the talk of Hays! Everyone knew her parents. Everyone would know Amelia had cheated with Cyrus. Sarah refused to go to church or to the grocery store. She was afraid to tell her friends. As they slowly found out, they were supportive, but not one of them could relate. That sort of thing didn't happen to them. Which made the shame worse.

Hays is one of the few major towns along Interstate 70, which runs the breadth of Kansas. In these towns, divorce does not happen often. Or, more precisely, a kid who grows up in Hays is simply not exposed to divorce. Kids are taught the sanctity of marriage. Four of Sarah's five best high school friends were engaged by nineteen. Every Sunday the *Hays Daily News* wrote up the local weddings; Sarah knew every couple, and they were all her age. This is the way you move ahead with your life, if you stay in Kansas. It's the way you make something happen. In one of her college classes, Sarah was the only one who was not engaged or married. The mayor of her college town once passed a proclamation officially condemning immoral life choices such as cohabitation and divorce. When you get divorced in Hays, it's not a stretch to believe the whole town is shunning you.

The whole family was suffering, yet not everyone in the family could participate in the decision making. Only her parents got votes. And her mom had the veto. If Mom wanted a divorce, if Mom wanted to marry Cyrus, the rest of the family could not overrule her. It felt fundamentally unfair. The rest of the family could only sit back and endure the consequences. At this most crucial time in their family history, Sarah was cut out of the executive council. Whatever happened to all those years of sitting down and making decisions together?

Even if her mom *needed* to get divorced, Sarah still didn't see why it had to happen so *fast*. If she had a vote, she might accept the divorce, but—darn it!—*slower!* Did she really have to see Mom and Cyrus together so often? Did Mom really have to try to push Cyrus on the kids when they weren't ready? And then Dad, scared of ending up all alone, started to look for women to date. And he found Jan right away! Couldn't anybody wait? Couldn't anyone respect a proper grieving period? Sarah desperately needed time to give up her attachment to The Way It Was.

It did not help to see her father holding Jan's hand. Why the affection now, when Mom had asked for it for years? That night, during another fatherly confession, Sarah was overcome and threw up into a trash pail again. Norman realized they needed counseling.

The counseling was semi-constructive. Everyone in the family went alone to the same therapist for a couple of months. The therapist was able to reveal how others were feeling and suggest how to handle the stress points. For instance, the therapist convinced Sarah not to say anything mean to Cyrus that she would regret later. And the therapist confirmed that it was okay to stay away from Mom and Cyrus if Sarah did not feel like being with them right then.

But why was "managing the breakup" the goal of the counseling? Why not "getting back together" as a goal? Why hadn't they gone years ago? These issues were never addressed. After a couple of months, Sarah stopped showing up at her appointments.

In November, Norman and Amelia went to court in Salina to have a judge finalize their divorce. Norman took Jan along and set her up in a hotel room. He wanted the support. Sarah thought it was tacky. That night Sarah came out of a sorority meeting and found out that her sister, Leslie, needed a ride to the hospital immediately. Leslie had lost her medicine for migraines, and now she was losing feeling in her arm and was unable to talk. It took hours for her parents to arrive at the hospital, which felt just plain wrong. To top it off, both Cyrus and Jan showed up at the emergency room. Amelia became furious that Jan was there (ignoring that Cyrus's presence might have been equally upsetting to her kids). An argument ensued over whose house Leslie would stay at when she was released.

"My sister was in the ER, and the moment couldn't be *just* about her," Sarah explained. "The moment had to be co-opted by my parents, Mom's boyfriend, and Dad's girlfriend. It seemed so selfish. I was sure the rest of my life would be like that. Family time would never be just hanging out. In every instance, one parent would win and one would lose."

Sarah and her siblings spent Thanksgiving at Cyrus's house with their mom. This was hard to accept. Sarah felt numb. These were not her relatives. This was not her house. This was not how it was supposed to be: *No, my dad makes the turkey, my mom makes the dressing, and I make the cranberry sauce. No.*

Sarah felt angry, righteous, offended, and rushed. But she had not found the space to grieve. Anytime she got near it, something happened that demanded she get indignant again. Then she and her longtime boyfriend, Tony, broke up, once and for all. Suddenly grief overwhelmed her. It was like she was in a prairie fog; she couldn't see beyond the reach of her arm. She couldn't think. She stopped eating and dropped twenty pounds.

Did she project her grief over her parents onto her own breakup? Possibly. "But I think Tony had long ago replaced my father as my source of emotional support," Sarah reflected. "Tony gave me what my father couldn't." She had leaned on him hard the last few months. When they broke up, she had nobody in her corner anymore.

Grief defies all stereotypes. It can surprise anyone with its gloomy power. As scary and isolating as it feels, something healthy happens when it takes us over. Every day feels like a week. And in that state, we open up to what we've been missing. Every smile from a stranger feels like a great gift. Every kind word sustains us for another hour. We find people who seem to know what we've been feeling. Not that we talk about it; it is more like a look in the eye. *He knows. He's been here.* Grief is somewhat of a secret, unspoken language. We join a club we did not know existed. It's almost shaming, this feeling; we regret having been so unaware. Grief puts the miracle of empathy in our hearts. Grief opens us up to seeing the world from other people's point of view.

In this way, Sarah found herself talking to her dad one night about her breakup with Tony. It was at his house (their old house). She never would have talked to him about boys before. But she could see the look in his eyes. *He knows.* And she finally understood what he had been going through the last six months. How hard it had been on him.

"When your mother and I split, I thought the world wouldn't go on," he said.

Yes, yes. It was so surreal—her own father, relating to her like a friend.

And then she noticed: Sarah was not the only one who had lost weight. Her dad had matched her, pound for pound.

"Dad, you've got to eat. *Please.* For me. Eat."

"Okay," he said. Then, "You're not doing okay, are you?"

"I don't know why it's so hard for me, Dad."

"Would you go talk to the counselor, Sarah? Would you? For me?"

"Okay." And she did.

On the day before Christmas, Sarah chose to work at the clothing store. She got a call from Cyrus. Now her mother was in the hospital with appendicitis. On the way, in her car, Sarah appealed to God.

"Why, God?" she asked. "Why Tony at the same time as my parents? It's okay, but show me the reason." In asking, she felt the answer. She *knew* the answer. *To understand how my parents have been feeling.*

Sarah took a seat beside Cyrus in the waiting room. They ended up getting lunch in the cafeteria together and sharing breakup stories, including the story of his divorce. For the first time, Sarah found herself thinking, *Maybe Cyrus is going to be okay.*

That night, Christmas Eve, she was all alone. Her sister was at her boyfriend's; her brother was at his girlfriend's. She ate spaghetti by herself and watched television. The family always used to order a pizza on Christmas Eve. On the verge of it becoming another depressing evening, her sister called and invited Sarah over. They played board games late into the night.

The next night Sarah was at Jan's house for Christmas dinner. Jan was a widow with two children, one of whom knew Sarah from school. Sarah found them all laid-back and fun. They drank wine with their meals, which never happened in Sarah's family. After Christmas dinner, they liked to go out to a bar. Sarah went with them. She could not believe it when her dad didn't stop her.

In this way, each day was rescued from despair. Sarah went back to church, less afraid of that dreaded question *How's it going?* She suddenly saw, in the congregation, not a bunch of people who were religious and therefore likely to disapprove of her family, but a bunch of families who had experienced grief and were able to commune with others in pain.

When she discovered that she was allergic to wheat, it was her dad, of all people, who took an interest and created a wheat-free recipe book for her. And when her dad suddenly noticed for the first time what kind of music his daughter listened to (contemporary country), he turned her on to Arlo Guthrie, James Taylor, and Bob Dylan. She decided to attend Kansas State in the fall. She had wanted to go two years before, but she had lacked the courage to leave home, so she had attended Fort Hays State. Now that seemed silly. Kansas State was just a few hours away.

In the late spring Sarah told everyone not to remind her father of her forthcoming birthday. She wanted to see if he remembered. He did, and he had a surprise. He took her flying. Norman had taken some flying lessons in college, but he gave them up when he met Amelia. Now he was taking lessons again. Sarah was thrilled. His best friend flew as copilot. It was fun to see her Dad with a buddy. She couldn't remember the last time he'd hung out with friends.

After their flight, they had a burger.

She asked him, "Why did you stop flying when you met Mom?"

"She felt the lessons were too expensive. Your mother and I rarely saw eye-to-eye on where the money should be spent." Then, afraid Sarah would take the remark as unsolicited criticism, Norman added, "I don't miss your mother, Sarah. But I do miss the unit, the family unit. The *us.* I miss that foundation."

"Why can't you and Mom get back to that feeling you once had?"

"I'm not sure we ever had it, Sarah. You know, we were young when we met. I was going to be a lawyer, and Amelia's father was a lawyer, and it seemed like such a nice picture. Her family loved me. And we went ahead on that."

"You don't think you were right for each other?"

"Now I don't. But I didn't get that until just this year. All along, I thought what we had was normal. I thought it was normal for the feeling to be gone after a few years. I thought it was normal to not be affectionate. I was willing to stick with it. But now that I know? I'm glad we didn't, Sarah. I'm grateful for the new life your mother has given me."

"You are?"

"This might be a weird thing to hear, coming from your father. But I think I'm a different man than I had led myself to believe."

Sarah went back to school that evening. She liked this new dad who confided in her. For years Sarah had imagined her wedding day, in all its possibilities. There was always one element that was hard to envision going well: the dance with her father. When she tried to imagine dancing with him, it felt so unnatural and forced. That night, she pictured it again. This time, it didn't feel weird. It felt sweet.

In May, Sarah moved out of the dorms at Fort Hays and back into her childhood home with her father and Jan. Norman had put the house up for sale to pay off Amelia and the legal bills. It sold in June, right around the time that Amelia and Cyrus eloped to Reno. Norman and Jan moved into a new place and gradually moved everything over. Sarah refused to leave their house. It was not a rebellion. She just couldn't let go.

"It was inexplicable," she said. "I thought I was doing fine. Things had never been better with Dad. I had done two stints in counseling. I should have been okay."

Norman did not force her. The sale did not close for sixty days. But he kept moving the furniture, then the appliances. The water was turned off. Still, Sarah could not leave. She asked that her room not be touched. The electricity was shut off and the air-conditioning no longer cooled the house, so daytime temperatures climbed to one hundred degrees. Sarah ordered pizza every night. She fell back into a funk. She did not know what she was after. What she wanted was impossible. She thought if she just smelled it, one more time, by wandering the old rooms, she could keep it with her forever. The vomiting erupted again, this time every hour, until she realized it wasn't depression that made her feel so sick—she had food poisoning, courtesy of three-day-old pizza left to fester in the heat. A friend took her to the hospital for fluids.

After that, she moved into her dad's new place. Jan had her own rules. Sarah found herself arguing frequently with Jan over the mess in her bedroom. It infuriated her to come home and find that Jan had been in her room, picking up her shoes. With two weeks left in her summer, she cleaned out all her possessions and left for a friend's house without telling her dad. This *was* a protest, though against what, exactly, Sarah could not articulate.

It broke her heart when her dad did not call that night to ask where she was, or why she had left.

For ten days she waited for her father to break the silence.

Finally her sister, Leslie, came with a message.

"He can't call you," she said. "He's heartbroken."

"From what?"

"From you. He said, 'Sarah knows how hard it was, for my wife of twenty-six years to leave me. But for my daughter to leave me, it was ten times worse.' Sarah—he needs you."

Sarah went to her father and embraced him. She couldn't stop crying.

"Why?" he asked. "Why did you leave?"

"I don't know."

"It's not about the shoes, is it? It's about me and Jan getting married?"

"I finally know the real you. I like the new Dad. Now you're getting married, and I'm going away to school. I'm going to lose you."

"Sarah, I'm going to be in your life more than ever. You watch me."

"Okay."

"And Jan is not taking me away from you. She helps me be easygoing, not the strict and conservative guy who kept to himself."

"Okay."

"We're getting married at the courthouse in two weeks. I want you there, Sarah. We're not having anybody else come. We just want our kids there. And I was hoping—I need someone to sign the license as my witness. Will you be my witness?"

"Okay."

Sarah came out of that hard year the way any parent would hope a kid might. Her depression ultimately gave her a sense of purpose by giving her a way to relate to society's troubles. She is pursuing her master's degree in public administration. She volunteers for a crisis hotline as a police response advocate; she drives out to the families that have called in and helps them take advantage of county services. She now loves new experiences. The scarier the better. She's been skydiving several times and rides motorcycles with her dad. She spent a summer in Boston. She is not scared of love—she's fallen into it twice since her parents' divorce. I spent the day with her in Topeka, where she has an internship with a state senator. That evening Norman and Jan flew in from Hays, and we had dinner.

Afterward, Sarah and I hung out on the edge of the airfield for hours. She had brought some lists she had made for me—things she wanted to make sure she said. Things she was afraid she had not communicated in our previous conversations.

"I thought I had lost my family as I knew it. I felt nothing would be the same. Both those feelings were correct—*fortunately*. I got a better family out of it. I never would have had the great relationship I have with my parents today if it were not for my parents taking the initiative to change their entire lives and start over. They could never be their true selves together. Staying married would have just meant more unhappiness.

"We used to act so formal around each other. I always wished I could be like some of my friends who considered their mom or their dad one of their friends. Now my parents are the first people I call when I need advice about relationships. I share things with them I never thought I would, and vice versa. I used to coach my boyfriends for when they came over to my house, which was rarely. Now I relish the chance to take a boyfriend to Mom's or Dad's. Mom always wanted to have real conversations over dinner, with the television off. She has that now, with Cyrus. My brother eats there every Sunday. He talks. My brother never used to talk. All of this has come about the last year. I never could have imagined that something so tragic was just what my family needed."

"You worry about other families in that situation?"

"Our society pumps out this message that parents should stick together for their children. But it's not always the right choice. You think you're giving your children stability, but you have to be really careful what you might be unwittingly teaching them."

She looked at her list. "I was being taught all these things were normal, as sure as Dad makes the turkey, Mom makes the dressing, and I make the cranberry sauce. I was being taught that you shouldn't talk about your love life. I was being taught to keep it a secret that I went to parties and had a good time. I thought it was normal not to invite friends over. Normal not to have friends. Normal that the romance wears off. Normal that love is like a business relationship. I thought change was bad, or threatening. I was being taught that men are not emotional. I thought it was normal not to hug my dad. I thought it was normal not to even want to hold hands with my boyfriend."

"Tony?"

"Yeah. We hung on to each other for years, because we thought what we had was normal. We had a loveless, businesslike relationship. We should have been just friends. And I didn't know we both deserved better. We hung on to it, because it looked just like what my parents had."

I looked down at her lists. By then I understood all of the references, except one.

"What's 'Trip to New Mexico'?"

"That was our last family trip, before it all blew up. We drove to New Mexico. The front seat was dead silent the whole way. They had nothing to say to each other. I was sitting in the backseat, and I started writing this essay in my journal, about whether I would ever know who my parents really are. I wondered what their hopes were when they were my age. Surely they wanted more from life than this, more than a silent ride into the desert. We're finally free of that now. We're not trapped in that car anymore. It scares me to think I was once so attached to that old way of being a family."

What makes a good divorce?

I interviewed a family in Blaine, Washington, which is just miles from Canada. They had been divorced seven years. The husband had remarried; the mother had not. The four daughters carried their hurt around for a long time. Finally, in advance of last Christmas, the daughters (now fifteen through twenty-four years old) ganged up on their three parents. They were sick of having to split time on holidays between Mom's and Dad's; they were sick of the animosity between the parents that flared up whenever the splitting of time had to be negotiated. One day, one of the daughters realized, "It doesn't have to be this way, just because we've been doing it like this for seven years." She got her sisters together. They went to their dad and stepmother and gave them an all-or-nothing ultimatum: Mom must be invited to their house on Christmas Eve or the four daughters would not show up. It was tense for a couple of days. The stepmother felt that her feelings and her turf were being disrespected. But unable to separate the girls, who stood firm, the three parents tried a Christmas the way the girls wanted. Ever since, the three parents have gotten along smoothly, no matter how often they are in the same room. Forcing the former spouses together has helped both to drop their old view of each other and made them see what they have both become: mature, interesting people.

It was not the divorce that caused the pain, the daughters learned. It was being caught in the middle. At the very least, a few times a year a family needs to come together and recharge their relationships. The opposite had been happening. It's no wonder the charge had been running low. It's no wonder that two of the daughters were saying things like *I'm not sure I want a family of my own.*

Sarah Iverson's story is a good example of how a family weathers a crisis. There's a phase where it feels like they are all trapped in a school bus without any brakes careening down a windy road. They seek professional help. They seek religious guidance. They try some brutal honesty to get things out. Then there's a phase where small moments of jeopardy are rescued by random kindness—which feels like the universe is looking out for you. The family tries some constructive behavior modification (they hold their tongues). They start to see the problem from one another's perspectives, which leads to a first attempt at forgiveness. Their lives move on, and they get new hobbies or new friends or new lovers, and these become stepping-stones forward. One day, they will be grateful for how this crisis has made them better people.

In some families, that arc can take twenty years. In others, it can take two generations. Sarah's family was able to get through it in a year and a half. But this is no race. Everyone who finishes gets a prize.

Sarah's story, though, is not just about divorce.

There are many families out there riding in silent cars to the desert. Silence is the most common coping mechanism in families. Not temporary silence, which is in any healthy family's bag of tools and offers a good way to defuse a heated situation. In this case, I mean prolonged silence that goes on for years. Pretending "it" never happened. Holding all those emotions in. We've all been actors in our own homes, playing the part of who we used to be.

We live in an age of confession. Turn on the television and on every other channel somebody is revealing shocking and intimate truths of his or her life. In the pages of this book, there's a lot of that, too. Are there secrets left? In interviewing seven hundred people about their families, I was trusted with hundreds of secrets. Some of these were explosive, but by far, most of these secrets were of a single variety: The people I interviewed revealed their true character to me but withheld it from their family. That was the secret they were hiding.

Why didn't they feel free to expose their real nature?

The explanation commonly offered was, "Well, my whole family is just *that way*. We don't show our feelings." From so many of these people, including Sarah Iverson, I met with absolute silence when I asked to meet with their parents. The notion that parents would be open with me was inconceivable to most. In several cases it took a long time before people I had been interviewing told their parents about me and provided me with their parents' phone number. But I found that parents were easily as forthcoming as their now adult children. Maturity had worked wonders. In many cases the parents were far more revealing than the children.

The willingness is there, more often than people suspect.

Silence has become a habit and has made many of us numb.

Every single family struggles with the trade-off between familiarity and authenticity, between security and free expression. Between calm and honesty.

When I started my research I would have said that authenticity trumps all, but I now see that was a bias I had, and easy for me to say. For instance, I befriended a Pakistani man in Birmingham, England, who lives with his parents and sister. He has been unable to tell his family he's gay. He's twenty-six years old and works in finance. His family has moved from Islamabad to Abu Dhabi to Beirut to England. His parents are traditional and closed-minded and oppressive, but they've stuck things out through some unbearably hard times. He has remained in the closet, not to protect them, and not to save them the shame—but because he values their love and the security they provide so much. He's not yet ready to give up his support system, even if it's based on a spurious premise. He knows he has to confront the silence eventually, but who am I to say that time must be now?

When it comes to the trade-off between authenticity and security, it's not one or the other. A family needs both. Getting there, and establishing both, is one of the rites of passage a family must complete if it wants to survive. Confront the silence.

It is not a race. Everyone who gets there will be rewarded.

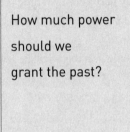

How much power
should we
grant the past?

Home Front

Steve and Gamze Ligler

Gamze Erokay had absolutely vivid memories of her childhood. But was this a blessing or a curse?

Gamze is Turkish and was born a Sunni Muslim. Her earliest memory is of going on a pilgrimage to Mecca in Saudi Arabia with her mother and great-grandfather. They drove the whole way down from Istanbul. They entered the Great Mosque, al-Haram, with its irregular colonnades, and joined the vast crowd circling the Kaaba. Some fifty feet high, the granite cube was draped with a black silk cloth. The floor was tiled with marble. Gamze was only four years old. As the crowd prayed and walked their seven concentric circles, Gamze only pretended to pray. She knew it was important but didn't understand this holiest of Muslim rituals. Instead, she was fascinated by the endless variety of people who had come from all over the world. In particular, she remembers the women from India, who wore chains that draped from their nostrils to their earlobes.

When Gamze got home from Mecca, her mother and father went to England for six months so her father could attend language school. Gamze understood that her father had graduated from medical school in Turkey and he had been offered a fellowship in New York City at Columbia University. This was considered a great honor back in Istanbul. Gamze stayed with her grandparents. Six months later her mother came home, and her father went to New York. They waited for him to send for them.

A year later he did, but he brought them to Chicago, not New York. They lived in an apartment tower on Nordica Avenue, above Elmwood Park. It was not a good neighborhood. Something was different about her father. He was frustrated by his inability to pass the medical boards, primarily due to his trouble with English. He became an extremely controlling father. Gamze was terrified of him. Spilling a cup of milk could mean physical punishment. Speaking her own mind could trigger his temper and lead to yelling and screaming. When she didn't eat, she was put in her high chair out in the hallway, with the door closed. She remembers neighbors walking by, afraid to say anything. Her father's research was in pediatric nutrition; he had theories. She was his experiment. She thought of him as the Mad Scientist. She remembers many unusual physical and emotional punishments. One time, when she refused to eat a cup of mushroom soup, her father responded by refusing to talk to Gamze for six months.

They shielded her, forbidding her from leaving the apartment other than for school. Gamze was denied her own feelings, denied her own thoughts. She was not even allowed to pick a favorite color. She was told what color to like, and told what kind of cars to like. Forget about being able to choose her own clothes. Nor could she cut her hair; it hung past her waist.

When she was in junior high, Gamze went to visit relatives in Istanbul. One day her paternal grandmother opened a closet full of Gamze's father's old things. One of the items was an issue of the national newspaper. On the front page, there was Gamze's father, mouth gaping, yelling at the prime minister. Her father, the accompanying article said, was a professor at the only medical school in Turkey, and he demanded the government build hospitals in rural villages. Her grandmother explained that Gamze's father became a populist figure, and there was talk of him running for Parliament. Instead, he took the scholarship to go to the United States.

Gamze couldn't reconcile this brazen and heroic image of her father with the broken man who scared her so much. It shocked her.

Gamze was the outsider, the watcher, the silent one. She was unable to confront anyone. When a teacher made an error grading her test, she could not dispute it. When a salesclerk overcharged her, she was incapable of protest. If friends at school got mad at her, she hoped they would never bring it up. When they did, she felt like she was melting into the ground.

Her father always insisted that Gamze would marry someone Turkish and Muslim. Marriages outside their faith did not work. If she did not do so, he vowed many times, he would kill her and commit suicide.

It surprised Gamze that her parents let her choose a college in another city—the University of Wisconsin at Madison. The night before college began, her parents drove her to school and helped her get situated on the third floor of her coed dorm (with boys living on the second floor!). They departed the next morning. She considered that day her "very first day of freedom." Gamze had to register for classes. She took the timetable down to the dorm lounge, and within minutes she had been introduced to a white guy named Steve Ligler. When they met again that night, she understood he was interested in her.

She was frightened. She had never been on a date in her life and was wary of his intentions. "This is very serious for me," he insisted. She didn't understand why. *Why would anyone be interested in me?* He had never met anyone from a foreign country. He told her he was on an ROTC scholarship. She had no idea what that was, and even though he wore a navy uniform every Tuesday, the import of this didn't sink in. They began dating, and in October, just two months after their meeting, Steve proposed. They were not formally engaged, but he wanted Gamze to know his interest was genuine. Needless to say, Gamze did not mention this to her parents.

That first Thanksgiving, she met Steve's parents, and that spring break, Steve invited her to visit his home. She was reluctant—she was afraid his parents would figure her out and it would all be over. Before she got to college, she'd had a fantasy that she would marry a man whose family had all tragically died. She couldn't handle more family than she already had. But Steve kept asking. Finally she put it out there:

"What if your parents don't like me? What are you going to do?"

"Nothing. I would not do anything. They are entitled to their opinion, but it won't influence mine."

That shocked her. She had never met someone who did not rely on the opinion of his parents. So she agreed. She told her parents she had to remain on campus for special tutoring during the break. They drove for five hours—the longest she had ever been in a car. Steve had grown up in a place called Trego, Wisconsin. Only two hundred people live there, every one of them of German Lutheran ancestry. It was so remote that the nearest stoplight was twenty miles away. When they reached his parents' house, a gutted deer was hanging from a tree in the front yard.

Throughout the week, Gamze was alternately enlightened and confused. If a guest ever came to her own parents' house, her mother would cook for two days in advance, and the guest would be served using the finest china. The slipcovers would be off the couches. Everything was for show; Gamze hated visits from guests because her father was especially attuned to maintaining the façade. Gamze always feared saying something that would haunt her the rest of her life.

So when they got to Steve's house, she had to ask Steve, "Didn't they know we were coming?" At first she was sort of insulted. Not one special preparation had been made. The house had not been tidied. They did not ask what her father's profession was. Gamze was shocked. Did they not have any social graces? His parents were laid-back. They were not interested in judging her. When their dog jumped on the couch, nobody yelled at it.

After dinner, she asked Steve if he wanted to go for a walk.

"Now? Is the moon out?"

The moon was not out, but what did they need the moon for?

She soon found out. It was so dark she could not see her hand in front of her face. Before them lay 160 acres of wilderness, entirely invisible. To find their way back to the house, they had to walk backward. Gamze had never been out of a city before. She had never seen the pitch-black. She had only ever seen jumbo jets and a pink reflection of Chicago in the sky.

After a couple of days Gamze began to acclimate.

My world, this is what a family can be like?

Steve's parents told wonderful stories about him. They adored him. Since he was age seven, his nickname had been "Little Professor." He had made up that phrase. It said a lot about the way his mind worked, the way he figured things out for himself.

"It's so cool the way they feel about you," she said to Steve. "They treat you like an adult, a human being."

"My family's *not* perfect," Steve tried to assure her. "We're not as free of dysfunction as it seems. But they do let me have my own mind."

Gamze recognized that she helped Steve break the Wisconsin-boy mold. He relished telling his friends and family that his fiancée was Turkish and Muslim. And he was genuinely curious and open-minded about where she came from. He begged her to tell him about the Middle East, about everything she wanted to forget. She could not bear to talk about it. Gamze did not like being exotic. She hated it. In high school she'd been the only Muslim out of twenty-five hundred students. She just wanted to fit in.

Steve was the love of her life, but because Gamze was so scared of doing the whole family thing, her commitment was tenuous. Steve felt it. She constantly told herself, *If this gives me strife, I'll walk away.*

Steve was one year ahead of Gamze. As he approached graduation, he was scared he was going to lose her. He wanted to get properly engaged. It was time to break the news to her parents. Gamze couldn't do it directly. She told her mother, who told her father. Their daughter was going to marry a white man, a Christian, and to top it off, he was an officer in the U.S. Navy. Gamze's father hated the American military.

Gamze's father was livid. He cut her off financially and swore he would hunt her down and kill her. Gamze moved to an apartment off campus and refused to give her mother the address. She had to take out student loans and get a job to support herself. Only then did Steve really understand what kind of childhood Gamze had had. Steve decided to do this properly, and so, as a sign of respect, he wrote her father a letter asking for permission to meet him and to marry his daughter. For a long time, her father never wrote back.

Finally word came that her father would consider accepting Steve if he converted to Islam.

Gamze told Steve, and he answered without hesitation, "If it's important to you—okay. I'll do it." He was afraid of losing her. For several years he had feared Gamze would decide it wasn't worth the hassle with her parents.

"But it's not important to me," Gamze said. "It's only important to them."

"Having your parents' blessing is important to you. It would make it a lot easier on you."

"That doesn't sound like the Steve I know. The Steve I know would ask what *I* really think about God."

"And what *do* you think?"

They both admitted that their faith was tempered with skepticism. She did not accept the Koran as literal truth, but rather as moral tales, and this was exactly how he felt about the Bible. So many of the stories in the Koran are similar to stories in the Bible. She was Muslim, he was Christian—"as different as the right hand is from the left," according to her father—but those were labels. In truth, their spiritual sensibilities were nearly identical. They should not let those labels keep two people who love each other apart. Too many wars had been fought over religious ideology. They had the chance to declare peace and learn to live with it.

"But what about my father?" Gamze asked.

"He's just making those threats because he's angry, right? He wouldn't really do anything, would he?"

"I don't know," Gamze answered.

"We'll take some precautions. We'll be all right."

Gamze's mother came to their wedding and read a poem. Gamze's father refused to attend. He learned to hold his tongue, but he was not ready to accept this fate for his daughter, which he was sure would end in ruin. Steve's interpretation of the situation was accurate. Gamze's father expressed his displeasure only by cutting them off. Nevertheless, the old threats loomed in Gamze's mind.

After he graduated, Steve moved four times during the year that Gamze finished her accounting degree. At the end of that year he was commissioned in Seattle. Gamze received a job offer from an accounting firm there. They lived in an ugly white building across the Magnolia Bridge. It was an old army barracks that had been converted into five apartments. Navy housing, but they were not on base, so Gamze did not yet get the full blast of what it's like to be a military wife. She did get a taste, though. Steve's ship was in Bremerton, on the peninsula across from Seattle. Her first month, she received a bill from the Wives' Club. Gamze called the club office to say she wasn't going to participate in their meetings because she was down in Seattle and her accounting job had her traveling frequently. The next month, an overdue notice was in her mail. Again, she had to call and explain. Eventually the captain's wife had to authorize Gamze's choice. Over time, Gamze would feel that she was always being watched. Not because she was Turkish, but simply because there are certain expectations held for officers' wives.

As the New Year unfolded, Steve prepared to mobilize for the First Gulf War. He was stationed on his first ship, a tiny wood minesweeper. The war ended so fast that his ship never left port.

Gamze and Steve stayed in Seattle for three years and began discovering what it meant to be married—balancing the demands of two careers in two very different worlds, both traveling a lot. When Steve was gone, it was easy for Gamze to check out, throw herself into her accounting work. It was hard to shift gears when he returned. Gamze was determined to prove her father wrong—to show him that being from two countries and two faiths was not going to cause troubles in their marriage. But having a good marriage means speaking up and communicating—and speaking up is something Gamze had never done.

It was very hard for her to grasp the notion that the quality of her marriage depended on her complaining at least a little—making sure her needs were met. If your needs aren't met, you can't give in return, and the well runs dry. Gamze had spent so many years afraid of her father's hand. She expected wrath every time she opened her mouth. So if something Steve did bothered her, she would hold it in, then all of a sudden explode over the most meaningless and misdirected offense. Yet she wouldn't voice her real concerns, because even the worst moments with Steve were so much better than the best moments of her Chicago childhood. She had escaped her father's physical harm, but her war was not over, for now she had to undo his emotional harm.

Gamze began therapy, and she found out that men could listen to her without being angry. Steve was similarly levelheaded and cool—he never lost his temper. Steve did not heal Gamze, but he created a supportive environment that afforded her the chance to heal herself. He was patient and never pushed her. Slowly, through being in the regular company of a variety of good men, Gamze rewired herself. She learned to discern her feelings and talk about them. This took years. She slowly let go of her anger at her father.

Gamze was not ready to be a mother for many years. She did not have confidence that she could give a child the kind of bottomless love he or she would need. She was afraid she was beyond repair. So at first she bought a plant. When the plant did not die, she got a dog. When the dog did not die, Gamze said, *Okay, I'll try.* They had been married eight years. The navy had moved them away from Seattle to several locations around the country, but by then the navy had moved them back to Seattle again.

Gamze's pregnancy began to bring her family back together. They talked about seeing one another. When she was three months pregnant, Steve's family invited them back to Trego, Wisconsin. They also invited Gamze's parents up from Chicago for a few days. Gamze could not look directly at her father. But her parents responded to the culture of Steve's family exactly as Gamze had, ten years prior. They loved it. Her father was ebullient and complimentary. "Steve is so great," he told her. "They are so laid-back, it's refreshing. I've never seen anything like it. They are so nice." His words were sincere, but oddly it only made Gamze angry that his prejudice had kept them apart for so long. She could not express any of this anger.

Later in the pregnancy, Gamze's parents visited Seattle. Again, her father kept repeating how great Steve was. There was hope this baby would put an end to the chasm. Gamze's father wanted to visit and be there for the birth. Gamze wasn't quite ready for that. Her mother came.

A week after Katherine was born, she developed jaundice and wouldn't nurse. Gamze had to take her back to the hospital and have her cared for in the neonatal intensive care unit. There was risk of brain damage. The doctors had to remove Katherine's blood and give her fresh blood. A memory came back to Gamze, how when she was growing up and wouldn't eat, her mom would utter an old Turkish cliché. Its translation: "May God grant you a child that will be worse than you, so that you can suffer the way I've suffered." Standing outside the window at the N-ICU, Gamze grew enraged. To her mother, she said, "Well, I guess your prayer came through. She's not eating, just as I wasn't. You feel good?"

Katherine survived, but she did not reunite the family. Prior to the birth, Gamze had come so close to forgiving her parents. She anticipated that having a child would help explain how her own father could have beaten her. But once she held Katherine and she felt the absolute innocence of this child, she could never imagine laying a hand on her. Gamze had dealt with her anger at her father, but not at her mother, who had stood by and never intervened when Gamze was a girl.

She asked her mother to go into family therapy with her when she next visited Seattle. Gamze desperately needed some acknowledgment from her mother. It was difficult for her mother to do this, but she admitted that her behavior had been wrong; she should have intervened, but she had felt powerless. Gamze wanted to know if her mother had been beaten as a child. She had not, but Gamze's father had. (Gamze always assumed so.) The sessions worked; they allowed Gamze to move on with her mother. Gamze told her mother that if her father wanted to reunite, he needed to go through this same process with her—with a counselor present. Regarding this proposal, she heard nothing in return. Now and then her father would call and ask to see his granddaughter. "Can't we get over this?" he would plead. He wanted to make the past the past, pretend it never happened. Gamze's answer was always the same: "I'll meet with you in a therapist's office."

In the meantime, as Steve's career moved them all over the country, Gamze began raising Katherine. When Katherine turned two and began having tantrums, Gamze was terrified that she would repeat the pattern—that in one hot moment she would find out the monster was in her, that it had been stashed away in her brain stem for ten years, dormant, waiting to strike as she had been struck. She read books on how violence gets passed down in families, and how the urge is uncontrollable. She felt this surge through her every time Katherine threw a fit. Gamze learned to stop giving Katherine time-outs and instead gave *herself* the time-outs, by locking herself in the bathroom while Katherine pounded on the door.

As the century turned, Steve was moved from one ship to another, and for some period of every year the ships were at sea, positioned to defend freedom if violence broke out. Back at home, Gamze was struggling to prevent the same war from erupting inside her. Throughout humanity's history, violence has been used to control others who anger us. Whether it is on a political scale, as in the Mideast, or on the scale of one parent and her child, it's the same thing. Ending the cycle is one of those rites of passage for families.

They were living at the Fort Leavenworth army post in Kansas on September 11, 2001. It was a surreal time. The year before, when they were stationed in Tennessee, Gamze had gotten nervous about using her name in the South, so she'd taken the nickname "Emma." She had brought this name with her to Fort Leavenworth. She didn't tell people she was Turkish. So she heard the most vile and prejudicial statements around the base. At the same time, the base culture was a world unto itself. The quarters were close, and the gossip was thick. She might as well have joined a sorority. "Where'd they get the money for that car?" people would sneer with skepticism. The women tended to take the rank of their husbands, practically expecting to be saluted. Gamze got the impression there was a lot of sleeping around. Marital counseling was pushed on all the officers and their wives. She discovered this truism about human nature: When people are similar, they create their differences. Gamze was glad that she and Steve were different to start. She wasn't interested in any of it.

She had her own battles with Katherine, who was four years old.

While Steve was "protecting freedom," as it is termed, Gamze was home protecting the free will of her daughter, making sure Katherine had a mind and desires of her own. She stood duty, watchful, ever attentive, waiting for the enemy to appear in her own raised hand. Out there, the world was still primed like lit gasoline. But at home, the war was over and won. Here, in the living room, peace was found. When Katherine turned five, the tantrums abated, and by the age of six they were gone. The threat was over. Gamze marveled at how her daughter developed and grew into a robust child, always asking questions, asserting herself. It seems so small sometimes, such a quiet victory. Could anyone realize how proud Gamze was to hear Katherine say her favorite color was pink? And then the next month, change it to purple, then blue, all of her own free will?

Steve was next commissioned in San Diego. He was a damage control officer on the USS *Boxer,* an amphibious assault ship that calls Naval Station San Diego its home port. He bought a nice home in the hills of Chula Vista, south of San Diego. His ship was sent to Kuwait for the invasion of Iraq. The whole world watched. Meanwhile, far from attention, Gamze got a phone call from her mother in Chicago. She had a brain tumor.

Her father's English was still too awkward for him to make the hospital arrangements, so Gamze had to accomplish this by phone. When she talked to her father, he said he hoped this tumor would bring the family together. Gamze did not respond to this. She flew to Chicago with Katherine, but she was not intending to leave Katherine alone with her father, so Steve's mother drove down and took Katherine back to Trego. In the meantime, Katherine had two days around her grandfather, in the apartment and at the hospital. They were strangers to each other, but they found their connection. Gamze watched as they began to play with each other on the couch, tickling each other and spinning each other in the recliner chair, giggling. Gamze was so nervous her father would snap that she did not feel any joy in this sight. She couldn't even talk to her father. Her mother's brain tumor was the size of a lemon. But it was benign, and it was removed. Her mother went back to work, and Gamze went back to San Diego with Katherine.

Nine months later Gamze's mother had a nervous breakdown. She was hallucinating and paranoid. It was believed to be a consequence of the tumor. Again, Gamze arranged for her to be seen at the hospital, this time in the psychiatric ward. She was in care for a week when Gamze's father called. "You need to come out to Chicago," he pleaded.

For the first time in her life, Gamze stood up to her father. "All of this is *your fault,*" she hissed forcefully. "All of this is your doing. This is what you did to me. Now what's happening to her is a result of *you.*"

"Okay, you're right," he said. "I made mistakes! Let's get over that, let's be a family, come on, come help us." It was the closest he had ever come to taking responsibility, but Gamze was unsatisfied—his confession felt hollow, like cutting corners just to get her to Chicago. He didn't seem to mean it.

The next day her father's best friend telephoned. "Your dad is trying to make up with you, Gamze. We're stubborn old men. But he'll always be your father."

Gamze returned, "You were around me a lot growing up. Did you ever think anything was wrong with our family?"

"You know, I always thought something was wrong with the way you were treated. But I didn't know what it was and I didn't want to ask."

"So after thirty years you call me up? And tell me to go befriend my father?"

She hung up angry.

Her mother recovered quickly. Gamze told her that putting up with her father all these years—taking it and never fighting back—had caused it. She made her mother see a counselor. Her mother told the counselor that all her problems would be solved if Gamze just came back into the fold of the family.

Was it time? When she thought about it, Gamze grew angry. *What is the cost-benefit on this?* she debated. *Who has anything to gain?* Gamze didn't need her father. She needed acknowledgment. She needed him to confess his sins. She had made this clear for years. That he denied her this, when he knew how badly she craved it—all the while begging her to return to the family—was that not just another form of manipulation?

Seeing her father hurt made Gamze feel good. He should know the pain he caused. But seeing her mother hurt did not. Should she do this for her mother? Was there any risk anymore? She wanted to blink and make it all go away, but she couldn't. As a child, Gamze had been the silent one in her family. She could not go back and be silent again. She could not pretend it never happened. When she closed her eyes, it was still vivid.

The war wouldn't end, neither at home nor over there. The USS *Boxer* returned from Kuwait, but not for long. They redeployed for another six months. Always these wars. Perpetual. When would it end? Who would end it? The next time Steve returned, Gamze decided it was finally time to take her family to Chicago. They could go for Christmas to Trego, then stop by Chicago on the way home. She wanted to drive, and to take their three dogs. So it would be a short stay, and they could leave anytime if Gamze couldn't handle it.

She barely could. She was still unable to look her father in the eye for two days, and she could not talk with him individually. She felt bad about it. His reversal had so thrown her off. He said such nice things about Steve's family again. They had seen one another on the Fourth of July. Gamze always thought of her father as socially inept, and she couldn't imagine him holding a conversation with Steve's parents. Even now he sat there, in his leather recliner chair, unable to interact. He was better with her dogs. His sister was visiting to help with Gamze's mother, who could no longer drive. Gamze's aunt was into reuniting them. "Can we try?" she prodded. "Can't we get over this?"

"I've always made it clear what it would take," Gamze responded.

Then Katherine, who was eight now, began to spin her grandfather around and around in the recliner chair. He laughed loudly, and Katherine squealed. Then he moved to the couch. He'd pop up, and

Katherine would push him back down. Pop up, push down. Squealing. Goofing. Tickling. Laughing.

The next day, it was time to leave. Gamze's parents came down to the car to see them off. At the last second, Gamze went to shake her father's hand. He began sobbing, his mouth wide-open. He took her hand in his, and she knew he wanted to give her a hug, so she leaned her right shoulder in and put her left hand on his shoulder. He was sobbing uncontrollably, and for a moment she was able to raise her eyes and look at him without fear, without anger, and without pain.

Next year, she thought, *we'll take Katherine to Istanbul.*

How do we accept
what we cannot
understand?

The Unexplained

Kraig Emery

This is the story of a man's attempt to cope with the sudden and unexplained death of his son, who, at two and a half years old, did not wake up from his nap one day.

Kraig Emery is a humble man. He lives in a duplex north of Concord, New Hampshire. Every bit of his life has been hard, but nothing in his prior experience prepared him for this, a tragedy of biblical magnitude.

His son Kalahan had always had special meaning for Kraig. Kalahan embodied Kraig's great second chance at life—the intentional part, the conscious part. The previous part was wound up like a dog chasing its tail, a flurry of action without any headway, Kraig constantly unable to escape his past. When he was six, his mother's drinking had caused her death. His father quietly scratched out a paycheck as a dishwasher. Kraig spent a lot of time at friends' houses. He began working at age fourteen, and he was out of school and working full-time when he was sixteen. For most of his life, Kraig worked at Market Basket grocery stores, beginning as a stock boy. By the time he was twenty-one, he had three children with his first wife. He grew up with those kids. "Children raising children," the experts call it. The odds were against them, and eventually, the odds prevailed—the marriage lasted six years.

But after that, Kraig felt like his life was finally getting somewhere. He was making good money as a head cashier. He had matured. He prayed for a second chance, and God listened. He and his girlfriend, Heather, gave birth to a rosy-cheeked, honey-haired boy named Kalahan. This was his chance to get it right.

Even though the relationship with Heather got screwed up pretty quickly, that did not taint Kraig's feelings about Kalahan. Kraig was old enough now to really accept the gift of a child. His love for Kalahan dwarfed any feelings he had ever had for a woman. He could give his full attention to Kalahan in a way he never had to his three older children. It felt *right*. It felt like he was not screwing up his second chance, despite doubting himself, and that gave him a pride that was raw and satisfying.

Then, one day, something completely mysterious took Kalahan away. It was not the nap that killed him, they know that. It was not a poison or suffocation or anything that modern forensics can test for. The only explanation for what killed him is the old-fashioned one—sometimes these things happen. Which elicits a question that has been asked this same way for tens of thousands of years: *Why?* Why do these things happen? What are we supposed to learn from it?

When we spoke the first time, by telephone, I couldn't believe how well Kraig could talk about what had happened. At the time of our first conversation, it had been two years since Kal's death. Kraig neither wore his pain on his sleeve nor hid it deep inside. He was emotional, but not to the point of choking up, and he was honest without hesitation—even in answer to intrusive questions I had to ask. He was a good man born into some awfully tough circumstances. Yet he was doing something right, all by himself, living among people who simply put their heads down and plow on, and who largely do not talk about their pain—they look forward to payday and are grateful there is dinner on the table. I wanted to know what it was that Kraig was doing to heal, and whether the rest of us might learn it from him. I wanted the extraordinary wisdom of this ordinary man.

Most people would simply crumble, or run, if they lost a child in such a mystifying way. That's pretty much what happened to the boy's mother, Heather. Kraig tried to find someone to help her, but she withdrew and shut down, then fled. She moved to Manhattan, then Florida, then New Orleans, then back to New York, then somewhere in New Hampshire. Kraig has not been able to find her for a year.

Several times Kraig has even been able to say to me, "As tragic as my son's death is—and not a day goes by I don't feel the hurt—I am grateful for the good it has brought into the world. If every time someone hears Kalahan's story they go hug a kid—well, I'm proud my son's short life is helping other kids out there get hugs."

Being able to get to the point where he could say this is a kind of miracle. It is a textbook example of what psychiatrists call *thriving,* defined as finding new growth in your life and being able to have new meaningful relationships.

I have known Kraig for two years. We have talked monthly over this period. I have been to New Hampshire to meet his father, his friends, his kids, and their mother. I have had the benefit of watching him get better and become a better father, and a new man.

The first year was hell. Did he turn to drink? Yes, on his lunch hour. Some parent would bring a kid into the store and Kraig would fall apart. He would sneak into the back room of the grocery store, drink a six-pack, and bawl his eyes out. When he returned to his roost at the register, he thought he was okay. His co-workers said nothing and almost never talked to him about Kalahan. They gave him a wide berth. Once in a while one would suggest, "You might want some mints, Kraig—you smell like beer." He was grateful for this small offering, this implicit recognition of his grief. The hours are long in a grocery store— a manager is paid for forty-three hours a week, but he has to put in sixty-five hours, including every single Saturday and one fourteen-hour double shift during the week. In addition, his store was an hour's drive from home. Though Kraig took a week of paid bereavement, he couldn't afford to take unpaid family leave.

While some people told him to seek counseling, that simply was not Kraig's inclination. There was no time in his week to do so, and it wasn't part of his culture. It was hard to see the merit of sitting on a couch and spilling his guts. That was not going to make Kal come back.

His best friend, who drove a dump truck, has always stood by Kraig, but he is a lot more comfortable gabbing about the Patriots than listening to Kraig's feelings. Kraig could sense that people avoided him because they did not know what to say—they didn't want to be the one who brought it up, but they also didn't want to act like it didn't happen.

So how do you deal with the worst of all tragedies when you don't have the benefit of costly counseling and videos and books and support groups? How do you process grief when you're the kind of person who has never used the words *process* and *grief* in the same sentence? Who do you go to when your mother is dead and your father works nights and everyone you know is scared of saying the wrong thing?

Eventually Kraig was able to transfer to a store closer to home and limit his time to forty-five hours. He also moved to the duplex he rents today. He had to get away from the place where his memories of Kalahan were too bright. When he would clean, he would find himself wiping away his son's handprints or footprints. He brought one undusted bookshelf to his new home. It stands on the landing of the staircase, between floors, and is full of Red Sox memorabilia.

At the time Kal died, Heather lived with her parents. She and Kraig shared Kalahan amicably, but their relationship had deteriorated.

The Wednesday of that week, Kraig had Kalahan all day. They watched *Bear in the Big Blue House,* then ran some errands. Kalahan got a Happy Meal at McDonald's with a Beanie Baby rainbow snake as the toy. That afternoon, they played with Kalahan's Little People Barn and farm animals. The snake joined in.

When it was time for Kalahan's nap, Kraig put in a video of *Toy Story.* They climbed into the recliner's plush seat together. Kalahan fell asleep clutching his "cuddly," a rabbit-like plush toy named Carrots. In the late afternoon Heather came over to pick him up. Kraig woke Kal up and carried him through the snow out to her car. He had to get the car seat from his own car, which Heather strapped in. Kraig put Kal in the seat and Heather buckled his harness. Kraig kissed him and said good-bye. Kal's hands were full of toys he wanted with him. Heather drove off.

When she got to her parent's house twenty-five minutes later, she went to unbuckle Kalahan and found him limp. In a panic, she carried him to the porch and performed emergency CPR. He revived quickly. She called 911 and then left a message for Kraig. Immediately the word got out—around there, everyone is a volunteer firefighter—and neighbors showed up in their four-by-fours, offering to take them to the hospital. Kalahan seemed fine, briefly, but in the ambulance on the way to the hospital he again passed out on the paramedics. Again, they revived him. There was not an available room on the pediatrics ward, so they wheeled a bed into the toy room. Kalahan was lethargic and tired. Kraig had a pizza delivered. Kalahan ate a slice.

Kraig was given the third degree. What did you do today? What did he eat? Where in the apartment were you? Did Kalahan go near the cupboards?

The hospital began running tests. Over the next two days, they found absolutely nothing unusual. Kalahan had not suffocated or inhaled carbon dioxide, and he had not choked. By Thursday night he was completely himself again, pulling all the toy drawers out of the cabinets in his makeshift hospital room. On Friday afternoon the hospital discharged him. Neither Kraig nor Heather was happy about this, but the doctors insisted they could not keep Kalahan any longer. Heather took him home to her parents' house, which was near the hospital.

Late Sunday morning Kraig called Kalahan on the phone. Kalahan told him he was tired and was going to take a nap. He told his dad he loved him. Kraig said he would see him later.

Kalahan's nap lasted two hours. Heather and her parents and her sister remained on the couch downstairs. Heather went up and checked on him every fifteen minutes. The last time, she asked her sister to go check. Her sister screamed. He was not breathing. Heather performed emergency CPR, but it was too late.

Kraig got the call from his father.

Even with the most senseless tragedies, you at least know how someone died. You struggle with why, and what you could have done differently. But you know the cause of death. Kraig did not have the benefit of such a cause. Kalahan was too old for sudden infant death syndrome, which does not happen to babies older than twelve months. And in the absence of a medical explanation, devastating rumors surfaced in his community about Heather. In his heart, Kraig was convinced she did nothing wrong. But for that first year, he could not help but be suspicious. The detective on the case told Kraig that he was investigating Heather. Friends recounted incidents where she had seemed to be an unwilling mother. An incident in which Kalahan had gotten food poisoning and vomited became fodder for speculation.

This niggling suspicion ate him alive.

Kraig telephoned the New Hampshire medical examiner every week. "Did you find something?" he would ask. Usually he just talked to the receptionist, but he had to try. During the autopsy they had ruled out choking, suffocating, and obvious poisons, but they continued to run one toxicology test after another on the blood and tissue samples. They told him it would take four months to run all their tests. He continued to call, and they never minded. A year went by, and the police investigation was closed. Finally, Kraig got the medical examiner on the line.

"I've just got to ask, Doctor. I have these scenarios planted in my head by friends—scenarios that they think your tests would never pick up—"

The examiner cut him off sharply. "Listen to me, Kraig. Before I became the medical examiner here, I spent fifteen years doing this in New York. I've seen every possible case. Everything your friends could imagine, I have seen. Down there, parents kill their kids more often than you want to know. We have tests for everything. I guarantee you, if there was something to be found, we would have the police and the television cameras on her in an instant. I am not ignoring your son. The toxicology tests have been run by some of the best hospitals in the country. You need to put your suspicions aside."

That phone call was a pivot point. The scenarios stopped looping in Kraig's mind. The examiner's statement took their place, a mantra to heal by: *If there was something there, he would have found it.* It was reassuring. It got him off the hook. The doctor gave him permission, perhaps, to accept that he may never know the answer. Finding the answer to what killed Kal was something Kraig could never succeed in. Accepting that it was a certifiable mystery was hard, but it was within his control. Kraig found the strength to stop drinking for lunch.

There were other things that helped Kraig survive.

Let me start with two you might overlook, because they seem so ordinary.

1. He had three kids who needed him.
2. He believed in Heaven.

Though Kraig had stopped going to church regularly after his mom died (because she was the one who had always taken him), he always believed in God, and for whatever reason, when Kal died Kraig never looked at it like God had done something to him. Maybe more importantly, he firmly believed in heaven. The morning after Kalahan's death, Kraig was lying in the darkness unable to sleep, and he asked God to send him a sign that Kalahan had made it to heaven and was all right. A moment later a light shone through every window of the room. Kraig started crying and felt a satisfaction and indescribable warmth. He did not really believe in miracles, and if this had happened to anyone else, he would suspect there was a truck outside with its headlights on. All that mattered was that Kraig believed his son was in a safe place, and that one day, after his own death, he would be able to see his son again. You can imagine how much this helps him.

This belief was probably worth a thousand hours of therapy.

Kraig does not attend church. He was invited by many people to attend their services, but he doesn't really like being part of a group. This is somewhat out of character, because Kraig really enjoys company. But he prefers connecting with God all by himself, in his own way. Every night for years he has walked his dogs, and during that time he says things to Kalahan, and to his mom, and to God, and he feels like he is close to them.

As for his three older children, they gave him a reason to stay alive. His oldest daughter, Alyssa, put her grief into worrying for Kraig. She would spend her school lunch money on telephone calls from the pay phone in the school hallway, just to make sure he was okay. She now lives with Kraig.

His middle daughter, Kaitlin, kept to herself and guarded her feelings. She was hard to read. But his son Alex had it really hard. He was already a child with a nearly traumatizing fear of darkness and claustrophobia. After Kalahan died, Alex was afraid to fall asleep, for fear he, too, might not wake up. Ultimately he needed to be treated for sleep deprivation. He gets counseling through his school.

Their mother says that Kraig has turned into a great parent since Kalahan died. Before that, providing for the kids was a much higher priority than spending time with them. When they were young, he couldn't wait until they were eighteen and he would be done being a parent. There is no doubt that before Kalahan died, Kraig looked at his first batch of kids like you look at a first batch of pancakes—with the guilt that you could have done a lot better. When Kalahan died, he was suddenly grateful to have kids to embrace. Now he builds his life around their schedules, coaches Kaitlin's soccer team, and spends countless hours playing catch with Alex. He also looks for occasions, like AIDS walks, to take his kids to so that they can learn that they are not the only family that has suffered.

Recently one of his friends with a newborn said with some envy, "Man, in a few years you're done!"

"I don't ever want to be done," Kraig answered. "I want it to last forever."

We all have a need to tell stories, and in these stories we have a need to connect the dots, to pin down causation. It is particularly true with a story like Kraig's, because nobody wants to imagine this could happen to their child. By forcing an answer on the mystery, we defuse it. We get our distance from it. I've found that when I tell Kraig's story to people, they either don't ask any questions at all and change the subject or they drill down, looking for the clue that allows them to attribute blame. And if casual listeners feel this, imagine how Kraig felt. Imagine how intense his need was to have his son's death explained.

But in every family, there are pieces of the story that are ultimately inexplicable. We can't blame our parents for everything. We can't blame ourselves for everything. In the same way that marriages can survive better if we expect there will be differences, we can heal from the past better if we accept that crucial periods might never be explainable. Being in a family teaches us to accept events beyond our understanding, and if you can do so, you will be more comfortable with your experience of everything outside your family, too. Kraig really only began his healing process on the day he was set straight by the New Hampshire medical examiner. On that day he stopped trying to make life answerable to his desire for it to make sense.

A couple of months later, the New Hampshire medical examiner called Kraig with a suggestion. He said a study had been done on a few dozen cases like Kalahan's. A new term was being used: *sudden unexplained death in childhood.* It's a diagnosis of exclusion. It's important to use it as a surrogate diagnosis to help with future analysis. Frequently medical examiners write down "suffocation" as the cause of death when they have nothing else. If they wrote down "SUDC," then those cases could be tracked and studied—and maybe one day potential causes might be understood.

Kraig logged on to the SUDC website that night. He wrote the organization an e-mail asking them for any kind of support they had to offer. He was particularly concerned with how Kal's death had affected his three older children. He really did not think this organization would have the time of day for an uneducated cashier in New Hampshire, but it was worth a try. To his surprise, the SUDC director called him at home that very night. She listened to his story for two hours. During that conversation, Kraig's life began to change. He was realizing that it would be okay if the worst thing that ever happened simply did not have an explanation. And he could see, for the first time, how some good might come from Kalahan's death. Not enough good to ever balance out the loss, mind you, but *some* good. It helped him so much to know that he was not the only one in the world to have this happen, and he wanted to be there for the next person who needed to know that.

People close to Kraig could not see the point. Only forty cases had ever been classified as SUDC. It wasn't like Kraig or the organization was ever going to prevent a senseless death. To Kraig's friends, it seemed like nothing more than a way to wallow in the morbid past.

The SUDC organization began hosting online chats for parents. Kraig would log on to the computer and just observe, afraid to type. Kraig felt as though he had found a home among parents dealing with the true unknown. It gave him somewhere to put his energy.

He wrote me at that time, "People say that when you lose someone, a piece of you dies as well. I wonder, in some way, whether you don't gain something as well. Sort of a connection you wouldn't have had otherwise. I wonder if too much emphasis is placed on the loss and not enough, if any, on that which we gain. If life were easy we wouldn't have an appreciation for the good times. There would be nothing to compare them to."

If there is something to learn from Kraig, I think it's the way he let this idea steer him—that something good should come from Kal's death. Nobody told him to do this. He didn't read it anywhere. It just felt right.

One of the places Kalahan loved was the Carter Hill apple orchards up the mountain from Concord. They welcomed visitors and had several short trails through the woods. Kraig wondered if one of these trails might be dedicated to his son. He contacted the owner, who gave the okay. The trail begins beside a perfect pond that reflects the skyline of the trees. It empties out onto the back side of the orchards. The setting is picnic-perfect. Since Kalahan was cremated, this has provided Kraig a place to reflect on their time together. Every year, on Kalahan's birthday, he brings the kids here to let loose some balloons.

There was always someone in his life saying he was going about it wrong. He has friends who did not agree with how much he cared about this trail. They thought naming a trail was merely symbolic and he was using a superficial project to avoid dealing with the hurt inside. A lot of people wanted him to stop, stop everything, and get counseling. But just because many people heal that way doesn't mean everyone does. Kraig needed life to go on. He needed projects, and he needed the company of people. He is a person who heals from the outside in. Many do.

To Kraig, having this trail dedicated to his son feels like a monumental achievement. The people who get things named after them are governors and mayors, civil rights leaders and tribal chiefs. Famous people. People whose lives had a real impact. To have Kalahan included in that group seemed not insignificant. Kal had made a difference in his short time here, even if it was just in the heart of his father. It meant a lot to have that impact publicly recognized.

So how else, he wondered, might something good come of it?

Ever since the tragedy, he found himself wishing he could make a difference in the lives of children. Ideally, he wanted to be a schoolteacher. This desire led him to begin a difficult journey, away from the security of the grocery chain where he had worked since he was fourteen. His first step out was a failure. He took a job as a dump-truck driver, on the promise that his hours would be short and he could take community college classes at night toward a teaching credential. The hours were not short at all; he never had time for a class. So he quit that and started a combination of part-time jobs, including substitute teaching, summer-camp counseling, and doing odd jobs for his landlord. His income had fallen by two-thirds, and it was on faith alone that he persevered. Then he took a job at the local racquet club—at first just for a little extra cash. But it has grown into a full-time job, and he has given up the other work. The club runs a summer camp and after-school programs, so he is with kids daily. He has full benefits and enjoys having less stress in his day. His hours are flexible. Plans for college have been scrapped until his kids have moved on.

Staffing the sign-in counter and handing out sweat towels may not sound like such a great outcome. But at the time Kalahan died, Kraig was working sixty-five hours a week and commuting two hours a day. Now he works thirty-five or forty hours just minutes from his house. This has allowed him to be with his kids whenever they need him. He has the mental energy to focus not so much on what he is doing with his life but how he is living it. He treats everybody with respect and can enjoy an impromptu conversation.

Kraig has always needed to talk about his experience, right from the very first day. He wanted to telephone everybody, while Kalahan's mother didn't want to call anybody. Kraig insisted on a wake, while she couldn't bear to be seen in public. Even today, when someone asks him how many kids he has, he will answer "Four," and when he is asked their ages, he explains the early exit of his youngest. Complete strangers get walloped with something they are never prepared to handle. He doesn't push his story on anyone, but he rarely conceals the event just to maintain pleasantries.

Is this healthy?

His friends grew weary of hearing him bring it up. They feared he was stuck in the past. They wanted him to move on. I think they were being unfair. It makes them uncomfortable to be constantly reminded. They *can* push it away. Kraig can't. Pushing something like that out of his mind is simply impossible for him. So he has taken a strategy that is different from theirs, but more effective for his circumstances. He has integrated Kalahan's death into his identity. Rather than trying to forget, he has let it shape him. He is not stuck in the past; rather, he is focused on making sure something good comes from his time here on Earth. He could have just been a cashier, a crummy dad, a drunk, and a broken man. But he is not. His life means something now. He feels he has a purpose, and that purpose is to bear witness to what happened.

For the last year Kraig has been raising money for the SUDC foundation. This has taken him to some interesting places. When General Wesley Clark was in Concord to campaign for president, Kraig heard he wanted a place to swim laps. So he hooked Clark up with the racquet club, and he was rewarded with three minutes of face time to tell the candidate about SUDC. Then Kraig got to attend a convention in New Jersey on SIDS, where he met many other parents who had lost a child. Every year, the radio host Don Imus does a fund-raiser for SIDS, and Kraig took his oldest daughter down to staff the phones. Through those contacts, he learned that Don Imus runs a camp for kids who have lost a sibling. Kraig applied to attend, and last summer he and his oldest daughter went to the Imuses' ranch for a week. He figured it was a big summer camp with dozens of kids, but instead he encountered five kids with their five parents, sitting at the dinner table every night with Don Imus and his wife. Kraig revered Imus. He had listened to his show for years. Now he was sitting at dinner with the guy!

Over the last two years, Kalahan has begun to rest easier in Kraig's mind. The fund-raising has provided an appropriate outlet, so he doesn't need to bring it up at times when it just makes everyone feel awkward. The trail is a permanent memorial, softening the need for him to be the guy who always remembers.

His second chance at life did not die with Kalahan. Kalahan gave him *this* chance, through both life and death, and Kraig has not screwed it up.

Kraig had a girlfriend last year. I met her and spoke with her separately. In many ways, she was great for him. She worked at the state hospital counseling troubled kids. She fed him studies on how death in a family affects children. She encouraged him when he talked about attending college. Around her, Kraig didn't feel pressure to always be one of the guys.

But over time, she was a great source of agony, primarily because she came from a world of professional intervention, while Kraig had pursued his own layman's way. She warned that if he did not put his life in professional hands, he was a living time bomb. It was clear to her that she was a distant third after his kids and Kalahan's memory. From her point of view, Kraig was blocked from embracing the rest of his life—principally, her. She made him feel bad enough about this that he decided to find a grief counselor—just to shut her up. His insurance would pay for it. A doctor at the racquet club highly recommended a doctor in Concord named Rick Axtman. He had dealt with a lot of families in which someone had committed suicide.

Kraig started seeing the grief counselor. Eventually, Dr. Axtman told him he was fine and doing well, with one exception—he needed to take a break from his girlfriend.

"You just need a little validation, someone who supports you and recognizes you're doing something positive."

Kraig took his advice.

Nobody has a monopoly on healing.

Kraig still sees Dr. Axtman once a month. It's now on his dime. Dr. Axtman has told him several times, "You don't need to come anymore, you know."

"That's okay," Kraig said. "I like having someone to talk to."

"All right. What should we talk about today?"

"Can I tell you about my dad?"

"Sure. What about him?"

"After Mom died, my dad worked hard, at menial jobs, to provide for me, but wasn't around to do any parenting. After work, he always had a beer in his hand. He was the guy in the shadow of the bar, a faint presence, kept to himself. He never talked about Mom. If he tried, he always choked up. I knew the barest of facts. But about a year after Kal died, he started opening up. He told me how they met, and about her homeland in Hartland, Vermont, and how involved she was in the church choir and church suppers. And he started to change, to seize his life finally. He met a woman online who lives in England. You know how suspicious that is, but she visited here several times, and she is really nice, and now Dad is moving to England. My dad! He's happy! I thought I would never see it. And I have to think Kal had something to do with that."

———

One well-known writing exercise recommended by the teacher John Gardner in his book *The Art of Fiction* instructs writers to describe an old barn from the point of view of a man whose son has died, without ever mentioning the son or his death. The goal of the exercise is to learn to describe objects in such a way as to convey the psychological state of the observer. I would do the exercise every year to test my progress.

There are a lot of old barns in the sleepy hamlets of New Hampshire. And I can report now that when Kraig looks at a barn, he doesn't notice the aging wood any differently than you or I. The colors are not more vivid or more dull. He doesn't think the barn can never be repaired. Those are literary projections. All those exercises I wrote were bunk. Kraig just sees a barn, like any of us, and he thinks only one thing: *Man, Kalahan would have liked to go in there.*

Kraig would want something good to come of his story being in this book. If he were standing in front of you right now, he would feel bad that you had to hear about such a terrible event. He would sympathize with you, with the strange feeling in your gut. Tonight, when he walks his dogs, he would pray that you're doing well and making it through whatever troubles you.

Maybe you are one of those many people who have come to him and admitted they lost someone they loved. If so, he wants you to know you are not alone.

Maybe right now, you feel like you haven't been through anything. If so, don't worry that you don't know what to say. Saying something is not necessary.

Maybe you are someone who has been through something and can't even explain what it was. You can't even explain what caused it. If so, he wants you to know that this doesn't have to be the end of the story. Rather than just try to get past it and move on, ask if anything good can come from it, anything at all. He doesn't believe that everything happens for a reason, or that God has time to put it right in front of you. You have to go looking for it. You have to look hard.

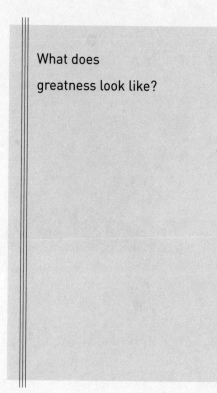

What does

greatness look like?

Some Thoughts

Mary Naomi Garrett

The most amazing thing is that, for all the people profiled here, not one thought that his or her life was the kind of story that deserved to be in a book. They were amused by my continued interest. They knew I was interviewing dozens of potential stories, and most doubted they would make the cut. To be in a book, they figured, you were supposed to be famous. You were supposed to be worth billions, or be a special witness to history, or be a doctor with a revolutionary new theory. *Books aren't written about people like me, are they?* they wondered.

How easy it is to forget what is truly worth celebrating.

In the end all books boil down to one thing: They offer a philosophy of how to live. My beliefs are simple: The quiet journeys depicted here are worthy of commemoration and celebration. Their triumphs are as noble as anything that brings fame and attention. These people indulged me not for the glory of being in a book, but because I convinced each of them that their story would help other people in similar straits. They were unsure how it might do so. They felt their lives were too troubled to be models. Most of the time that is exactly what appealed to me—the struggle. Yet there were times I lost my bearings on what constituted a worthwhile story, and I wondered whether I ought to include people whose lives had been so hard.

Consider the example of Mary Garrett. She is eighty years old. She grew up during the Depression, in a tar-paper shack in the Cincinnati neighborhood of Lincoln Heights. Her mother cleaned houses. Mary got herself educated and she was intending to be a schoolteacher, when she met her husband, Leonard, in a bar. She ended up having eight children in eleven years while working at the post office. The neighbors warned she would end up on welfare. Instead, Mary found scholarships for her children to attend the best private schools in Cincinnati. Mary never pushed her kids. All she did was ask them, "Did you try your best?" She gave her best, and they gave their best, and six of her eight children ended up getting scholarships to Ivy League colleges. She taught them to transcend race and poverty. She treated each child individually. One was interested in television and radio, so she sent him to a good vocational school. Today he is a cameraman for ESPN. Another loved art; he went to Williams as an art major and is a musician today. The other kids are doctors and managers—and more important, flat-out great people.

Mary, meanwhile, didn't forget her promise to become a school-teacher. At the age of thirty-seven she began teaching, and she gave thirty years of service to the neediest of Cincinnati's public schools. The day after she retired, in 1999, she was right back at her school, William Hart Taft Elementary, putting in a full day's work as a volunteer.

Their challenges came by the dozens. Through it all, there was never a spell of years when Mary lost hope or stopped trying. There was no villain in the picture, no antagonist to prove wrong. Her husband died in 1983. Mary just kept showing up, trying her best, day by day.

She is not done living up to her promise. Today Mary lives in Atlanta in order to be near her daughter and grandchildren. Three nights a week Mary tutors her grandchildren. Every other month she rides the Greyhound bus to Orlando to help her oldest daughter with her boys. The Garrett family is spread from Seattle to Switzerland, and they are all independent, but they are emotionally close, and they talk by telephone constantly. They support one another financially when necessary. Neither the great distances nor their great successes have pushed them apart. Mary still tithes to her church in Cincinnati. They've even hung on to their old phone number. Today it rings in the home of Mary's son.

Mary, in my estimation, is one of the greatest mothers in the world. Her children think so, too. They are ages forty-two through fifty-two, and they still call her "Mommy."

Here's the thing: Mary was a little confused by my interest in her, because there were details that clouded the picture considerably. Details that might have disqualified her, if I was looking for the goddess mother who embraces all, who soothes all, who torments none. I'll give you three examples. Ask yourself whether these disqualify her, in your judgment, from being a great mother.

First, Mary is one of the quirkier women I've met. She has a set of traits that would drive many people crazy. To start, she refuses to fly in planes. She also refuses to drive—she has never once in her life driven a car. She gets everywhere by city bus and Greyhound. She has worn makeup only once in her life, causing her daughters some torment when they wanted her to be presentable at a big event. She also has terrible phobias—she has claustrophobia, which is why she hates planes, and she has unreasonable fears of snakes and thunderstorms. She is an unusual bird. One of her favorite meals of all time was a hunk of cow liver sautéed in Vaseline. Her favorite activity is to attend a basketball game. Her second favorite activity is to watch a basketball game on the television. Does she drive her kids crazy with all her oddities? A little.

Second, Mary never hugged her children, and she never told them she loved them. She still has a hard time doing so today. When I learned this, it completely threw me. It was inconsistent with the imaginary "great mother" I have in my mind's eye. Mary said she came from an era where people didn't do those things, and they didn't know that doing so was important. So I checked with her children, and they made it clear to me—yes, their mom never pronounced her love out loud, but her love was *never* in doubt. They always felt loved. It took me a while, but I got over my perception problem. I've learned that greatness can defy expectation.

Third, there is the mystery of what happened to Mary's son Timmy. The Garretts do not know if Timmy is alive or not. He was an exceedingly bright child who went to Brown University and wanted to be a lawyer. During law school, he developed some form of mental illness. Mary tried to get him help, but he threatened to kill her, demanded money from her, robbed her house, and fled to New York. They have been looking for him ever since, assuming he is either destitute or dead. You can imagine how much this hurts.

For a long time I found this piece of the story wildly distracting—it did not fit in with the rosy picture of this family rising out of that tar-paper shack and becoming such notable people. It wasn't like I saw anything to blame in Mary's actions. They all tried to help Timmy, but he ran and disappeared. Still, it was an unseemly detail—not the sort of event, I once thought, that goes on in great resilient families. I took nearly a hundred pages of notes on Mary, but for months I wondered if I could put her in this book. I didn't know how. How could I tell her amazing story without also telling the truth about her quirks, her reserved love, and her missing son? Would anyone still think she was so great?

We all have an imaginary great mother in our mind's eye, just as we have an imaginary definition of a great family. We imagine what it would be like to belong to such a family. No fights over the holidays. No getting on one another's nerves. Respect for individual identity. Mutual support, without being intrusive.

So many people believe they are disqualified from having a better family experience, primarily because they compare their own family with the mythic ideal, and their reality falls short. Is that a fair standard to judge against? By that yardstick, Mary Garrett would not look so great. Yet her deeds are unassailable. I have realized this book needs her, quirks and all.

This is how the three years of working on this book have changed me the most: What I hold in my mind's eye is no longer a naïve myth. By studying actual families and sorting for the great ones, I've discovered they do not resemble the imaginary family that once resided in my mind's eye. I've learned that painful and troubling things happen, even in great families. I've learned they still get in arguments and they still get their feelings hurt, but over time they overcome most of the challenges in their path. They may not be tolerant, but they eventually learn tolerance. They may try to control one another, but they eventually learn not to.

I've learned that what makes a family great has nothing to do with whether you live in the family-friendly suburbs, or whether the grand-parents are still around, or whether there's never been a divorce. The ideal family does not fit any demographic test. Rather, most of our fam-ilies are on a trajectory, evolving into the form that fits into the ever-changing society around us. Some families are ahead, some are bringing up the rear, but the path is the same.

This has helped me. I used to compare my family with that mythic one in my mind's eye, and it was an unfair comparison. When I com-pare us with real families, though, I see we are doing okay. We are get-ting there. We are closer than I thought.

Was there nothing more earth-shattering? Is that all I have to offer, in this golden age of shiny ideas—a change in perception? How unfash-ionable!

Sometimes I'm a little embarrassed that after three years of research, all I have to offer are such quiet conclusions. I did not turn up a won-der drug that makes family trouble go away. I did not find some scien-tist with a miracle machine that promises to change family life as we know it. Counseling is the only new weapon we've created in a hun-dred years. But even in counseling, the tools we have are ancient ones. They are these: taking responsibility and granting forgiveness; discern-ment and awareness; willingness to change and acceptance that things won't change; honesty and tact; perception and empathy; compromise; listening; communication. That's really it. What we expect from family is changing, but the means that get us there aren't.

Another way I've been unfashionable is in telling these stories with hardly a dust of irony. Did I miss the memo that we like our family sto-ries funny?

Wrapping these stories in irony would have been like giving the Inuit the gift of snow. When it comes to our families, we already have all the irony we will ever need. It has become fashionable to use irony as our first and only reaction. We've surrounded ourselves with an early-alert Ironic Shields Defense System, making sure nobody gets through. We have accepted, too easily, that nothing is going to change—that the people who bug us are *always* going to bug us, as if we lack any control over our experience.

I hope what these stories demonstrate is love. Not fakey romantic love, and not love that's perfect or anything close to idealistic. Rather, how you get through life with the ones you love. This might lack the sizzle of a grand theory, but it makes up for it with veracity. It might lack the comfort of a temporary cure-all, but it makes up for it with integrity. In five years what I have written here will not be out-of-date. It will still come back to those basic rudimentary tools of engagement.

In the end, the little tidbits of wisdom buried in these stories won't be remembered, anyway. The stories will fade, and even the people will fade. What I will remember is the images. Those, I will never forget. James Louie finding that bracelet in his wall. Rosa Gonzalez touching her nose. Young Andrew Bennett running his hand along the chain buried in his elm tree. Brian Olowude inventing his imaginary palace to calm his nightmares. Andy Matsui's Standing House for his orchids. The silent car rides. The river of family life that sucks us into its holes. And this next one, the tornado that blew the roof off Charlie Taylor's home in Birmingham, Alabama. And Charlie Taylor, mowing his wife's lawn, earning his way back.

When should our love

be sympathetic and

when should it be tough?

The Tornado

It seemed just a second ago.

Could it really have been so many years? Charlie Taylor wondered.

Just a second ago, Robin was eight and Paul was thirteen, and they were all at the beach in Gulf Shores. Charlie had put his work down for a week—really put it down, didn't touch it. He remembered Robin running up and down that beach, giggling, deliciously happy despite nothing more to entertain her than some white sand and two-foot surf. The next day he rented a flats boat and taught Paul to catch the flounder that were migrating from the bay out to deep water. They used finger mullet, and they hooked six flounder (only got two to the boat), three reds, and a small bonnethead shark, which Paul wanted to keep. Man, that was a day to remember. What Charlie remembered more than anything was the look on his wife's—Susan's—face. All week long she had this look, as though she were a happy white cloud. There are a few things that go straight into a man's heart, and one of those is seeing the weight of it all gone from his wife's face.

He would get back there. Charlie vowed he would find a way back. His situation did not look good, he had to admit. It looked downright abysmal. But he had given Susan twenty-one good years and two great children. And he knew that no matter how hurt she was, in the end those twenty-one years would count for something.

Man, he had screwed it up. There was nothing else to say about it. He had *screwed it up!*

When they got through this—whenever that would be (one year, five years, ten years?)—he would take Susan back to Gulf Shores. More than just one week a year. He would find a way. And he would buy a boat. Not a flats, maybe a center-console V-hull, get out on the water, nothing like it. Nothing like that feeling of heading home over blue water. Salt spray tossed around by a ten-mile wind, a bait well full of kings, a family smelling of sunscreen, a smile on her face.

He would get back there.

Nothing else mattered. Not the baby grand in their great room, not the fancy antiques they had spent years collecting, not being senior vice president at the firm—none of that tripped Charlie's trigger anymore. Not even his 6,100-square-foot house. It was just stuff. Stuff! Susan could have all of it. But eventually, he would convince her to get rid of all of it. Sell it, donate it, whatever. Get lean and mean again. Just like he was here, at the Chardonnay Apartments, with a Wal-Mart card table for a dining table, a single couch Susan had let him take, and a mattress on the floor in the one bedroom. They could live like this again, couldn't they?

Despite the walking wreck he had turned into, Charlie was doing one thing right. He made sure he saw both his kids every single day. He drove them to school in the mornings, and he coached Robin's soccer team. One day Charlie took Paul fishing on the Cahaba River, which runs right through Birmingham.

"Is there anything your mom needs?" Charlie asked his son.

"You asked me that yesterday, Dad. I don't think she needs anything."

"How is she?"

"She cries for days, Dad. But she doesn't talk to me about it. She says it's between her and you. She says it's got nothing to do with me and Robin."

"She's right."

"I still think I should have come to you when I read those e-mails."

"No, you did the right thing, going to your mother. You were protecting her."

"I didn't know it would turn into this. I thought you guys would just have a fight."

"Paul, you did the right thing. *I'm* the one who screwed up. But I love your mom and I'm not going to let her take off."

"She's pretty pissed off, Dad."

"I know that."

"I don't see what you can do about it."

"I promise you, Paul. I promise you I am not going to let her take off."

"All right."

A minute later Paul sent Charlie right back to square one. "Dad, how could you do this?"

"Paul, you're sixteen. It's easy for you to look at me and ask how with disbelief. But when you face the challenges a grown man has, you'll understand better why. I don't always make the right decision. I don't always do the right thing."

When Charlie dropped Paul off that night, Susan opened the front door for her son, probably just so she could give Charlie an icy look that said *Eat shit and die.*

Susan had always made it absolutely clear to Charlie that if he ever cheated on her, she would divorce him. She had watched her mother put up with her father's affairs for fear of being out on her own without any money. Susan's mother let herself be trampled, and Susan was too tough to let that happen all over again. She vowed to protect herself and the kids financially. She did not relent in insisting on a full and formal divorce: half of everything.

Charlie pleaded with her. *It was only four times. I don't love her. She came after me. I'm a guy. It was flattering to know I still had it at forty-four. I was vulnerable. My dad's dying of cancer, Susan—it was an escape from thinking about my old man wincing in pain. I screwed up, Susan. We can find the best marriage counselor in Birmingham. Please, Susan.*

Susan had no intention of ever being with Charlie again. *You killed my feelings. I don't know you anymore. I thought you were different from all those men out there. If a man I loved could do this, then men are worse than I thought.*

Susan was getting all sorts of advice from friends, too—most told her to welcome Charlie back with open arms.

"No!" she insisted. "That's not the way it goes."

Charlie realized he had only one option: to give Susan exactly what she wanted. He would respect the vow she had made to herself and he would not fight the divorce. The sooner the divorce was finalized and the sooner Susan felt protected, the quicker he could get her to let him back in. So he fired his lawyer and he sent all of his financials over to Susan's lawyer with the instruction "Take all you want." Then he went to Canterbury Methodist Church and kneeled before God and begged for forgiveness and bargained for his life. You do not normally kneel at the altar in a Methodist church, but nobody said anything because they thought Charlie was praying for his dying father.

"God, if you can see me through this, if you can put it back together, I will never do it again. It seems crazy to let her go and divorce me, but I'm trusting you that it's the right thing. Thank you for making me a good husband again and a good father again. Please, God, thank you for making this work. I am in your hands. Please, God, don't take Susan away from me."

The divorce was finalized by a judge in the fall. On the way out of the courthouse, Charlie asked Susan if he could take her on a date.

"Call me," Susan said. "I'll let you know if I can fit you in."

The next morning Charlie was parked in the driveway, ready to drive his kids to school. That afternoon he came by to clean the pool.

"What are you doing?" Susan demanded.

"The pool's a mess, Susan."

"Well. You can't come in the house," Susan said.

The next day Charlie was back to mow the lawn. Charlie knew his wife could ditch him and have a date the next day—she was that attractive. But she wasn't dating anyone. That meant something.

Soon the lawn had never been in such good condition, for Charlie was out there three times a week, pushing that mower, sweating, working for his forgiveness, every drop of sweat testifying to his commitment. Afterward, he sat on the steps of the garage. He must have been out there every day for a month when Susan finally came out with a mug of water. She sat down beside him. He got her to laugh, and then her anger came to the surface.

She said, "I want to hate you so bad. Why don't you just go away? You'd make this easier if you went away."

"I'm not going to go away, Susan. I love you, you love me, and we're going to make it."

Susan paused and tried to imagine it, but ran right back into her wall of pain. "I don't see how," she said sadly. "How could you do this?" she cried. "How could you hurt me this bad?"

"It's worth saving, Susan. I don't want another life. I don't want to be a single guy out on the prowl. I want to have dinner every night with my wife of twenty-one years."

The next week Susan and the kids were eating dinner while Charlie was out cleaning the pool. She took him a plate of food, covered in aluminum foil.

"Can I kiss you good night?" he tried.

"No. You go home."

He took his food back to the Chardonnay Apartments, where he had one fork and one knife, and sat at his card table. Hours later, he was in the driveway again, to take the kids to school. That became their routine—he worked for food. Charlie found a marriage counselor and made an appointment. The first appointment, Susan never showed. Nor the second. During the third appointment, Susan walked in. She was surprised to see that the counselor was a woman. She had figured it would be Charlie and another guy ganging up on her, making excuses for men.

"I went for the kids," Susan said several years later. "My kids needed two full-time parents. Paul was sixteen, and despite being a select-level player he hadn't made the high school soccer team, and I'd found some pot in his room. He didn't have a whole lot in his life but school, which he was never that great at—Charlie and I tutored him every night just to get C's. And Robin was eleven, and she was just starting to pull away from her friends, the future cheerleader crowd, and she was drawn to these other girls who wore black and smeared black eye shadow around their eyes. Nothing was wrong yet, they were just teens, but I could feel that they were vulnerable, that they were on the fence."

"Were you afraid Robin and Paul were reacting to the divorce?"

"I always insisted to the kids that they had a good dad and this was between me and him. Charlie was with them every day. We did what we could. We did not tell them we were divorced, but Paul found the papers in a drawer. We took Robin to a counselor to get her to try to talk about what we were going through. A divorce was unthinkable to her. She didn't want to hear it. She covered her face and her ears and refused to say a word."

So Susan relented and went to marriage counseling. One day the counselor turned to Susan and said, "I've met with this guy for several months. I think Charlie's genuinely remorseful. You've either got to get over it or tell him that you can't. In one direction or another, you've got to move on."

She turned to Charlie. "Everybody at church knows."

"Canterbury is not the only Methodist church in town."

Christmas of that year was upon them. Susan decided to let Charlie back into the house to sleep on the couch in the living room. At night, she locked the door to her bedroom.

Finally Charlie got Susan to go on a date. He drove her down toward Montgomery to the Wetumpka casinos. They got a room with a hot tub and ended up making love. Afterward, Susan cried and cried and cried.

In February, Charlie moved back upstairs into their bedroom.

"I give God the credit," Charlie said. "I give Susan the credit, too. She must love me a lot, because I really hurt her. We are closer for what we went through. She had a vow to herself, and I respected it and I took the consequences. That eventually impressed her, and she let me back into her life."

That spring Charlie bought a 1,900-square-foot condo at Gulf Shores. To afford it, he had to rent it out all but a few weeks a year. But he would figure it out. It was a stake, a foothold, and a sense of direction.

On Valentine's Day a year later, Charlie and Susan went back to Canterbury Methodist and remarried. They went alone, without the kids, using the associate minister as their witness. When they walked out of there, Charlie figured they had put their bad times behind them. They had hoped to go to lunch together, but they had been called the day before by Robin's school and were asked to come in for a meeting. Apparently Robin, despite scoring nearly perfectly on her tests, had stopped doing any homework or classwork and was about to receive F's in every class. Also, the day before, Charlie had found a hollowed-out pen stuffed with pot on Paul's desk. Charlie had denied him use of his car for a week and had given Paul a speech about how Charlie had been a teen once, too.

Maybe they weren't in the clear just yet, Charlie realized.

In Charlie's gut he felt like he had scared his kids to death and he had knocked himself off the pedestal they put him on, but despite that, some good had come of it. *Because he and Susan had made it back.* In so doing, he had showed his kids how not to run from a problem, how to work through it, how to hang in there and be there every day and just keep trying. Charlie hoped that when his kids did run into hard times, whenever that was, they would remember their dad in the backyard, mowing that lawn, sticking it out. He hoped they would remember that. He hoped that would sink in.

If there were a motto for Charlie Taylor's life, it would be *He never saw it coming.*

Charlie is an insurance broker. The main point he tries to impress upon his clients is that no matter how you might think you have it all figured out, *you don't.* Life sends things your way that are simply not in the playbook. His own life is a shining example.

Charlie Taylor did not have a screwy childhood. His parents might as well have been Ward and June Cleaver. For fifty-seven years they lived happily married in one single house. "I put my parents through absolutely *nothing,*" Charlie insisted. Any trouble he tasted, he managed to keep out of their sight. Charlie went off to college at Auburn, and he thought he had it all figured out—"the stupidity of youth," he laughs. He proposed to his college sweetheart upon graduation, and he figured they would marry and have kids and spend at least fifty-seven years together, same as it ever was.

The marriage was all planned. Betty had been given her wedding shower and unwrapped the gifts. Charlie had paid for the bridesmaids' dresses. Twelve hundred cocktail napkins had been printed with CHARLIE & BETTY in the wedding colors. The last thing Charlie ever expected was that he would find himself thinking about this woman who lived downstairs, Susan. He'd had pizza with Susan a couple of times—just a friend—and then she stayed away from him because he was getting married and it wasn't right. Charlie wondered: Was he just experiencing cold feet? Was there something special about Susan? He told his preacher first. When he told Betty, she slugged him.

But he married Susan not four months later.

Just like Charlie, Susan came from a middle-class, small-town Southern family. They thought they would get pregnant right away, and they did—but the egg implanted in the tube, and that tube collapsed after the surgery. Then a cyst took the other tube. The surgeons were in Susan every six months. Her stomach was carved into a smiley face. Charlie remembers the hurt on Susan's face, and the guilt she wrongly carried. At church, Susan would have to get up and leave during christenings for new children. Charlie took her to the best doctors he could find. For two years, those doctors tried to unblock the first tube.

A lawyer arranged for them to get Paul. They got the call to meet at a Hardee's—in one hour. They rushed there in their van. Paul was two days old, bundled up in a hospital blanket.

Five years later they got Robin through St. Peter's foster home. Robin was three weeks old.

"When we got Paul and Robin, I smacked myself on the head. Now I get it. Now I understand. Maybe this is what we went through all that for. Because if it had gone like clockwork, I wouldn't have *my* kids."

Charlie Taylor kept trying to live a perfectly normal life, but surprises continued coming his way. The trick to life, for a guy like him, is learning to embrace all the pieces that don't go according to plan.

A good example was the tornado that hit them right before dinner, a few years back when they lived over in Oak Grove. There was no siren warning. The lights flickered, the sky went black, and the windows starting sucking in and out. Charlie had about three seconds to act. He pushed Paul and Robin into a windowless bathroom, then he tackled Susan and pinned her to the floor. They heard a sound like a train. Lumber shot through the air, impaling the walls. Then the roof exploded and disappeared. Charlie rose up and yelled out to the kids. Paul returned, "Yeah, we're okay!"

Charlie had never been so grateful—never so absolutely in touch with what really mattered. The story of his whole adult life was encapsulated in those eight seconds. When those eight seconds began, Charlie considered his house his bragging right, a monument to all he had accomplished in his career. When those eight seconds were over, the house was meaningless rubble, but he had never loved his kids so hard.

The tornado spared the house right next door. A few gutters were torn off; that was it.

"You never know why it hits one house and spares another," Charlie counseled. "That's life. You do everything you can to prepare. You think you have the angles covered. And stuff still happens."

Birmingham, for instance, was supposed to be one of the top places in the country to raise kids. Among the neighborhoods and suburbs of Birmingham, Mountain Brook was supposed to be *the best.* It had the kind of houses you want, the quiet streets you want. It's safe to play on the sidewalks, you know your neighbors, the schools are good—when you raise your kids here, you think you're doing right by them. You think your kids can't possibly get in much trouble here.

"But then," Charlie warned, "there are a lot of parents around here who work too hard and then feel guilty about it and just want to be their kids' friend. So these kids are spoiled. They've got a lot of cash in their pockets, despite nobody making them work. And it starts to become common for these kids, if they want to party, to rent the field house or the country club for celebrations. And it steamrolls, until parents are renting out the country club for every birthday. Soon Robin's fourteen-year-old girlfriends are renting limos for dances. Everyone's drinking, everyone's screwing—and you finally wake up and say, *Damn, Charlie! A kid can get into a whole heck of a lot of trouble in*

Mountain Brook! In fact, when your kids get to a certain age, it seems there isn't a single thing to do here *but* get in trouble."

Charlie always worried Paul might fall in with the wrong crowd. Like many teens, Paul had long ago decided his parents were idiots. If Susan commented on how nice a day it was, Paul would retort, "Oh, she thinks it's a *nice* day." Paul was a decent kid, but not a natural student. He wasn't going to college. If there was an antidote to trouble, Charlie figured, it was having a job. Paul had been working at the Fairfield Inn since he was sixteen; Charlie insisted on it. Paul could build a nice résumé in the hospitality business. When he graduated from high school, Paul went to full-time at the Marriott Courtyard and moved in with his girlfriend in the West End. Charlie figured his son was doing all right. Whose kid doesn't try pot? Charlie didn't know that a maintenance guy at the Courtyard had given Paul coke in exchange for using his car to make drug pickups. Charlie didn't know that his son had been beaten and robbed at his girlfriend's apartment, or that he had found another source in Tarrant City and was blowing an eight-ball every night. Charlie just knew that Paul showed up one day saying his girlfriend had dumped him.

"Where are your clothes?"

"I'll get them next week," Paul said. In truth, Paul was afraid to go near West Birmingham again.

The Taylors welcomed their son back.

The motto had never been more appropriate. Charlie never saw it coming.

One day Charlie and a friend were headed to the range for target practice. Charlie kept a .357 magnum in the house. That gun, which was ten years old and in mint condition, meant a lot to him. When he found it missing, he went straight to Paul.

"Where is it!"

"I don't know," Paul said, cowering.

"You sold it, didn't you?"

"Yeah."

"After all we've been through, buddy? I can't believe it."

"I'm sorry. I'm sorry."

"I know you're broke, Paul, but if you need money you need to come to me!"

"I'm sorry, Dad."

"Can I buy the gun back?"

"No. It's gone."

"I can't believe you put another gun on the streets of Birmingham. Someone's probably going to get killed because of you. Did you think of that?"

What do you do, when you discover your son has stolen from you and put another gun on the streets? Charlie stewed for several sleepless nights. Was he wrong believing his son was basically a good kid? Charlie always thought Paul would be fine. The kid *knew* how to apply himself. By the age of eight, Paul was a black belt in karate. He was a darn good soccer player, and devoted to the game—Charlie had coached him himself. So was this just a phase every teen goes through? Or was Paul sliding into real trouble? Charlie had pulled a few fast ones on his own parents, but he could never imagine stealing from them.

Am I playing this right? Charlie kept wondering. *This is my son.*

Charlie had busted Paul for pot twice and drinking beer at least once while Paul was in high school. He'd taken Paul's car, and he'd grounded him, and he'd warned Paul how much the Mountain Brook police would love to find a drunk punk behind the wheel of a car. Charlie had tempered that toughness with kinship: "Paul, I was young once. You're not putting anything by me, you know? Just take it easy with this stuff." He let Paul know it was wrong, but he also let Paul know he was still loved.

Should he have been tougher?

A scary thought entered Charlie's mind. Maybe he was so grateful that Susan had forgiven him he was too willing to forgive his son. Susan had made Charlie suffer the consequences before forgiving him. Maybe if Charlie had been stricter . . . maybe if he had taken Paul to the police the second time he found pot . . .

Or, God forbid, had Charlie let it slide because he felt guilty?—

because he feared that his affair—those damn e-mails! Had they pushed Paul over the edge?

And maybe it was already too late! Paul was eighteen now; Charlie had no authority over his son. Charlie felt the best thing he could do was keep Paul close as long as Paul was willing. He believed he and his son had a bond.

In his gut, Charlie trusted his sense of things. He shook off those scary thoughts. He had played it right. Paul was just a kid who fell in love too easily, this time with a girl from a screwed-up family—a girl who had friends who shouldn't be Paul's friends. Charlie figured if it weren't for the girl in the middle, Paul never would have fallen into this crowd. He would be saving his money rather than blowing it on beer or pot. Charlie trusted his instincts.

How could he have known that the truth was far worse?

Paul got away with it for a while, thanks to the fact that Charlie never bothered to balance his checkbook. One day Susan got a phone call from the bank saying there was an overdraft.

"Overdraft?" Susan asked. "There's two thousand dollars in the account."

Susan went down to the bank to reconcile the matter. She realized Paul had been stealing checks out of the back of Charlie's checkbook. The checks were made out to the local corner store, and were cashed for sixty to a hundred dollars a pop with a forged signature. They added up to two thousand dollars.

For the first time they realized the extent of the trouble Paul was in.

Charlie was in the kitchen when Paul came home. When Paul stepped around the corner, Charlie knocked him flat on his back. Then Charlie jumped his son and started soft-punching him in the ribs.

"I can't *believe* you did this to me!" Charlie hissed.

"I'm sorry! I'm sorry!" Paul yelped.

Until that moment, Charlie had never touched his son in his life. He wasn't trying to hurt his kid—he held his punches—but he did make contact. Charlie needed to show Paul a level of anger that Paul had never seen—so that Paul would get the message and finally think about what he was doing.

"Two thousand dollars, Paul! Two thousand dollars!"

"I'm sorry, Dad!"

"What was it for?"

Meekly, embarrassed, "Coke."

"Cocaine? You're into *cocaine* now?!"

With every soft punch, Charlie just wanted to hug his boy. He couldn't believe he was losing his boy to a drug. It seemed like just a second ago.

Charlie got up, misty-eyed.

Paul screamed, "Dad, you beat me up!"

Charlie's anger returned. "I didn't beat you up. Can you get up? Are you hurt? If you think that was a beating, you're softer than I thought."

Paul left the house in a daze, sweating and crying, unable to recognize that any of this was his own fault. He was gone before Charlie or Susan realized letting him go maybe wasn't their preferred next move. Susan started calling Paul's friends, and soon she got him on the phone.

"Mom, I can't believe my own father hit me!"

"Paul, I am the most nonviolent person in the world, and *I* wanted to hit you."

When Charlie drove over to get Paul, he recognized the moment. He figured this was close to being the last chance he had with his son, possibly for a long time. It killed Charlie that he had not seen this coming. If he played this wrong, Paul might run and end up dead or in jail. He had to get through to his kid. He *had* to. For a moment, Charlie considered taking Paul to live with his grandmother—but what would keep him out of trouble there? Then he thought about the coast. Gulf Shores. The condo. He could move there, take Paul, take a year off, mentor his son every day. Should he do that? Was that the right thing? Somehow that didn't quite seem right. If Paul had spent two grand in just over a month, then he had a genuine drug problem, probably. He needed treatment. When Charlie landed on that possibility, it seemed right. *My son needs treatment.* He had seen ads on late-night television for a rehab center called Bradford. If nothing else, a place like that might scare Paul straight. But again, Paul was eighteen. Charlie couldn't make him go.

So when Charlie got Paul in the car and buckled down, he put it to his son.

"Paul, I love you and I always will. But you've got two choices. I can drive you right down to the Mountain Brook police station, and they will send you to jail for writing bad checks. Or you can go to Bradford, a rehab center. You tell me where we are going."

"Dad, let's wait until tomorrow. It's late, it's dark."

"No, Paul. Either way, it's happening *tonight*. I can take you to jail, and I will press charges against you. Or you're going to rehab."

"Dad, don't do this to me!"

"You've done this to yourself, son."

Charlie was serious that he would have taken Paul to jail, but he was not serious about pressing charges. Charlie is a city commissioner, which means he's on a development board, and he knew a couple of people down at the police station who could keep Paul overnight and put a good scare into him if need be. But that's not where Charlie wanted to go.

"Paul, you need help. If anyone knows weakness, it's me."

"All right." Paul nodded.

Charlie drove his son to Bradford's intake center. A counselor evaluated him and processed the paperwork for Paul to be admitted the next day to an outpatient program. It was devastating for both father and son. Paul had a powerful need to impress his father, and this was the most embarrassing thing he could imagine. Charlie was tearing himself up for not figuring it out sooner. Now he was trusting his son's life to strangers he had seen on television. Would they look out for his boy? Or were they a machine that preyed on innocent people in order to squeeze maximum dollars out of health insurers?

Paul's outpatient program required him to show up every day at a giant house. He was assigned to a group, which moved from room to room, listening to doctors and therapists. That was about all Charlie learned from Paul. The place was extremely strict. About a month into the program, Paul showed up five minutes late one day—and thus forfeited his privilege of being in the outpatient program. Or at least that's what Paul told Charlie. Charlie didn't know what the truth was. Maybe his son had failed a urine test? The next day Paul moved into an apartment with four complete strangers, grown men with lifelong problems. He would be in there for at least a month. Charlie was not allowed to visit. It was two days before Christmas.

Every few days, the phone in the Taylor house rang at seven P.M. This was Paul's only allotted call.

"I can't wait to get out of here, Dad. These guys are such bullshit. They keep us in meetings day and night."

"Maybe you need to be in meetings."

"Dad, I get it, all right? I'm in here with guys who are screaming all night long, aching because they want more stuff. Guys with no teeth. Guys who sneak out to get high. I don't want to end up like this. I'm done, man. I'm never touching coke again."

That was what Charlie wanted to hear. The ghost of Paul's future had paid him a visit at Bradford, and it had put the scare in him. Charlie figured Paul would be all right now.

Paul got out after a month.

"What are you going to do now?" Charlie asked.

"I don't know," Paul said. "I'm scared to go out at night, Dad. Every person I know gets drunk or gets high."

"Maybe you need to get out of Birmingham."

"Maybe I do."

"Do you think you can stay clean living on your own?"

"Dad, I told you. I'm never touching that stuff again."

"Then what about Gulf Shores?"

"You would let me?"

"Your mom gave me a second chance, son. I owe you a second chance. Don't screw it up."

"I won't."

"You'll have to pay me rent and make the utilities. I'm not carrying you. But with your résumé, you could get on with any hotel in two days."

It killed Charlie to make this offer. Here he was, a squeaky-clean workingman, twenty hard years into the financial planning business, and he couldn't get down to Gulf Shores more than a week or two a year. But his own son, an addict, a desk clerk at eighty-dollar hotels, a *screwup,* was about to have the life that Charlie had coveted for so long.

It took Paul less than a month in Gulf Shores to make a fatal mistake. He had the condo, he was meeting girls (and managing not to fall in love with every one who looked his way), and he had a decent job at the Residence Inn. Then he called some buddies, and he sorta blurted out how great his setup was, which they took as an invitation to come and ruin it. Charlie figured six hours of freeway was sufficient distance between Paul and his old friends. But trouble has a way of chasing you.

Charlie called Paul often. When Paul got fired by the Residence Inn, he told his dad that he had been "hired away, with a promotion" by another hotel. Charlie called that hotel. They'd never heard of Paul. Charlie knew something was up.

Several months later Paul pulled up in front of their Birmingham home when he saw Susan in the yard. She called Charlie right away.

"Are you sitting down?"

"What is it now?"

"Paul is in trouble. He's here."

"What's up?"

"He says he drove here to drop a friend off, to get him out of his life. Paul wasn't going to show up here, but he drove by and saw me. He's shaking, Charlie. He says he's drinking all the time."

"A lot?"

"At least twenty beers a day. Often more."

"Son of a bitch!" Charlie felt weary. How long could it keep on going?

On the way home, Charlie stopped by Canterbury Methodist again. "Is this how I pay back, God? Is this my mission, to learn to forgive the weak as I have been forgiven? Or is this just me and my own doing, God? Did I bring this upon myself? Because if I did, I will tell anyone you need me to. I will tell them it's not worth it. You bring me the man, and I will tell him."

That night he and Susan talked. Charlie had found another rehab center, for alcoholism, that was covered by his insurance. He knew he would be taking Paul there in the morning. But he needed to blow off some steam.

"Susan, you made it clear to me. *There would be consequences.* And there were. You forgave me once, but I know for damn sure you would not forgive me again. So why are we not kicking Paul out on his own? How many times are we supposed to bail him out? He's twenty years old! It's his life, not ours."

Susan just let him talk. Maybe after Paul got out of rehab they would send him on his way. In the meantime, they decided Susan would drive out to the coast first thing to make sure Paul's friends hadn't caused any damage to the condo. Charlie would take Paul to rehab at the university hospital.

"I don't need to go, Dad," Paul insisted.

"You've been drinking a rack a day, Paul."

"With my friends around! I got rid of them."

"You're my son, Paul. I'm not trying to punish you or scare you this time. I simply can't take the chance of sending you out into the world without treatment. I can't look in the mirror in the morning if I don't do everything I can."

The University of Alabama at Birmingham's rehab program was on the fifth floor. That day, Charlie said good-bye to his son, who was wearing a pajama top and jeans. Paul was surrounded by druggies and junkies. It killed Charlie to get on that elevator.

Susan called when Charlie was headed home. She was distraught. "You wouldn't recognize the place," she cried. "Charlie, it's *awful.*"

"We'll get it fixed up, Susan."

"The wallpaper has been peeled from the walls. Two windows are broken. There's vomit in the carpet, and the couches have been peed on. Who pees on a couch, Charlie? The electricity is off—I'm sure they didn't pay the bill. And cockroaches, Charlie. It's *infested*. I can't sleep here."

He felt violated—God, his dream home! His future!—but it was the hurt in his wife's voice that stabbed Charlie hardest.

Would it ever end?

Would they *ever* get back there?

It took eleven grand to repair the condo. Paul was kicked out of the UAB center on a technicality after three weeks. They were strict there. They had rules, and they enforced them, and if that meant writing off a twenty-year-old kid, so be it. Charlie begged them to continue counseling his son. They told Charlie to leave.

"Can he come to AA classes here?"

"Not here. Find somewhere else."

There's a theory about the brains of teenagers. Scientists have put dyes in their brains and then taken pictures with MRIs. These scientists speculate that there is a lobe of the brain whose purpose is controlling impulses, and that this part of the brain isn't fully developed until the early twenties. One day your son is a pot of water, boiling violently, and then seemingly for no real reason he comes off the heat and turns into a placid guy who seems to finally recognize the distinction between right and wrong.

Charlie doesn't know, but he considers this a possible explanation for why Paul got a whole lot better in the next six months. Another explanation is that not one single day went by when Charlie didn't call or see his son. And not one single day went by that Charlie and Paul didn't tell each other how much they loved each other. Charlie hung in there, despite never being sure whether he was hearing the truth or just a version of it dressed up to impress Dad.

Paul professed that he kept going to AA classes for six months. Charlie doesn't know. But that could be an explanation, too.

Yet another explanation is that Paul finally realized how badly he had screwed it up. "I had the good life in the palm of my hand," he told his dad by phone. "You set me up. I had the condo, the job, the girls, the pool, the DVD, the big television. I had *everything*. I kept it spotless. And then I screwed it up. I let it go to shit. Dad, every single morning when I wake up, I think about Gulf Shores. How good I had it. Where I could be in my life today if I didn't invite my friends there. It makes me sick to think about what I had, Dad. And what I lost. It makes me *physically* sick, Dad. Can you understand what I'm saying?"

Charlie was sitting at his desk in his office, looking at a picture of Robin running on the beach when she was eight years old.

"I understand, son. Believe me, I understand."

"I would jump at the chance to go back there. Someday."

Charlie wanted to say it. He really did. The words almost left his mouth. *We'll get back there.* But Charlie felt like if he said it, that might somehow feed Paul in the wrong way. It was good to hear his son have remorse. It was good to hear his son know the agony of having screwed up the best thing he ever had. That very same feeling had worked wonders on Charlie. It had changed him.

When he hung up that phone, Charlie knew the worst was behind him. Paul was going to be all right. Somehow, they had made it through his trouble. Not only had they made it, they still had a relationship. They still talked every single day.

It was worth it. It was worth every minute.

Charlie did plan a two-week family vacation that summer to Gulf Shores. But he would not fly Paul there. Paul had a job, and that was a good reason not to include him. Let him taste his loss a little longer.

Meanwhile, Robin was asking for her boyfriend to be included. His name was Jason.

Jason had recently celebrated his eighteenth birthday. Robin was only fifteen. Despite that, Robin was the responsible one in the couple. She was the parent and Jason was the kid. Robin was a straight-A student who loved to study but hated the immaturity of high school.

Jason, meanwhile, had flunked out of tenth grade and hadn't done anything to speak of in the last two years except visit his father in prison once or twice. That was just like Robin. She loved her projects. She brought home stray dogs when she was a girl, and she brought home stray kids as a teen. She also loved to shock her parents.

No way was Charlie bringing Jason to Gulf Shores.

This trip would strictly be a family affair. It wouldn't be like old times, not without Paul, but it would be good for all of them. Charlie half hoped that two weeks away from her boyfriend would help Robin realize that it wasn't her responsibility to save Jason.

Charlie suddenly wondered—was Robin trying to save Jason because Charlie had worked so hard to save Paul? Had he, inadvertently, taught his daughter to parent a loser?

Robin always related to people with problems, so much so that she would invent her own just to be part of the club. Every kid's gotta have an identity, and these days there's a badge of honor in having been one of the oppressed. So Robin reveled in her status as an adoptee. She believed her birth parents would never have been so cruel and uncool as Charlie and Susan. Her birth parents, according to this fantasy, would have been completely cool and let Robin have all the independence she wanted. In this way, Robin manufactured an aura of being oppressed by her troll-like parents. Robin would even make up stories about how mean Charlie and Susan were—one friend's mom was ready to take Robin in until the friend got wind and said, "Robin, I can't believe you told my mom all those lies! You've got the two coolest parents in Birmingham! You don't even know how lucky you are!"

It seemed like Robin had been looking for a reason to get distance from her parents ever since she was twelve years old. Robin had even come to the dinner table recently and said nonchalantly, "I need some time on my own. I should leave school, get a job, and get a place of my own."

Charlie knew better than to just say no. Or to laugh. So he took her proposal on its face and tried to shine some sense on it. "Robin, you aren't even old enough to drive a car. And the law limits someone your age to twenty hours a week of labor. At six dollars an hour, you can't afford a place."

After dinner, Charlie got out the newspaper and went through the apartment listings with his daughter. They did the math, adding in the cost of a bus pass and food. Robin was good at math. She didn't bring it up again.

So that was Robin. You had to think quickly in parenting her. You had to show her how the world worked, but if you became the dictator, you would play right into her strategy. What was he missing here? He was handing his kids the keys to a very good life. But they didn't seem to want anything to do with it.

"Do you think Robin and Jason are sexually active?" Charlie asked Susan after they caught Jason sneaking into Robin's window one night.

"I hate to think of it, Charlie. She's fifteen. But I've taught her a thousand times how important contraception is."

"Susan, we're talking about Jason here. You think he's going to be smart enough to use a condom?"

"I can't even believe we're having this conversation."

"Me neither. But we need to."

"You think we should put her on the pill?"

"I don't know, Susan."

"It just wasn't like this when I was her age."

The very next day Susan got a telephone call from Robin's school, reporting that Robin was not in classes. A mother's instinct kicked in. Susan drove over to Jason's house. She knocked on the front door.

"Don't hide from me, Jason! Your car is in the driveway. If Robin is in there with you, you better open this door!"

Jason continued to pretend he wasn't there.

Susan looked down and saw a screwdriver. So she began stabbing at the door with the screwdriver, plunging the head an inch deep into the cheap wood. If that boy didn't open the door, she would ax her way in. Anyone who crosses Susan Taylor ends up regretting it.

By the time Jason opened the door, he and Robin were both dressed. "Mom!" Robin fumed.

"Jason, you are eighteen years old. A fifteen-year-old girl is underage in Alabama. Do you get what I'm saying? You stay away from her!"

Susan dragged her daughter to the car and drove straight to the doctor. They told the doctor—a friend of Susan's—that Robin's periods were irregular and painful and they wanted birth control pills to even her out. He gave Robin a sample pack to try—one month of pills. If they were agreeable to her system, he would write a prescription when those ran out.

Robin agreed to begin the pills. The Taylors were headed to Gulf Shores in two weeks, as soon as Robin's sophomore year was done. The time away couldn't come fast enough. Susan decided she would drive out to the coast a week early.

The night before she left, Susan was on the back patio when Robin came to her. She looked strained, ready to burst.

"Robin?"

Robin couldn't say it. So she threw the sample pack of birth control pills in Susan's lap. Susan saw right away that none of the pills had been taken. Anger did not come to her. Only sadness.

"Are you already pregnant?" Susan asked.

Robin nodded. "I think I am."

"You think?"

"I took a test at a friend's house."

Susan sighed. "I had a feeling you weren't taking them. Come here, baby."

Robin climbed into Susan's lap, and they cried for a while.

Then Susan got serious. "We can't tell your dad when he's here. He'll kill Jason, and then your boyfriend will be dead and my husband will be in prison. We're going to wait a week, until he gets out to Gulf Shores and he can't go after Jason. I'm going to drive out to the coast tomorrow exactly as planned. Okay?"

While Robin was great at keeping secrets from her dad, she was terrible at keeping secrets from everyone else. She told her brother, who—by now thrilled with his newfound command of right and wrong—decided Charlie needed to know.

"I hate to tell you, Dad. But your daughter is pregnant."

Charlie didn't know how to act. He flipped out, but he didn't do anything except go into the garage and start smoking Susan's cigarette butts. He had never smoked a cigarette in his life. He felt panicky. Then he went upstairs to see his daughter. He had no plan. He had no plan at all.

"What's wrong, Dad?" Robin asked.

"Why don't you tell me what's wrong?"

"Huh?"

"Paul told me."

"Told you what?"

"Robin, are you sure you're pregnant?" He felt like crying.

Caught cold, Robin went for the shock value. She pulled out the three pregnancy tests she had taken and showed her father the blue line.

Charlie hugged her and could no longer hold back the tears. He was sure his daughter's life was ruined.

"I guess you have some choices ahead of you," Charlie said, broaching the topic as gently as he could.

Charlie believed in a woman's right over her own body, but he was devotedly antiabortion. His kids wouldn't be in his life if they had been aborted rather than given up for adoption. He was sure of this stance. But that night, it ate at him. There was an easy way to nip this in the bud, to make it all go away. It was not a theoretical question anymore. The life course of his fifteen-year-old daughter was at stake. If she had this baby, her youth was plumb gone. If she kept this baby, all her potential for a full life would be sidetracked.

He didn't sleep. He felt crazy. He got a phone number and gave it to Robin and told her it was for an ob-gyn, and she needed to make an appointment for when they got back from Gulf Shores. All day long, he bugged her. "Did you make that appointment?"

"What's it for, Dad?"

"You gotta see an obstetrician if you're pregnant, Robin."

Robin's instinct told her that wasn't what this was about. Her instinct told her that her father was sending her to a doctor who would offer her the choice of having an abortion. And Robin was right. Charlie's official position was that he would be supportive of whatever Robin chose. But right then, still feeling panic, he hoped Robin would choose the quick out.

"Dad, you know me. You know I have always told you that if I ever got pregnant I would *never* have an abortion. That baby could grow up to be president, or discover a cure for cancer. Dad, what if my mother had aborted me?"

When Charlie heard those words, his mind relaxed a bit. Robin was right. He couldn't support an abortion, and he already regretted that he had even considered it. It was good to have that off the table. One less decision to fret over.

An hour later Charlie and Robin left for the coast. They talked the whole way, and it felt good.

At the beach they made an important decision the very first day, so that it wouldn't hang over their vacation. They were afraid Robin would drop out of school with this big distraction. So they would be proactive. They would take Robin out of school and Susan would homeschool her through Jubilee Christian's program. Robin was too smart a girl—she had too much potential—to risk her academics. Susan was game for it, and when they shared this idea with Robin, she was, too. She hated high school anyway.

The happy white cloud never quite came over Susan's face those two weeks. But it came close. They enjoyed themselves. Their troubles were in Birmingham. The day before they left, they were sitting at the dunes looking at the water when Charlie saw Susan was crying.

"We'll get through it, Susan."

"I'm not ready to care for a baby again, Charlie. I'm ready to be a grandparent, and I will be a *great* grandparent. But I am *not* ready to be the mother of this baby. If Robin keeps it—you *know* she's not responsible. You *know* who will end up taking care of it."

"Well, we're just going to have to make that absolutely clear to Robin. She'll have to factor that into her decision."

Susan was quiet for a while. She was thinking about all that they were going to go through in the next nine months.

"I hate to leave here. I love it here."

Charlie sat there for five minutes, trying to think it through.

Finally he offered, "Why don't we move here?"

"What?"

"Why not? Not today. We'd have to start a process. We'll have a plan. We'll get Robin's baby out, and we'll sell the baby grand piano and all those antiques—we'll sell the house, scale down to a rental condo. A year from now, we can be living here."

"What about your job?"

"I don't need to be in Birmingham every day. I mostly talk to my clients on the phone. I can gradually build a business here."

"Are you serious?"

"Susan, I don't want to wait until we are in wheelchairs to do it. I want to do it while you and I are still young enough to take a ten-mile bike ride."

Tears of joy came to Susan's eyes. "Man, I'm all over it," she said, laughing with relief.

They had something to look forward to. That made such a difference. It didn't hurt to leave when they took off the next day.

They would be back.

They would.

They had a plan.

Sure enough, something unexpected happened.

Charlie never saw it coming.

Charlie grieved over the loss of his daughter's youth. He was soaked with regret for this very sad thing that was happening to Robin. But then he bothered to notice something about his daughter. Robin was responding miraculously to the sudden responsibility she carried. The change in her was undeniable. She used to drink, and she probably smoked pot, but Charlie wasn't sure. Now she wouldn't go near it. If her friends were driving and got reckless, she made them stop and she got out of the car and waited for her dad to pick her up on the side of the road. Robin was always smart—but not until now did she have a reason to not act stupid. Not only was she in church every single Sunday—swollen, proud, beaming, shocking everyone—but she went Thursdays as well, to youth night, something called "Fuel" that the Baptist church was doing.

Rather than having to choke back his anger at his daughter, Charlie found himself saying, "Robin, I'm not proud of how you got into this situation. But I sure am proud of how you're handling it."

And she was racing through school! Susan was paying sixty dollars a month to Jubilee Ministry for the booklets. She had Robin at the kitchen table from darn near the moment she woke up straight through lunch. Without all the distractions of school, Robin soaked up every detail. She was burning through her studies with such commitment that she had finished her entire junior-year program by September! Every couple of weeks, Robin went down to Jubilee's center in Irondale to take the tests on the material. She walked out with straight A's. Charlie could hardly believe it. His daughter was supposed to drop out of school—that's what happened when a teen got pregnant in Birmingham. Who ever thought she would use this chance to study harder than ever?

"You sure must be a good teacher, Susan."

"I'm not doing anything but turning the phone off and keeping her at the table through lunch, Charlie. It's all Robin."

Robin loved to go to the mall and walk around showing off her little belly. She loved telling every friend and every stranger that she was pregnant. It drove Charlie crazy, but he respected it, too. She was maybe owning up to it a little too much, he thought. Maybe he was old-fashioned, but he still thought there were a few things in life you kept hush-hush. Some of his clients found out. He got over the shame.

And who would have known that Jason was a decent kid at heart, after all? At first, it was dicey. Charlie did want to kill him. He had gone looking for Jason a few times, after they got back from Gulf Shores. Jason hid at his mom's. But then he showed up the second Sunday to take Robin to church. Charlie stopped him in the driveway. He looked him in the eye, hard. He wasn't sure what he was going to say, or what he might do. But you couldn't beat a kid up on his way to church, could you?

So Charlie said, "Listen, Jason. Here's the deal. You don't have to do this. You can walk away from Robin and that baby right now. It doesn't have to be your responsibility. I don't want you hanging around out of some sort of guilt, then leaving later. If you're going to leave, leave now. I will never come after you, and we will never demand anything from you as the father. But if you're going to come around here, take my daughter to church and all, then you've got to *stick* around. You can't be here one week, gone the next. You can't waffle. You either need to be here for Robin or *not*. You understand?"

Jason did not have the smarts to respect Charlie. To Jason, Charlie was just another grown-up trying to order him around. But Jason liked having this responsibility to help make order of his life. So he went to church twice a week with Robin, and he attended every single doctor's appointment. Charlie wanted to chase Jason away, but he knew if he did, Robin would get her fur up and make them miserable and end up with Jason anyway. Charlie figured he had to let their relationship run its course, as doomed as it seemed. Charlie signed Jason up for GED classes and paid for the three hundred dollars out of his own pocket. If there was any chance he was going to be in Robin's life, it made sense to stake him. Jason went out and got himself a job—in the warehouse at EBSCO, making eight dollars an hour. Then Robin got a job there too, part-time, and the two of them imagined themselves to be having a regular adult life going. They could almost imagine being parents.

They told Charlie they were leaning toward keeping the baby. Robin was about five months pregnant then. Charlie was not surprised. He knew Robin would not want to put her baby up for adoption. In hanging on to her baby, Robin would redeem the mother who had not been able to hang on to her, sixteen years before.

Charlie was ready. "I'll support you in whatever decision you make. But if you're leaning toward keeping the baby, you should know what your expenses will be."

Charlie gave them a magazine with apartment listings, and then he made a list of all the things they would need to care for the baby: tubs of formula, packs of diapers, a crib, a stroller, a cold air humidifier. He sent them to Target to price this stuff out and to see if they could swing it on jobs that paid eight dollars an hour. Even at Target prices, it added up fast. Wandering the aisles, Jason remembered back to his child development class, back when he'd bothered to go to high school. There was a poster on the wall he used to look at. It said a baby cost ten thousand dollars a year, for twenty years. They imagined all the Friday nights they could never go out because they could not pay a babysitter. The movies they would never see.

It really burst their bubble to realize they couldn't afford their own baby. It was a brutal accounting, and it made them feel guilty and worthless. At the heart of Robin's decision were her feelings about her own adoption. For whatever reason—and despite all the evidence—she believed her life had turned out worse for being adopted. So how could she doom her baby to the same fate?

Robin did not say any of this out loud, but she did not have to— Charlie and Susan knew what their daughter was thinking. So they decided it was time to tell Robin everything. They had a file on her adoption. Robin was on the couch when they dropped this file on her lap.

"We were going to keep this for you until you were eighteen," Susan said.

"But we thought you might want to see it now."

Until that moment, Robin knew only one thing about her birth mother: that she was very young. Robin had always imagined that "very young" meant eighteen or nineteen. She pulled the top sheet off the stack in the file and scanned the page.

NON-IDENTIFYING BIRTH FAMILY INFORMATION

FOR ▮▮▮▮▮▮

DATE OF BIRTH: ▮▮▮▮▮
TIME OF BIRTH: 8:26pm
WEIGHT AT BIRTH: 6'13"
LENGTH AT BIRTH: 19"

Copies of medical reports are attached.

	BIOLOGICAL PARENTS	
	MOTHER	FATHER
AGE AT TIME OF ADOPTEE'S BIRTH	12	
NATIONALITY/ETHNIC BACKGROUND	Irish/Indian	Mexic
RACE	White	
RELIGIOUS PREFERENCE	Baptist	
EDUCATIONAL LEVEL	6th Grade	
HEIGHT	5'2"	
WEIGHT	130	
COLOR OF HAIR	Blonde	
COLOR OF EYES	Blue	
COMPLEXION	Fair	

OTHER INFORMATION:
The Birth mother has dimples and a pug nose. She enjoys video games and ▮▮▮▮▮
OTHER CHILDREN BORN PRIOR TO BIRTH OF ADOPTEE: NONE
(All ages given are at adoptee's birth)

HEALTH HISTORY OF BIOLOGICAL PARENTS AND OTHER BIOLOGICAL RELATIVES:
The birth mother has had all childhood diseases and has frequent She wears braces on her teeth and has a sister who wears glasses. Is high blood pressure on both sides of the family and an uncle alcoholic. The maternal Grandmother has sinus trouble and migra headaches. The paternal Great Grandfather had diabetes, heart & and cancer.

"My mother was twelve years old when she had me!" Robin screamed with horror. *Twelve.* Robin looked back four years and tried to imagine having a kid while in sixth grade. No way could she do it.

No way would my life have been better if I was never adopted.

The file was brutal, too.

"God, they were all fat!" Robin blurted, looking at the heights and weights of her birth family. "Not one person in the family had more than a sixth-grade education!" Robin kept reading. Her mother had had a brother who died at fourteen. Throughout the family there was a history of alcoholism. Very little was known of Robin's birth father except his age, sixteen. Robin understood that the lack of information meant her father wasn't around.

Charlie looked at his daughter and remembered back to the judge who signed their adoption papers for Robin in family court. Robin's birth mother was the youngest the court had ever recorded. "This little baby girl is so fortunate," he said.

For the first time in her life, Robin recognized this, too. And she finally realized that her baby could have a better life as someone else's child.

They used the very same adoption counselor who had brought them Robin. She recommended Robin use an open adoption process, in which the birth mother gets to meet the adopting family and is allowed to continue visiting the baby until the baby is three months old. The theory here was that Robin would end up with less guilt and regret later. She found a very nice professional couple who already had a three-year-old daughter. A meeting was arranged.

Charlie showed up at the house to take everyone to the meeting. He was flabbergasted. *Robin had dressed up.* The bolt was missing from her tongue. Her purple hair had been dyed back to its natural color. Not once in Robin's life had she dressed to impress. If clothes had a purpose, it was to shock people. Robin had always ridiculed Susan's taste, and she never touched the clothes Susan bought for her. But here she was, for the first time in her life, trying to make a good impression, wearing khakis and a sweater.

Right then, Charlie knew his daughter was going to be all right. He knew the worst was behind them.

Their 6,100-foot house was put up for sale. Some doctor bought it. The baby grand was donated to a school. The antiques were scooped up by a dealer.

Robin kept whizzing through school. She was on track to graduate by May—a year ahead of schedule. She took the ACT test and almost won a full-ride college scholarship on her first try. She planned to move in with Jason when her parents moved to Gulf Shores, and go to college at the University of Alabama at Birmingham.

Baby Emma arrived two days early. Susan called Charlie, and he rushed to the hospital. It was a surreal moment. Charlie had never been in a delivery room in his life. Charlie was holding one of Robin's legs.

Jason was holding the other. Susan was at Robin's head. The nurse was there to catch. Robin was pushing . . . pushing. . . .

Look how brave my daughter is!

A voice was screaming inside Charlie Taylor.

This was not the plan!

No, it's not, my old friend, Charlie told the voice.

This was not the plan!

But it sure is beautiful, isn't it?

In the last moment before Emma came, nose out, Robin looked over and saw her father, the man she had been trying to get away from for five years. She had spent years testing this man. Years rebelling against him. Years seeking her independence. But there he was, holding her leg, *crying,* tears draining down his face, all confused and full of joy, and she finally understood.

She finally got it.

He's not a monster. He's not an ogre. He's not my jailor or a hardhead.

He's been at my side, holding my leg, all this time.

For five years, she had been looking forward to the day she could have nothing to do with her parents.

But now she knew differently. She and Jason would go to Gulf Shores, too.

He's just my dad.

Every girl needs a dad.

And with one last push, Emma came.

It hit them like a tornado, and it blew for six years. They fell like dominoes, one right after the other. First Charlie, then Paul, then Robin. They never saw it coming. Everything was fine before, and everything has been fine since. It gives Charlie the shivers to think how close it came to taking his kids away.

But they survived it, and they're closer for it. A lot closer.

"If I had not had my own troubles," Charlie said, "I would have judged what Paul and Robin did far more harshly. It taught me to love them through it. If I hadn't gone through what I did, I might have pushed them away."

A little later, he added, "I don't feel like we're a success story. I don't think I'm a model of anything. I don't know what we did right or what we did wrong. Half the time I think we must have screwed up as parents, for our kids to do this. I must have spoiled them, been too supportive, too lax, too forgiving. I think I gave them too many chances. But the other half of the time I worry I was too strict. I must have come down too hard. My love was too tough. I think I overreacted early, and I pushed my kids into rebellion. So which is it? I don't know."

That's the usual way to think about it: *Should I be more strict, or will that cause them to rebel?*

But there's another way to think about it. Maybe Charlie and Susan were neither too strict nor too forgiving. Maybe what they did right had nothing to do with where they fit on that spectrum. Maybe the one thing they did right was this: They established a *precedent* for how you work through trouble. In working through their separation, divorce, and remarriage, Charlie and Susan showed their kids a very simple lesson. You don't have to run, no matter how ashamed or rejected you feel. You can get through it.

"In your darkest times, life takes care of itself if you just don't lie down, don't put your hands up and say 'Woe is me,' " Charlie believes.

It was established, in the Taylor family, that despite a picture-perfect setting for a picture-perfect life, things will not go according to plan. And when that happens, you figure it out. You stay together in some way. You work through it.

That is how Paul and Robin explain making it through their hard times. "I saw my parents go through something just as tough," Robin said. "And they made it. They set an incredible example." Paul echoed this. "When I was in Bradford and wondering how I'd ever make it, I just remembered my dad out there mowing the lawn every night, cleaning the pool, refusing to go away. I'd gain strength from that."

Maybe we shouldn't try to create perfect childhoods for our children. We shouldn't agonize over every detail, hoping that if we do it right our kids won't run into trouble. The most important thing we can teach them is how to work through problems. Kids need practice distinguishing right from wrong and learning how to stay away from bad influences. Rather than hide our own problems, maybe we need to let our kids see us work through them.

Trouble finds everybody. Couples who have never learned to fight through a challenge, *together,* are often woefully unprepared when their time comes. They often have no idea how their partner will respond— Can he be truthful when the truth hurts? Will she run? Will he put his head down in denial, changing nothing? Only then will it be revealed that the "perfect" prelude to marriage doesn't look so perfect after all. By contrast, the couples who worked through some conflict *before marriage* developed the necessary skills to resolve differences.

We all wonder how we're going to handle situations like the Taylors found themselves in. How might we handle it when we learn our spouse has been with someone else? How will we react when we discover our son is trying drugs? What will we say if our teenage daughter tells us she's pregnant?

We wonder: Will we hug them? Will we be furious? Will we *act* furious, to send them a message?

But maybe these are not the real questions we should be wondering about.

Instead, we should ask this: What precedent have we set?

What precedent *can* we set?

The weather was clear. A ten-mile wind blew from the southwest. Charlie made it out to the one wreck he knew of by about noon. He found several large schools of bait in the area, which was a good sign. He tried trolling for about an hour with Clarks and Drones but had no luck. He finally anchored off a reef and went after the topwater. The amberjacks found his plugs irresistible. He hooked five, all on light tackle—not one under twenty pounds.

He released them all.

He would come back tomorrow to catch them with Paul, who was flying in that night. Paul had managed to get hired at the Marriott.

His son was coming.

That, too, is one of the things that goes straight to a man's heart: having his whole family around. Robin was in college there. Jason was working at Wal-Mart. Susan was the white cloud.

With plenty of time before the sun went down, Charlie released his anchor and pointed the boat toward shore. It was times like this that a man did his best thinking. Sometimes it hurt like hell to think that he had given away his first grandchild. That was usually his first thought, on days like these. But then he would think about what he was headed for, right then. How lucky he had it. How good he had it. Tonight he would fall asleep beside his wife, with the sliding glass door wide-open and the sound of the ocean in their dreams. Sometimes it felt so good he *had* to say something; his love drummed so hard in his chest that he could not fall asleep unless he let a little out in a whisper.

"We made it, Susan. We made it."

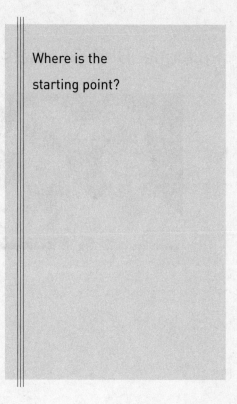

Where is the

starting point?

Epilogue: Blue Blankets

I'm humbled by the people here. Nothing comparable has ever happened to me. My mother never left me in a movie theater all day because it was cheaper than day care. My father never failed to claim me. I never slept in a floorless house with no heat. Nobody denied me the right to choose my own favorite color.

But I still feel like my own journey is in these pages. In the stories of others, I recognize myself. My beats are softer, but they echo what these people went through. They have lifted my story back to the surface of my consciousness.

So I offer this last one, not to compare, just to share.

There was a time in my life when I was on top of the world, but I was all alone, and extremely cold.

This was ten years ago, in Peru. My older brother, John, was getting married. His wife, Patricia, is from a very strong family in Lima. The wedding reception would be held at their house in the La Molina district. The wedding would be at a five-hundred-year-old Franciscan monastery in the Rimac, a historical neighborhood of Lima.

I did not have a lot of enthusiasm for the trip. I felt out of place among my family, fifteen of whom were going. My older brother did not involve me in the planning of the wedding, and we barely talked until the night before the big event. But my younger brother, Steve, asked me to meet him in Cuzco a week early to hike the Inca Trail to Machu Picchu. I almost made some excuse and turned him down, but I learned that two of my cousins were going on the trek. They were eager and willing; they weren't making excuses. To them, a family member getting married in Peru was a great chance to explore. *What is wrong with me?* I thought. *Why am I so hesitant to be around my family?*

I was filled with dread, Mister Worst-Case-Scenario. I was afraid the airline to Cuzco would lose my reservation. I was afraid my younger brother would get hurt in the Andes doing something crazy. I was afraid my parents would embarrass us in front of my sister-in-law's Peruvian family.

But you know what I was *really* afraid of?

I was afraid of being surrounded by family and still feeling all alone.

In the face of things I could not control, I was a worrier. I remember the challenge of packing my bag—I needed both a tuxedo and four days' hiking gear. I did not know if I would be able to store a bag reliably, so everything had to fit in a single pack I could carry up a mountain. There was no room for a big parka to stay warm.

Then I was worried about the overnight flight from Miami. I don't sleep well on planes. I bring a neck pillow and an eye mask, but I rarely actually use them, because I'm ashamed to look silly. Then, when I boarded this plane, I was surprised to find two of my aunts in the row behind me. One had come from Boston; the other, Seattle. They were in their pajamas and each had brought a bed pillow from home. It was a riot and a relief to see them this way. I pulled out my eye mask and joined the crowd. By morning, I had grown attached to the blue American Airlines blanket that had kept me warm all night. I decided to steal it and bring it with me to the Andes.

At noon I was in the Plaza de Armas in Cuzco, waiting for my brother Steve. He was coming from La Paz, Bolivia, or from the jungle in Brazil, I couldn't remember, but he was supposed to have made it to Cuzco a day earlier. He was only an hour late—an hour in which I feared something had happened to him.

Once in his company, all my dread left me. Steve had put a lot of planning into the trip. His command of the city put me at ease. I fed off his confidence and excitement. Cuzco's altitude is eleven thousand feet, so we spent the next two days acclimating to the thin air. We had nothing to do but goof off in the ruins of the Urubamba Valley. Twice a day we bumped into an aunt or a cousin.

For so long, my love for Steve was clouded with guilt. He was seven when my dad moved out. Mom had to work; our afternoons were un-policed. Growing up, Steve constantly presented me with a challenge—should I be like a friend, and watch him party himself to annihilation, or should I be like a parent, only to push him away with warnings to take better care of himself? He was a decent student, and he was a good athlete, but he was reckless. He played to an audience of his peers. If money ever found its way into his pocket, it was spent in a day. The thing he seemed to be missing was the instinct for self-preservation. Mom says I protected him for years, particularly when we lived at Dad's. When I left for college, I stopped looking out for him. I had to save myself, get out of there.

Dad tried to give him structure. At his high school, he was supposed to write in a journal for ten minutes every morning. His counselors dis-covered he'd been drawing pictures instead. In these pictures he was stabbing our Dad in the head with a big Excalibur sword, with bombs going off all around. Then he moved in with Mom, who tried to woo him with trust, but he just took advantage of it. I couldn't bear to hear these stories. They made me feel so powerless, so neglectful.

I drove him to college in San Diego. I was supposed to stay a few days and make sure he had settled in. But within hours of arriving, he had met some other guys on the soccer team and been invited to a toga party on the beach. He found his element quickly. I thought he was all set, so I left—another toga party didn't interest me. It turned out that the toga crew drove down to Tijuana and lost track of Steve in some bar. In the middle of the night, he had to hitchhike back to San Diego with no wal-let, no pants, nothing but a sheet over his shoulder. That was his first day of college.

In his twenties he switched careers annually and had his heart broken a couple of times. His most recent attempt at a career was to follow our dad into the insurance business. But he had quit right before coming to Peru, without another job lined up. *Here we go again,* I figured. This was always an awkward conversation between us. I'd switched jobs even more than he had, but I had been sustained by a passion, writing. Ear-lier that year, my first novel had been published. My years of devotion to my craft were finally paying off. I'd made it, while Steve was back in the starting blocks.

But was he? In Peru those jobs meant nothing. All we had was our character, and in the narrow streets of Cuzco my brother's incredibly giving nature was emerging. It was fascinating to watch him with people. He turned other tourists into friends quickly. He elicited their stories easily. He never left a shopkeeper without a bit of conversation.

Then, with my cousins and aunts, Steve seemed to know all the details of their lives—like the names of their friends, the situation at their jobs. He'd been listening to them, too. I was ashamed. I didn't even try to catch up on their lives, not wanting to call attention to how little I kept track. Afraid of embarrassing myself, I asked no questions.

"You seem so distant," Steve told me the night before our trek.

"No, man, I'm having a better time than I have in years."

"Then why were you so reluctant to come here?" he asked.

"It's hard to explain. I'm sorry I was lame about it."

He kept pushing me. "Why don't you let us in? We're your family."

"I don't know why. I lose myself around my family. I feel like wallpaper."

"Because you never say anything."

"I never know what to say. Talking about my life, it feels like submitting a book report, it's so remote. Who cares?"

"*We* care," he insisted adamantly.

"But why? Why would you care about the details of my daily life? It has nothing to do with you."

"Because it has to do with *you.*"

I just did not get it. I lived a thousand miles away from these people. I loved them, but I did not know why. I had my life, they had theirs; what was the connection?

By dawn, our bus was climbing into the Urubamba. We hiked five kilometers along the river, and then seven more into the mountains, where we made camp near a village called Huayllabamba at about nine thousand feet. There were ten people in our group. The porters were Quechua. Our guide was a native of Cuzco who spoke Spanish and some English. He warned us to get some rest. The next day's hike was grueling. We would climb to Dead Woman's Pass at nearly fourteen thousand feet, then have lunch before continuing down the other side. Going up, our feet would feel heavy. Painful headaches were likely. Rest often, he advised. The climb took most people five hours.

By the time we broke camp, waves of hikers were already on the mountain. I'm not sure where they came from.

I got frustrated quickly. We hiked single-file up the trail. The pace was slower than the crawl of window-shoppers. My legs felt trapped.

"C'mon," I told Steve. "Let's pass these people and get in front."

To pass people, we had to jog a few paces off the trail. My breathing was clear and I felt strong. Around every corner, there was another group to pass. So I just kept powering up the mountain, alternating long strides with jogging steps. People thought I was crazy, because the trail is steeper than a staircase, and in places it *is* a staircase of well-placed flat stones. But I got into a zone. I loved it. I just wanted to keep moving. I lost sight of my brother behind me fairly quickly. I didn't even stop to tell him I was going on alone. I just went. That was so typical of me, and that climb up the mountain was so emblematic of my life—I had started out alongside my family, but I soon left them, and attacked life alone. Instinct took over. I had to go. I couldn't be held back.

Halfway up the mountain, the trail ducked under the canopy of a cloud forest. Stumpy trees covered with moss flashed by my eyes. The blur of other hikers' legs. With my head to the ground, I glimpsed their shoes, not their faces. I was drenched in sweat and loving it. When I came out of the cloud forest twenty minutes later, I looked up and saw that only local porters were ahead of me. Soon I had reined them in as well. How many hikers had I passed? Two hundred? I wasn't really trying to be the first to the top—I just wanted to be able to hike at my own pace. As I climbed, the thin air took its toll. I enjoyed the sensation, vaguely astronaut-like. My feet felt heavy as paving stones. I was supposed to breathe deep between every step. I didn't. Time slowed way down. I'd been on the mountain for ninety minutes. The next thirty minutes felt like three hours. I began to appreciate the *puna,* the high grasslands. Snowpacks gathered in a few hollows another thousand feet up the mountain, so my brain registered that the air was probably very cold, but I was ablaze from the exercise. I could see the pass. Just twenty more steps. *Twenty more. Twenty more.*

The pass turned out to be a false pass; the ridge was another half a mile up. *Twenty more. Twenty more.*

I made it to the top in just under two hours. I found this incredibly satisfying, but I don't know why. I sat down on the ridge and looked back down the chasm, then collapsed.

A strong wind blew right up the valley at me. Within minutes I realized I was getting cold, quickly. From my shirt to my socks I was drenched in sweat. I had to get out of these clothes. I tore them off and put my third day's clothes on. The bitter wind cut right through. I was shivering, and my teeth were chattering. My hands could barely work the zipper on my backpack. I reopened it and layered up with my last set of clothes. It did no good. The fire in my belly had gone out. I had burned every bit of fuel coming up that mountain. I needed food and water. Without it, I had no metabolism.

Surely someone would come up the mountain soon, and I could borrow some food.

Still, not a person in sight.

I got my backpack open once again. My sleeping bag wasn't there. I had agreed to carry the group's iron skillets, and to make room I had given my bag to my cousin.

The tuxedo? No way. The blue American Airlines blanket! Thank God for the blanket! I pulled out my jackknife and stabbed a slit in the middle of the blanket, then put it over my head like a poncho, stuffing the tails into my belt.

I sat down again and made myself into a ball under the poncho, trying to will some heat out of my muscles.

That was stupid, I scolded myself. *Why did you have to run up the mountain, exactly?*

What did you think you would do when you got here? Hang out in your T-shirt and shorts at fourteen thousand feet?

"What is wrong with me?" I said. "Why do I run away from the people who love me?" There was such pain in me, such confusion about life's most basic elements. The thing I seemed to be missing was the instinct to stick together.

Where were those porters I had seen? They must have stopped to make lunch or set up another camp.

With no sugar in my blood and little oxygen in the air, I began to suffer delirium and panic. Had I taken a wrong turn? Had the weather turned people back? Should I go back down? My watch kept me sane. *It's only been fifteen minutes,* I assured myself. *Okay, twenty.* I contemplated busting out the tuxedo.

Finally I saw a hiker come over the false pass half a mile below. He—I thought it was a he—was coming very slowly, a full breath between each step and a minute's rest every ten steps. But he made progress. Then a big cloud filled the gully, and he disappeared. Five minutes later, he reappeared two hundred yards below me. He looked kind of like a porter, because he had some poncho thing over his shoulders. Then I realized.

That's not a porter.

That's my brother.

I whooped, then I crept down to meet him. He was exhausted. He needed me as much as I needed him.

The poncho thing over his shoulders?

A blue American Airlines blanket, slit at the neck.

"Did you take that from the plane?" he asked.

"Yeah. You?"

He grinned broadly. "It doesn't look like it's doing you any good. You're blue."

All those years I thought I was going to have to rescue him, but it turned out he was the one to rescue me. Not from the cold—he did give me a sweater, and we warmed up under his sleeping bag, but the cold was not going to kill me. He rescued me from ever again wondering what the connection was between us. That *was* killing me.

We did not know it then, but when we stepped over that pass, arm in arm, our lives split into Before and After. Behind us was the tumult and confusion of growing up. In front of us, a haven. After that trip to Peru, Steve and I took control of the experience of our family. That's the only way I can think to say it.

What does that mean, that we *took control of the experience*?

Well, before that trip, the spine of our family was our dual relationships with each of our parents—which were very often in conflict, and full of disappointment. My relationships with my brothers and my cousins were branches off that cracked spine, peripheral to my central experience.

After that trip, Steve's and my love for each other became the spine, quite overtly and consciously. During the next few days of our trek, we agreed that our relationship with each other would be the primary focus of our energy. When I thought of "my family," I would think of Steve, and vice versa. When I considered flying home to Seattle, I was flying to see Steve. We agreed that I would always stay with him, on his sofa, so that I would never again feel like I had to choose to stay with one parent or the other. It did not matter that Mom had a nice bed and a refrigerator full of food, while Steve's sofa was too short to lie flat on. I would stop splitting time between my parents. If Steve and I went to dinner, all our parents were welcome to eat with us. But I would not split nights—one dinner with Dad, the next with Mom. I would hang out with Steve's friends, sneak into his soccer games. Put him first.

It might sound like a mental trick, but it did not feel like one. I started flying home four to five times a year, and I did not feel out of place as I used to. My parents were on the periphery, which took the pressure off those relationships. By leaning on Steve, I no longer put much expectation on Mom and Dad. Disappointment no longer got in the way. It felt much healthier. Steve became my protector when I got frustrated. I was always able to stabilize myself with this principle: *Spend time with the person in my family I love the most, and I will learn again to love my family.* We took control of the experience, and the experience was good.

Everything changed over the next few years. Our new Peruvian relatives taught us how important family was to them. Steve discovered his calling in nursing, and he soon met his wife. We bought houses the same year. When I remarried, Steve and I became fathers to young boys within months of each other. Not even brotherhood prepared me for the sacredness of fatherhood.

When we think of "family," we so often think of it as an amorphous tribe—as "those people." Floating loosely in that tribe, it is very easy to get lost, to lose the connection. If you've lost it, remember this: All it takes is one other person to create a spine on which to build. A spouse, a child, a brother, a friend. If you put your energy there, it will breathe new life into the whole endeavor, and you will never again lose the sense of what family is all about.

There was a time in my life when I was on top of the world, but I was all alone, and extremely cold. Then my brother stepped out of a cloud.

‖ Author's Note

Please visit my website, www.pobronson.com. There you can write me about your family experience, and you can write these families a thank-you letter. I want them to know how their lives have touched others.

On the site I also have around two hundred pages of facts and statistics comparing families around the world and throughout history. You will find many curious details there, such as:

- In the United States 62 percent of households have no children under the age of eighteen in them. Thus the "typical" American household has zero children. Not 1.8 children, and not 2.4 children. Zero.
- In Arab societies more than 95 percent of people who are forty-five years or older have been married. Sounds like a different world, right? Not as different as you might think. In the United States, of those who are sixty-five and older, the percent who have been married? Ninety-five.
- Today one-third of all babies born in the United States are born to unmarried mothers. However, they're not necessarily doing it alone. Forty percent of unmarried mothers live with the father of their children. A considerable number of these cohabiting couples eventually marry.
- In the middle of the eighteenth century more than 40 percent of American women were pregnant at the time of their wedding.
- Between 1960 and 1990 the European labor force grew by thirty million people. Twenty-five million of those were women.
- In the United States, if your daughter has been living with some guy

for three years—and this is the first guy she's lived with—the chance they'll finally marry is 58 percent.

- In Seoul, South Korea, in 1960, less than 2 percent of Korean women had not married by the age of thirty-four. Today it's 18 percent. And their parents are freaked! Yet most do seem to marry in the next ten years—less than 3 percent haven't married by age fifty.

- A Dutch couple will, on average, experience a one-quarter to one-third drop in their purchasing power when they raise children, compared with what they had before having children.

- People used to abandon their children when they couldn't care for them. It's remarkable how common this was. In 1835 France, 121,000 infants were abandoned—in that year alone.

- Of the women who graduated from American colleges from 1900 to 1919, more than 50 percent did not have children by age forty.

- Number of adoptions in the United Kingdom in 2003: 5,354. Number of adoptions in the U.K. in 1974: 22,502.

- Average number of children for a Japanese woman in 2000: 1.35. Percent of Japanese children of preschool age who are in private or government preschools: more than 90.

- In Roman times, a Roman could sell his wife and kids (up to three times); he could use his children as laborers, beat them, and even kill them with impunity. The wife was not a legal guardian and could not object to the sale or transfer of her husband's children, even after he died.

- The United States is one of the few countries without a period of history dominated by arranged marriage.

- The notion that one should marry for love (rather than for property or for family) is a fairly recent idea, historically. This "new romanticism" became the ideal for the first time in England in the late 1700s. It spread to Europe and became popular in the United States in the early 1800s. By the 1830s the American middle class began marrying for love.

||| Acknowledgments

I am eternally grateful to the families in this book for being willing to help others by sharing their experiences. You're my heroes. I also am indebted to my assistant, Anne Ferguson. She has been a great sounding board; she conducted many phone interviews; she kept track of all my subjects. The other person on my core team is my researcher, Ashley Merryman. Were it not for her constant digging and distilling, I would have been lost among my varied ambitions. My wife, Michele, was my first and most important editor. Thanks also to Alex Wellen, Noah Hawley, and Ethan Watters, for their friendship and their guidance in shaping stories. Constance Hale also made invaluable edits. At Random House, thanks to Brian McLendon, Gina Centrello, Geoff Mulligan, Jane von Mehren, Janet Wygal, Amelia Zalcman, and Jon Karp. Thanks to my agents, Peter Ginsberg, Shirley Stewart, and Dave Barbor. I am particularly indebted to Jackee Holder in London for sending potential stories my way.

Thanks to Dr. Rebecca Wendell in San Francisco, Dr. Wayne Bentham in Seattle, and David Dewine, MA, in Boston, for their professional counsel on the manuscript. Thanks to Rose Kreider at the U.S. Census Bureau for her consultation on bureau reports.

While not a complete list, some of the scholars whose work informed and transformed my thinking were:

- On parental involvement, home-leaving, and what it means to be a grown-up in the United States: Frank F. Furstenberg, Jr.
- On marriage and divorce: Andrew J. Cherlin, Frank F. Furstenberg Jr.
- On children: A. R. Colón with P. A. Colón.
- On division of household labor: John P. Robinson.

- On time use: Sandra L. Hofferth.
- On idealized views of the historical family: Lorena S. Walsh (for the colonial period), Darrett B. Rutman and Anita H. Rutman (colonial), Ray H. Abrams (1950s), Stephanie Coontz (1950s and 1960s).
- On the impact of education and careers on women historically: Claudia Goldin.
- On the impact of the Industrial Revolution on individual family lives from a contemporaneous point of view: Mary Ross.

In addition, I drew on countless reports and publications from the U.S. Census Bureau (particularly the Census 2000 Special Reports and Briefs, and Current Population Reports); the European Observatory on the Social Situation, Demography and Family; and the United Nations Programme on the Family, Division for Social Policy and Development, Department of Economic and Social Affairs. Other sources we frequently were looking to for data included the U.S. Department of Health and Human Services' Centers for Disease Control and Prevention and National Center for Health Statistics; the United Kingdom's National Statistics website; the Australian Bureau of Statistics; the Clearinghouse on International Developments in Child, Youth and Family Policies at Columbia University; James J. Ponzetti's *International Encyclopedia of Marriage and Family,* second edition (2002); Bert Adams and Jan Trost's *Handbook of World Families;* and the *Statistical Abstract of the United States.*

To all the hundreds of people I interviewed for this book, thank you for your time and your interest and your encouragement. Then there were people who welcomed me into their families and spoke to me at great length, but I ended up not writing about them. The cause was not lost; their experience dramatically shaped the stories I did write. Those are Mary Andreoli, Doreen Banaszak, Terri Bessette, Joy Brown, Julie Chang, Cassindy Chao, Kristy Chmelarsky, Philippe Cibelly, Lisa Clark, Erin Dabbs, Fabian De Jesus, Harry Dickran, Lyn and Mike Duggan, Lisa Fabbri, Annabelle Favet, Charley Fratantoni, Larry Guo, Doug and Roselyn Hardy, Khatun Holloway, Lolita Jackson, Julia Lancaster, Anita Mackenzie, Deborah Kay Marsh, Fiorella Massey, Kathy and Aki Matsushima, Fareed Osman, Zoe Panarites, Juliette Posner, Michelle Quarles, Jorge Sanchez, Kristy Scher, Lloyd Sieden, Katherine Shao, Jim Souls, Chris Starks, and Imran Uppal.

Bibliography of Favorite Reference Sources*

Note: These titles are ordered according to their influence on this book.

Adams, Bert N., and Jan Trost, editors. *Handbook of World Families*. Thousand Oaks, CA: Sage Publications, Inc., 2005.

Colón, A. R., with P. A. Colón. *A History of Children: A Socio-Cultural Survey Across Millennia*. Westport, CT: Greenwood Press, 2001, p. 384.

Census 2000 Special Reports and Briefs. Washington, D.C.: U.S. Census Bureau. http://www.census.gov/population/www/cen2000/briefs.html.

Coontz, Stephanie. "The American Family and the Nostalgia Trap." *Phi Delta Kappan*, March 1, 1995.

Fields, Jason. *America's Families and Living Arrangements 2003*. Current Population Reports, publication 20-553. Washington, D.C.: U.S. Census Bureau, 2003.

———. *Children and Their Living Arrangements and Characteristics: March 2002*. Current Population Reports, publication 20-547. Washington, D.C.: U.S. Census Bureau, 2003.

Goldin, Claudia. "The Long Road to the Fast Track." *Annals of the American Academy of Political and Social Science* 596 (November 2001), pp. 20, 23.

Kreider, Rose M., and Tavia Simmons. *Marital Status: 2000*. Census 2000 Brief C2KBR-30. Washington, D.C.: U.S. Census Bureau, 2003.

"Major Trends Affecting Families: A Background Document." Reports for United Nations Programme on the Family, Division for Social Policy and Development, Department of Economic and Social Affairs. http://www.un.org/esa/socdev/family/publications/mtrendsbg.htm.

Monitoring Reports on the Situation of Families in the EU Member States [by individual nation]. European Observatory on the Social Situation, Demography and Family. http://europa.eu.int/comm/employment_social/eoss/research_en.html.

Ponzetti, James J., editor in chief. *International Encyclopedia of Marriage and Family*, Second Edition. Four volumes. Woodbridge, CT: Macmillian Reference USA, 2002.

*For a complete list of reference sources, please visit my website, www.pobronson.com.

Ross, Mary. "Shall We Join the Gentlemen?" *The Survey* 57, no. 5 (December 1, 1926), pp. 263–267.

Tate, Thad W., and David L. Ammerman, editors. *The Chesapeake in the Seventeenth Century: Essays on Anglo-American Society.* Chapel Hill: University of North Carolina Press, 1979.

Furstenberg, Frank F., Jr. "Are Parents Investing Less Time in Children? Trends in Selected Industrialized Countries." *Population and Development Review,* December 1, 2004.

Cherlin, Andrew J. *Marriage, Divorce, Remarriage,* revised and enlarged edition. Cambridge, MA: Harvard University Press, 1992.

Robinson, John P. "Is Anyone Doing the Housework? Trends in the Gender Division of Household Labor." *Social Forces,* September 1, 2000.

Petersen, William. "The New American Family: Causes and Consequences of the Baby Boom." *Commentary,* January 1956, pp. 1–6.

Historical Statistics of the United States, Colonial Times to 1970, bicentennial edition, parts 1 and 2. Washington, D.C.: U.S. Bureau of Census, 1975.

Pinsof, William M. "The Death of 'Til Death Us Do Part': The Transformation of Pair-Bonding in the 20th Century." *Family Process,* June 22, 2002.

Sussman, Marvin B., Suzanne K. Steinmetz, and Gary W. Peterson, editors. *Handbook of Marriage and the Family,* second edition. New York: Plenum Press, 1999.

Furstenberg, Frank F., Jr., Sheela Kennedy, Vonnie C. Mcloyd, Rubén G. Rumbaut, and Richard A. Settersten, Jr. "Growing Up Is Harder to Do." American Sociological Association, *Contexts,* Summer 2004, pp. 33–41. http://www.asanet.org/media/furstenberg_adulthood.pdf.

Smith, Tom W. "The Emerging 21st Century American Family." National Opinion Research Center, University of Chicago, October 2001.

Koops, Willem, and Michael Zuckerman, editors. *Beyond the Century of the Child: Cultural History and Developmental Psychology.* Philadelphia: University of Pennsylvania Press, 2003.

Cleek, Margaret Guminski, and T. Allan Pearson. "Perceived Causes of Divorce: An Analysis of Interrelationships." *Journal of Marriage and the Family,* February 1985, p. 179.

Abrams, Ray H. "The Concept of Family Stability." Annals of the American Academy of Political and Social Science 272, Toward Family Stability (November 1950), pp. 1–8.

Bramlett, M. D., and W. D. Mosher. "Cohabitation, Marriage, Divorce, and Remarriage in the United States." National Center for Health Statistics, *Vital Health Statistics* 23, no. 22 (2002).

"Conference of Family Desertions." *Charities,* May 9, 1903, pp. 483–486.

"Family Structures." In *Encyclopedia of American Social History.* Three volumes. New York: Charles Scribner's Sons, 1993. Reproduced in the History Resource Center, Farmington Hills, MI: Gale Group. http://galenet.galegroup.com/servlet/HistRC.

"Family Life and Training: Difficulties of Household Education." *The New York Times,* 1875.

Juster, F. Thomas, Hiromi Ono, and Frank P. Stafford. *Changing Times of American Youth: 1981–2003.* Ann Arbor: Institute for Social Research, University of Michigan, 2004.

Kamerman, Sheila B., Michelle Neuman, Jane Waldfogel, and Jeanne Brooks-Gunn. "Social Policies, Family Types, and Child Outcomes in Selected OECD Countries." OECD Social, Employment, and Migration Working Papers 6: Social Policies, Family Types, and Child Outcomes in Selected OECD Countries (May 20, 2003).

Statistical Abstract of the United States, 2003. Washington, D.C.: U.S. Bureau of Census, 2004.

"The U.S. Family: How It's Changed!" *Life,* December 16, 1966, p. 4.

Wright, Henry. "Housing: How Much for How Much?" *The Survey* 57, no. 5 (December 1, 1926), pp. 673–677.

"Why
Do I
Love
These
People?"

PO BRONSON

A READER'S GUIDE

A CONVERSATION WITH PO BRONSON

This is the part of the book where the author answers questions put forth by an un-named interviewer, often the author's editor or publicist. Random House suggested that Po Bronson be interviewed by his brother, Steve Bronson, instead. Steve Bronson is an organ transplant nurse at the University of Washington Medical Center in Seattle. He is married with two young boys. This interview was conducted in the summer of 2006 on Vashon Island, where the Bronsons share a summer home with their cousins and aunts.

Steve Bronson: For the record, I liked the chapter about us. It really got to me.

Po Bronson: And your off-the-record opinion?

SB: No, that's how I really felt. But I have looked back at the chapter and I hear this guilt you had, and I just want to make sure that you don't still feel that way—so as a formal question, do you still carry that burden of responsibility around? For me?

PB: Not since those days in Peru. After that trip, I didn't seem to have that weighty concern anymore.

SB: Why didn't you put that story first in the book, so readers would know you better?

PB: My whole method is to learn from the real experiences of others. I felt putting my story first would have undercut that method.

SB: You were always so creative and imaginative when we were kids. But you didn't trust for a long time that writing could be your life, or that you would ever make a living at it, and you tried a lot of other professions. Why didn't you trust your talent?

PB: I had no role models for how it's done. In our family, we didn't have any exposure to artists, or writers, or college professors. Then Mom got a boyfriend who was a writer, and he took it seriously, but he never sold anything he wrote. When he didn't have enough money to buy a roll of toilet paper, she had to throw him out. Then she'd miss him, invite him back, and eventually get fed up and throw him out again. So even though I wrote a novel the first summer after graduating from college, and continued to write at night for years, I thought of it like playing the lottery. You could play the lottery, but you had to have a life and a job, and could only daydream that one day you'd win the lottery.

SB: Was your writing a factor in why you were isolated from the family for many years?

PB: Yeah. Dad was a practical guy, a business guy, and he's been as supportive as he can, but it was painful for him to watch me quit one job after another. Then Mom, after her boyfriend, had to watch me go down that path, too. So I had to get away from the doubt and pragmatism. I didn't have any success for a while, and that was a little shameful.

SB: Your son lives in his elaborate fantasy life, role-playing anywhere, just like you did. And he just started at a performing-arts elementary school. He tells you he wants to write with you when he grows up. So, what if that actually happens? How would you feel about him taking that risk?

PB: Terrified and proud, but probably no more so than I would be if he chose any other field.

SB: Okay, let me switch subjects. Honestly, tell me your method when you interview these people. How do you organize all the details? Do you use audio recordings?

PB: I take handwritten notes. The act of writing the notes helps me remember it better later—I can picture the page in my memory. Also, when you interview someone for ten hours—it's hard to look at a person eye to eye for so long. So writing notes allows me to lower my gaze now and then, makes it feel less confrontational. The first night in my motel room (if I am not staying in their house), I draw bubble charts to record my main observations. I write his or her name in the center of a piece of white paper, start making a family tree, add notes about those relationships, include a big bubble around an event that presents a dominant metaphor, a bubble for each key turning point. This becomes sort of a one-page version of his or her story. When I'm done interviewing someone, I have maybe sixty to one hundred pages of handwritten or typed notes on that person's life. So I break the life story into chunks and color code the notes with crayons. Underlined in yellow is everything about his mother. In red is the theme of rejection. In orange is everything that happened to him prior to high school. So when writing a section about him and his mom, I can look for all those things underlined in yellow and find every detail.

SB: And then you go to your writing closet and lock yourself away in that small space with just your laptop?

PB: Right. Every time I write, I go in the closet. It's dark, except for a tiny light so I can see the keys. I put a song on repeat, then disappear into the story. It sounds claustrophobic, but it's not—the closet is a portal that takes me back to the place where I recorded the story.

SB: I'm a nurse, and in the medical field we think a lot about maintaining professional distance. I had to get used to people dying. How do you deal with the tendency to get attached to the people you write about? Have you formed a professional distance from these people?

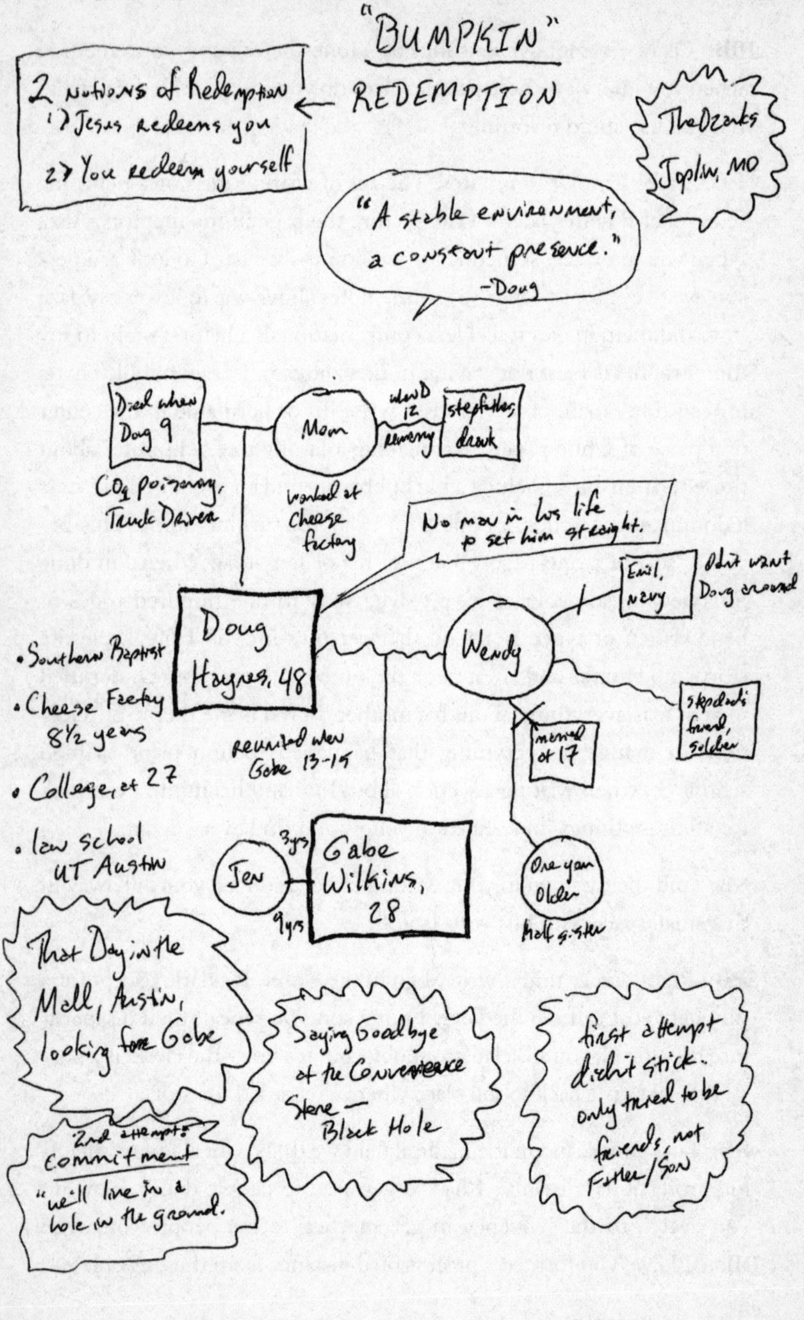

PB: The hardest thing about my work is to slowly back away after extensive interviewing. I don't have an institutional setting, like you do—your patients come to your hospital, and in that hospital there are doctors and orderlies all mimicking a similar distance. But I'm all alone, in their house. After someone tells me their secrets, they don't want to let me go. It's like they need me close so they can still guard their secrets. It might be hard for me to let go, but it's much harder for them—I, at least, get a lot of practice doing it.

SB: How did researching and writing this book affect your relationship with your family?

PB: With my wife and kids? Or with my extended family?

SB: All of us and them.

PB: Hearing these stories reminded me about the nobility of the journey. They made me feel good about being a son, a father, a husband, and a brother. They made me want to try harder. So I guess I became more patient, more resilient. I could handle more without getting peeved. And remember, no sooner had I finished the book than my wife's family lost their homes to Hurricane Katrina. If I hadn't done all my research, I wouldn't have even known how to have a conversation with those who've lost their homes to a hurricane. The research gave me the means of empathizing with people who've suffered every type of family crisis.

SB: What traits about our family did you realize defined us?

PB: Oh, we really like our heart-to-hearts, our one-on-one confessionals. And we don't let any tiff pass without everyone hearing about it in these sidebars and reenacting it and digesting it three times. And we're intense—we're pretty direct and don't use sly remarks or quips.

SB: Does healing always involve revisiting memories of the past?

PB: It's helpful for most, but not for all, and in some cases can be damaging.

SB: Why did you write this book?

PB: Because I wanted to write stories like these. Stories of redemption. Not fakey redemption. I have many writer friends who believe all redemption stories are lies. And many are. But I wanted to record redemption in the often imperfect, embarrassing way it actually occurs. Real redemption.

SB: If you could picture a person you were writing for, who would that be?

PB: Someone who has lost faith or is having their faith tested. Anyone who feels broken and worries that time alone won't fix things. Someone who is creating a new family and feels like the past is no guide.

SB: I would like you to write something funny again.

PB: I do write funny stuff. Usually to perform. Monologues, stories, speeches.

SB: No, a whole book story, a funny story.

PB: Where are you headed with this?

SB: Were you funnier when you were sad and screwed up and not so content with everyone in your family? Or did you just need to write this book to finally heal, to put the turmoil of our early years behind you, and now you can go back to writing stuff that makes me split my gut?

PB: Well, let's hope it's the latter.

QUESTIONS AND TOPICS FOR DISCUSSION

1. While reading, what memories of your own life came back to you? Do you see those events in a different light, having just read what other families have been through?

2. How did the fact that these are true stories, rather than fiction, affect the way you read the book?

3. People commonly invoke the phrase, "You can't choose your family." But in this century, while we might not get to choose who we come from, we do choose whether to live in the same state, how often to call, and whether to see our family once a week or once a year. In what ways have your relationships with various members of your family been your choice? In what ways have they not been your choice?

4. In "The Cook's Story," the Louie family's fate turns when they get to visit their childhood home. Have you had any interesting experiences when visiting your own childhood home?

5. In "The Trial," Vince Gonzalez writes to his mother, "Mundanity can be elevated to art by perception alone" (p. 58). What does this mean to you? Do you think the ability to *see* the beauty in the everyday and ordinary is key to healthy relationships?

6. In "Bumpkin," it takes thirteen years for Doug Haynes to go from a

young man who neglected his son to a very sensitive man who takes full responsibility for him. To pull it off, and to build trust, Doug becomes a listener, never telling Gabe what to do or ordering him around. How does your own father compare to Doug? How about your grandfathers? Has your father changed much over the years, becoming more tolerant, or a better listener?

7. Bronson writes in "The White Guy" that nearly every new couple today feels like they are bringing two different family styles into their marriage. Do you and your partner, if you have one, feel like you come from different family styles? How have you negotiated assimilating the two styles?

8. In the chapter "Jamaica?" Bronson raises the question, "When is it time to cut someone off?" We try to protect ourselves, and yet we don't want to run at the first sign of trouble. Has the book made you more inclined to hang in there longer with problematic relationships? Or has it made you more inclined to cut off people who mistreat you?

9. In "The Butcher's Wife," Bronson talks about two styles of forgiveness—one that puts the burden on the atoner, and one that puts the burden on the forgiver. The first voice tells us not to trust again, the second voice tells us how important it is to forgive if only to move on and let go of our enmity. Which voice is louder in your head? Has reading this book affected those voices—has it changed how you see forgiveness?

10. In "Some Thoughts," Bronson introduces us to one of the greatest mothers he has ever met, Mary Naomi Garrett. Then he admits that she never hugged her children, and that one of her children is missing (and might be dead) due to mental illness. Did that change your impression of Mary? Do you have preconceived notions of what a great relationship is supposed to be like? Do these notions ever blind you to the actual good that's in your real relationships?

11. If you were Charlie Taylor in "The Tornado," how would you have handled learning that your son has been stealing to support a cocaine addiction? Would you have been more strict than the real Charlie Taylor, or more lenient? What would you have done earlier, when you found pot in his room? Would you have suspected your son had much bigger problems?

12. In "The Tornado," do you think Charlie Taylor was more lenient on his children because his wife Susan had given him a second chance? How would you have handled learning that your fifteen-year-old daughter was pregnant? Would you have taken her out of school, as Susan did?

13. The chapters of this book are separated by questions that are meant to help us see all sides of family life. Two examples are "Do we need to have been taught what love is to give it to someone else?" and "Is it harder for them to accept you or for you to accept them?" Did these questions make you stop and think, either about the story you'd read or how it related to your own family?

14. Many of the protagonists in these stories are people who've made mistakes. Although they are portrayed as noble and Bronson clearly admires them, they have hurt their families, too—one neglected a son, several committed adultery, many of the parents disciplined their children physically, and several couldn't make their marriages work. Did Bronson manage to keep you from disliking these people or judging them? Is he simply recording the reality that nobody's perfect? Did you ever find yourself judging them when Bronson didn't? If these people were your friends, rather than strangers on a page, would you judge them the same way?

15. Bronson explains that some family problems are external, while others are internal. By *external* he means that the world has put the family in crisis, and they can either bond together or be broken apart by that which challenges them, be it poverty, culture, migration, or

discrimination. By *internal* he means that personality differences and actions toward one another cause the crisis. The families in this book have an abundance of both types of problems. Pick a story, and talk about which forces in it are external and which are internal.

16. For which person in the book do you most wonder, "What happens next?" What is it in his or her personality or story that makes you want to know more?

17. Instead of telling the stories of entire families, Bronson has chosen to focus on the relationship between two particular people in each family. Were there other family members you wished you had learned more about? Especially in his own story, "Blue Blankets," Bronson suggests that having a strong relationship with a single family member can save your relationship with the entire family. Do you agree? Do you have any personal experiences similar to that, where a family member is close to just one or two family members, but is estranged from the others?

18. Bronson has said that he hopes this book will give encouragement to those who have been dissuaded from having a family because of endless reports about rising divorce rates, single parenting, and so on. Are you one of the people he's talking about? If so (and even if not), do you think this book will help change that perspective?

19. Who in the book did you most expect you would relate to? Who did you least expect you would relate to? Did those expectations come true, or did you find yourself relating to people you did not imagine you would?

20. Most of these stories are built around an indelible image that works metaphorically—Andrew's tree, Jen's bracelet, Andy's greenhouse, silent car rides, a tornado, the river of family life, Brian's palace, Uma's boxes. Did it surprise you to find such a literary technique applied to a work of nonfiction? Which images do you think worked particularly well?

PO BRONSON's own family is spread out over three continents and several cultures, manifesting every modern variation on family. He lives in San Francisco with his wife and two children. This is his fifth book. Previously he has published two novels and two works of nonfiction. His last book, *What Should I Do with My Life?*, was a #1 *New York Times* bestseller. He currently writes essays for *Time* and has a regular column on social issues at Time.com.

For more about his research, visit www.pobronson.com.

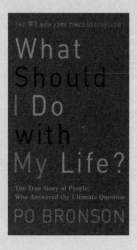